GW00599283

VICTOR MARTIN
MAR 91

Pascal by Example

An Introductory Course

Judith Ford

NCC Blackwell

MANCHESTER • OXFORD

British Library Cataloguing in Publication Data

Ford, Judith
  Pascal by example : An introductory course.
  1. Computer systems. Programming languages: Pascal language
  I. Title
  005.13'3

ISBN 0-85012-808-0

© NCC BLACKWELL LIMITED, 1990

All rights reserved. No part of this publication may be reproduced, stored in a retrieval system, or transmitted, in any form or by any means, without the prior permission of The National Computing Centre.

Published for NCC Publications by NCC Blackwell Limited.

Editorial Office, The National Computing Centre Limited, Oxford Road, Manchester M1 7ED, England.

NCC Blackwell Limited, 108 Cowley Road, Oxford OX4 1JF, England.

Typeset in 11pt Times Roman by H&H Graphics, Blackburn; and printed by Hobbs the Printers of Southampton.

ISBN 0-85012-808-0

Contents

Introduction

This book is intended to form the basis for a first course in Pascal programming. The reader is not assumed to have any previous knowledge of computers or programming languages.

The aim of the book is to teach good programming techniques in a practical way. Each chapter begins with a description of a particular programming problem. This is followed by discussion of how we could plan and implement a solution using Pascal.

In order to deal thoroughly with all aspects of the Pascal language, many chapters have a second section entitled 'more advanced topics'. These sections may enlarge upon aspects of the language raised in the main part of the chapter, or may discuss ways of improving the style or efficiency of programs. Students may find it helpful to leave out these sections on a first reading of the book.

The exercises and worked examples form an integral part of the text. Students are urged to attempt all of the exercises, particularly the programming examples. Exercises which require knowledge of the 'more advanced topics' section of any chapter are marked with an asterisk.

1 Introduction to Computer Programming

INTRODUCTION

In this chapter we will discuss the use of programming languages and, in particular, of Pascal. We will then look at the practicalities of running a Pascal program. Finally we will see how a language can be defined using a system of diagrams.

WHAT IS A PROGRAMMING LANGUAGE?

'High-level' programming languages, such as Pascal, are tools which enable us to 'tell' a computer what we want it to do.

A computer is only capable of performing very simple tasks, such as moving an item of information or adding numbers together. To do more complex jobs it must carry out a large number of these simple operations, one after the other. In order to tell the computer what to do, we must give it instructions in the form of a series of numbers, known as 'machine code'.

Giving instructions to a computer using machine code is very tedious. It is also very easy to make mistakes – and very difficult to correct them! For this reason we need a way of programming the computer (ie telling it what to do) which is easier for us to understand.

Programming languages have been developed to enable us to program computers without having to use machine code directly. In simple terms, we can write a program in a 'high-level' language, which can then be 'translated' into machine code. By a 'program' we mean a series of instructions which, after being translated into machine code and carried out one after the other by a computer, will enable it to perform a specified task. We might, for example, write a program to add up the prices of items on a shopping list, or to check for spelling errors in a document.

There are many different programming languages, which were each designed to suit particular purposes. Thus a particular type of program may be easier to write in one language than another. For example, Fortran was designed for scientific work and so has many powerful mathematical tools available, whereas Cobol is particularly suited to the manipulation of large amounts of data.

WHAT'S SPECIAL ABOUT PASCAL?

When Pascal was designed it was intended to be used in the teaching of computer programming. It was intended that it should:

1) Provide a language whose main features could be learned fairly easily. Hence there is a relatively small 'vocabulary' which you need to learn.

2) Make program design easier, and make programs easier to understand once they have been written. Hence there is a facility to 'break down' large operations into a number of smaller ones, so as to make it easier to see what is going on.

3) Make it more difficult to produce programs which do the wrong thing. Of course no language can prevent programmers from making mistakes, but Pascal, by having a very strict set of rules concerning what is an acceptable program, can alert you to the presence of some of the commonest errors.

4) Be 'portable'. This means that programs written for one computer system can be used on another, different system. For a program to be portable, the language it is written in must be 'standard'. That is, it must not differ from one system to another. Pascal is one of the most standard languages available. It has a recognised standard version defined by the International Standards Organisation – ISO Pascal.

DIALECTS

Versions of a programming language which differ slightly are known as 'dialects'. In general dialects of Pascal are very similar to one another. So programs written in one dialect will require only minor changes in order to run on a system which uses a different dialect. In this book, we will be concerned mainly with ISO Pascal. However, the most popular Pascal implementation for IBM compatible microcomputer users, Turbo Pascal, deviates slightly from the ISO standard. So both ISO and Turbo versions of the example programs are included wherever the two dialects are different.

GETTING YOUR PROGRAM INTO THE COMPUTER

Before your Pascal program can be translated into machine code and run on a computer it must be typed into the computer and stored in the memory. To do this you will need to use an 'editor'. Your computer system is sure to include one. Turbo Pascal has its own built-in editor.

An editor enables you to type in a 'file' of characters from the keyboard, which will then be stored in the computer's memory. If you want a more permanent copy of the file, you can then 'save' it on disk. The editor also allows you to display existing files on the screen, and to make alterations to them. You will need to become familiar with the use of the editor on your computer system before you can start writing programs.

COMPILING YOUR PROGRAM

In order to translate a program written in Pascal into machine code we need what is called a 'compiler'. This is a special computer program which enables the computer to 'read' a Pascal program, and translate each instruction into the equivalent machine code.

In order to run a program, once it has been typed in, you will need to 'call' the compiler. This means typing in an instruction, telling the computer to run the compiler program using your program file as data. The compiler will then go through your program (known as the 'source code') line-by-line, translating it into machine code. This process is illustrated in Figure 1.1.

The compiler will only be able to translate your program if it 'makes sense' to it. In other words, if it is written in correct Pascal. If the compiler finds an instruction which it does not understand it will display an error message. In some cases the compiler will stop as soon as it detects an error, while in others it will attempt to continue to the end of the source code and will then produce a list of all the errors that it has found. In either

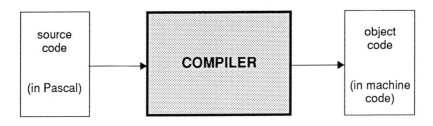

Figure 1.1

case, most compilers will display a message telling you approximately where in the program the error is, and what sort of error it is.

Since the compiler cannot be expected to know exactly what you were intending your program to do, it cannot always pinpoint accurately where an error has occurred. However, it is usually reasonable to assume that any error must be no later in the source code than the point indicated by the compiler.

This may be easier to understand if we look at an example of the way we detect errors in reading our own language – English. Supposing we are looking at a list of names. For example:

Mr. Fred Smith
Ms. J. T. Brown
Mis. Carol Ann Jones
Mr. A. Green

When we read this list we can see that there is an error in the third line. The rules (in this case, those governing the form which people's names must take) have been broken. However, it is not possible for us to know whether the mistake involves an extra 'i' in 'Ms.' or a substitution of '.' for 's' in 'Miss'. The compiler is in a similar situation when it finds a mistake in a program – it knows that something is wrong, but it cannot tell precisely what.

If we imagine that we have to read the list of names, a letter at a time, starting from the top, we will be able to 'feel' what it is like for a compiler attempting to translate an incorrect program. Everything seems fine until we reach the full stop after 'Mis'. At this point it becomes clear that there is something wrong, so we could report an error here. However, if the correct version is 'Ms.', then we have reported the error two letters further on than the point at which it actually occurred.

Once all the errors have been corrected, when you compile a program the compiler will make a file containing the machine code translation (known as the object code), which can then be used to run the program. Often you will be given a choice between compiling the program to memory or to a file on the disk. The advantage of compiling to disk is that you can then run the program whenever you like, without having to compile the source code again. This may save a considerable amount of time, particularly if the program is a long one. However, if your program is short, or if you are going to be constantly altering it, compiling to memory will probably be more convenient.

Below are listed two versions of a program written in Pascal. The first contains some errors. The second is the correct version.

Version 1.
```
program times8 (input,output);
var i : integer;
begin writeln ('8 times table');
for i = 1 to 10 do
writeln (i, '    ',8*i);
end;
```

Version 2.
```
program times8 (input,output);
var i : integer;
begin writeln ('8 times table');
for i := 1 to 10 do writeln (i, '    ',8*i);
end.
```

Practise using your editor and compiler by typing in version 1 and attempting to compile it. Do the error messages produced by the compiler help you to locate the mistakes? Correct the errors, so that you now have version 2, and compile the program again.

Once a program has been compiled it is ready to be executed (see below). Occasionally a computer system allows programs to be translated and executed using a single command.

RUNNING YOUR PROGRAM

To get the computer to run your compiled program (ie to 'execute' it), you will need to type in a command, possibly also specifying the file containing the object code. Try this using the program above, which you should now have typed in and compiled.

If your program is incorrrect it may either produce unexpected results, or possibly a 'run-time' error will be reported. A run-time error means that you have asked the computer to do something which it knows it should not attempt to do (such as dividing a number by zero). Usually the program will stop, and an error message will be displayed on the screen. Sometimes the part of the source code corresponding to the place where the error occurred will be indicated, but often your only clue as to where the error happened will be a number giving the position in the object code. This means that run-time errors can be difficult to track down.

Don't let all this talk about programming errors and the difficulties of correcting them depress you. Pascal is a particularly good language for detecting common typing errors at compile-time, thus avoiding problems during execution. And you will have plenty of opportunity to practise typing in and running simple programs before you have to tackle complex, error-prone ones.

DEFINING A PROGRAMMING LANGUAGE

It is only possible to write a compiler to translate from a high-level language into machine code if that high-level language is very precisely defined. This means that programs have to obey a strict set of rules or 'syntax'.

The Pascal language can be thought of as consisting of a number of 'elements', each with their own special syntax, which can be combined according to specific rules. These combinations of elements can be combined, again according to strict rules, to make more complex language structures, and so on.

In this book we will describe each language element as it is introduced, and give examples of what it is like and how it can be incorporated into a program. We will also use syntax diagrams, which are a pictorial way of describing the syntax of a language.

SYNTAX DIAGRAMS

Let's start by looking at the syntax of something in English. Suppose you want to describe all the possible forms that you might use to address someone, for example:

Mr. Fred Smith
Ms. J. C. Brown
Miss Ann J. Cholmondely
Mr. H. Gregory Hunt
Miss Black
Mrs. Jane Susan Beatrice Jones

We can see all of these consist of three parts: a title, followed (optionally) by a list of names or initials (or a combination of names and initials), followed by a name. Let's look at each of these in more detail:

- A title consists of one of the following: Mr., Ms., Mrs. or Miss. (We are ignoring uncommon titles, such as Rev., Dr. or Professor.)

- A name is a sequence of letters of the alphabet. An initial is a letter followed by a full stop.

We can represent the syntax of titles, names and initials using the syntax diagrams in Figure 1.2.

The simplest of these is the initial. You can discover what an initial

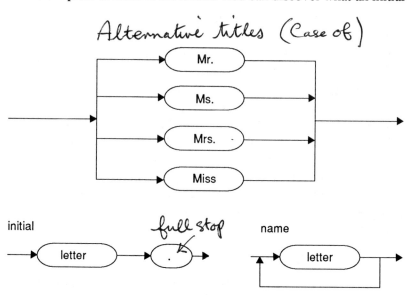

Figure 1.2

Syntax Diagrams

consists of by following the arrows from left to right, through each of the boxes in turn. We learn that an initial must be made up of:

a letter (from the first box), followed by
a full stop (from the second box).

Now let's look at the syntax of a title. In this case the arrow leading from the left branches into four alternative routes. This means that a title can have, as its first element, the contents of one of the four boxes (ie Mr., Ms., Mrs. or Miss). There are no further boxes, so a title must consist simply of this one element.

A name is a little more complicated. Following the arrow from the left, we enter a box containing a letter. We then have the choice of exiting (leaving our name consisting of a single letter) or following the arrow which goes back to enter the box for a second time. This means that a name may consist of:

a letter   *or*
a letter followed by a letter   *or*
a letter followed by a letter followed by a letter *or*
a letter followed by ... followed by a letter
                         (as many times as you like)

Now let's put these together to make a syntax diagram defining the syntax of a complete form of address. You will recall that a form of address consisted of a title, a list of names or initials, and a final name.

We will need to start with a box which tells us to put a title first. Up until now we have used round-ended boxes. These are used for actual characters (such as '.' or 'Mr.') which must be included and for other items (such as a letter) which require no further explanation. We will now use a rectangular box containing the word 'title', to indicate that we must look elsewhere to find the definition of a title. This is shown in Figure 1.3.

Next we have a choice between a name or an initial, or we may proceed

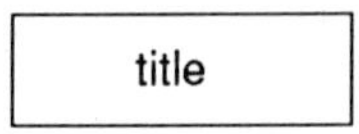

Figure 1.3

straight to the final name. So we need to split the arrow leading from our 'title' box into three, and put rectangular boxes containing 'name', 'initial' and 'name', as in Figure 1.4.

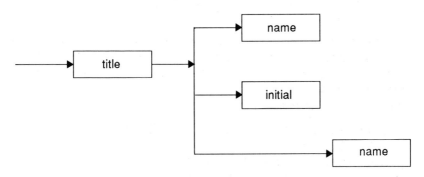

Figure 1.4

After a name or initial we may then include another name or initial, or we may proceed to the final name. In other words we have exactly the same choices as we had before entering the 'initial' or 'name' box. So we can complete the syntax diagram by drawing an arrow which brings us back to the position immediately before this box was chosen (see Figure 1.5).

form of address

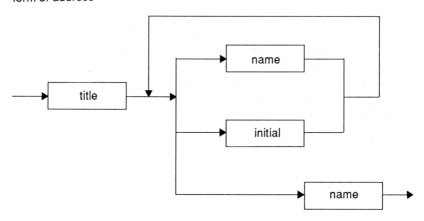

Figure 1.5

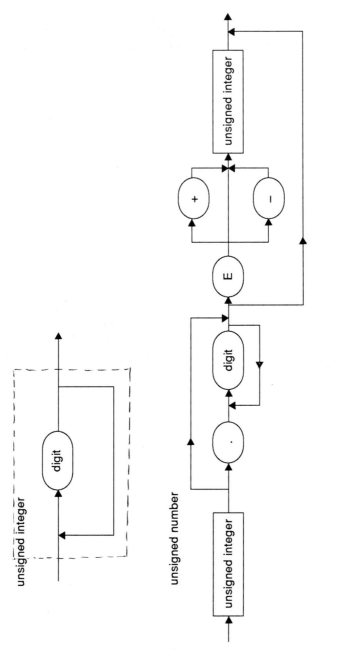

Figure 1.6

This completes our syntax diagram describing a 'form of address'. Check that it is correct by tracing the route which you have to take through the diagram for each of the examples which we started with (Mr. Fred Smith, Ms. J. C. Brown, etc).

EXERCISES

Study the Pascal Syntax diagram in Figure 1.6. (Don't worry if you don't understand what it is about!)

Now decide which of the following are syntactically correct 'unsigned numbers':

   i)   1

   ii)   123456789

   iii) 2a

   iv) E103

   v)   1.96

   vi) 00000.0000E$-$1

   vii) 34E+5

   viii) 76.E4

   ix) 5E97

   x)   22.1E$-$

2 Getting Started

INTRODUCTION

In this chapter we will practise compiling and running very simple programs to produce messages on the screen.

NEW PASCAL FEATURES

1) Program header
2) Comments
3) **write** and **writeln**
4) **begin** and **end**

'TALKING' TO THE USER

Whatever else we may want our program to do, we will certainly need to have some means of communicating with the user – perhaps by displaying words or pictures on the screen, perhaps by printing out a list of results, perhaps by making or amending a file on a disk.

Very often we will want to produce messages on the screen. We may want to ask the user to input information, or we may want to display the results of calculations performed by the program. So let's look at how we can do this using Pascal.

A program consists of a list of instructions (or 'statements') which, when carried out in sequence, will (we hope) perform our desired task. In order that the compiler, which translates these instructions, will be able to understand them, every program has to conform to a particular pattern. We will look at this general pattern, by considering a very simple example:

```
program Hello (input,output);
   {displays greeting on screen} begin
write ('Hello'); (* display greeting *)
end.
```

(If you can't guess what it will do, type it into your computer and try compiling and running it!)

Let's look at each line in turn.

THE PROGRAM STATEMENT

Every Pascal program must start with a program statement. This consists of the word 'program' followed by the name of the program, then a list of 'identifiers' (or names) enclosed in brackets, and terminated by a semi-colon.

The list of identifiers gives information to the compiler about any external files which will be used by the program. Further information about these can be found in Chapters 9 and 10, but for the time being, all our programs will begin with a statement of the form:

program name (input,output);

The semi-colon at the end of the program header tells the compiler that the end of a statement has been reached. Every Pascal statement must be terminated by a semi-colon or some other suitable 'delimiter'. For the time being, all statements will be terminated by ' ; '.

Figure 2.1 shows the syntax of the **program** statement.

program statement

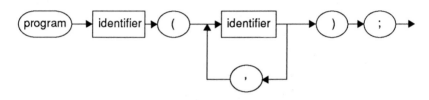

Figure 2.1

IDENTIFIERS

The program name and file names (or 'identifiers') must be of the following pattern. Each must start with an alphabetic letter. The remaining characters may be either letters or numbers, but must not include any other characters. Thus the following are legal identifiers:

x
a1
Tuesday

while the following are illegal:

1st   (does not start with a letter)
New price   (contains a space)
p–q   (contains –)

So an identifier must satisfy the syntax diagram in Figure 2.2.

identifier

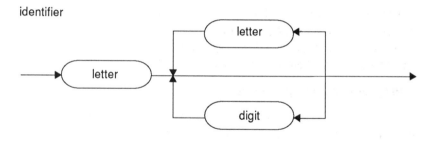

Figure 2.2

In addition, the identifier must not be one of the Pascal 'delimiter' words (see below). A full list of these is included in Appendix B.

In theory identifiers may be of any length, but in practice your compiler will probably ignore all characters beyond a certain length. Thus, the two, apparently different, identifiers:

extremelylongidentifier1234 and
extremelylongidentifier1235

may be treated as being the same.

Upper and lower case letters are treated by the compiler as equivalent. Thus, the identifiers:

Answer
answer
ANSWER

will *always* be treated as being the same.

In order to make your program easy to understand, it is useful to choose identifiers whose names indicate their function in the program. For example, a program to print out names and addresses might use the following identifiers: CurrentName, CurrentAddress and AddressList, to refer to the location of information about the names and addresses which are being processed.

COMMENTS

It is not always easy to understand a program, particularly a complex one, simply by looking at the source code. Using comments is one way of making it easier to follow a program listing. Comments are simply messages inserted within the source code to give additional information. They are divided from the rest of the program by being enclosed in curly brackets: { }, or by putting the combination (* before the start of a comment, and *) to terminate the comment.

In this very simple program a comment was not really necessary. However, it is always preferable to include superfluous comments than to leave a program insufficiently documented. Programs frequently require updating and alteration. It will be much easier to do this if the original code is easy to follow.

BEGIN AND END

The words **begin** and **end** are examples of 'delimiters'. These are special words, each with its own set meaning. The delimiters 'begin' and 'end' tell the compiler where a sequence of statements begins and ends.

The full-stop after the final 'end' in a program indicates that the end of the entire program has been reached.

WRITE

We use **write** in order to output information. In the example on p. 28, the word 'Hello' will appear on the screen at the current cursor position.

You can easily alter this program to print any one-line message you choose, by putting it between single inverted commas inside the brackets following 'write'. If you want to include a single inverted comma in your message then you must type two of these, like this:

write ('Don''t panic!');

If you were to put only one inverted comma then the compiler would think that this was the end of your message, and would attempt to interpret the remainder as part of your Pascal program. A syntax error would result.

So now we know how to write a program which will print any short message we like on the screen. This is all very well, but at the moment, our message always appears just wherever the cursor happens to be on the screen. And, if there is some text already on the screen, it can be difficult to see what has been written. To improve our screen display we can make use of:

WRITELN

If we modify our program to look like this:

```
program Hello (input,output);
begin
writeln;
writeln;
writeln ('Hello');
write ('This is my first Pascal program.');
end.
```

then our output will consist of:

2 blank lines
Hello (at the extreme left of the screen)
This is my first Pascal program (immediately below)

The cursor will be left at the position immediately to the right of the word 'program' on the final line of output.

As this example shows, **writeln** can be used either with or without a message to be printed out. Used alone **writeln** simply outputs a new line character (ie moves the cursor to the beginning of the next line on the screen). Used with a message, it outputs the message followed by a new line character. Thus, the same effect can be achieved by either of the following program segments:

```
writeln ('Hello');    or

write ('Hello');
writeln;
```

MORE ADVANCED TOPICS

Starting with a Clean Sheet

Our presentation would be further improved if we could clear the screen before displaying our message. Unfortunately this is often not easy using Pascal, since there is no standard way of controlling the screen display.

Some Pascal implementations include a special command to clear the screen (for example, in Turbo Pascal the statement **clrscr;** will do this). ISO Pascal includes a command, **page** (see Chapter 7), which is used when sending output to a printer to move on to a new page. Using this command may have the effect of clearing the screen.

Alternatively, the instruction 'write (chr (12));' may clear the screen. This is because the ASCII code 12 denotes a 'formfeed' character. This is often interpreted as 'clear screen' when writing to the screen. The Pascal standard function **Chr** converts from an integer value to its character equivalent. So **write (chr (12))** will output the character with code number 12.

Consult the user manual for your particular Pascal implementation and try some experiments for yourself.

EXERCISES

1. Which of the following are legal Pascal identifiers?
Result, 2nd, program, x, x+y, a1b2, M(1), NAME, BEGIN.

2. When the following program was compiled, the compiler reported a syntax error at the point indicated by the arrow (^). Correct the error and run the program.

```
program silly (input,output);
begin
writeln;
writeln ('*********************************');
writeln;
```

```
write ('Greetings! ');
writeln ('I would like to say 'welcome' to new users.');
                                   ^
writeln;
writeln ('**********************************');
end.
```

3. Write a program to produce an attractive 'title page' for a piece of software. You should include the name of the software package, the author's name, and a few words to describe what the package does.

3 Question and Answer

INTRODUCTION

In this chapter we will look at some programs which 'ask' questions and act upon the answers. Programs which do this are known as 'interactive' programs. They are useful because they provide an easy way of supplying the computer with the information which it needs during its execution. If such a program is well-written then even an inexperienced computer operator will be able to run it successfully.

NEW PASCAL FEATURES

1) Variable declaration
2) The **char** type
3) **readln**
4) **if**
5) The **boolean** type
6) The **integer** type

A SIMPLE INTERACTIVE PROGRAM

In Chapter 2 we learned how to write a message on the screen. Now we will look at a way of inputting the reply. The program below asks for a character to be typed in, and waits until this has been done.

program
header

program wait (input,output);

declarative
section

var
ch : char;

35

```
              begin
                writeln;
                writeln ('Welcome!');
main body       writeln ('Press "enter" to continue.');
                readln (ch);
                writeln;
                writeln ('Thank you.');
              end.
```

This program consists of three sections, as illustrated above. We have seen a program header and the main body of a program before, but we now need a new section: the 'declarative section'. We will look in detail at this below.

INPUTTING DATA FROM THE KEYBOARD

Let us look first at how we read in information which has been typed in at the keyboard. The command **readln (ch)** reads a line of input from the keyboard and puts the value of the first character into the particular area of memory which has been given the name **ch.** So, when we run this program, we would expect it to display this message:

Welcome!
Press 'enter' to continue.

It will then wait until the 'enter' key is pressed (signifying that a line of text has been entered), before moving the cursor to a new line and writing: **Thank you.**

THE DECLARATIVE SECTION

In order to allocate space in the computer memory for storing data, the compiler needs to know how many, and what kind of pieces of data you will require. So each Pascal program has a 'declarative section' immediately after the program statement, which includes this information.

When we want to store a piece of data we do so by declaring a 'variable' identifier. This means that we tell the compiler to allocate a space in the memory, and give it a name which we can use to refer to this particular space. Because different types of data take up different amounts of memory, we also need to tell the compiler what 'type' of variable we are using.

The Pascal delimiter word **var** is used to mark the beginning of the 'variable declaration section' of the program. It can be followed by any number of variable declaration statements, such as the following:

ch : char;
age : integer;
INITIAL1, INITIAL2, INITIAL3 : char;
readytostop : Boolean;
x,y : integer;

The three type identifiers **char**, **integer**, and **boolean** are the names of three Pascal types which we will need to use later in this chapter. They will each be described as they are introduced into our program.

The syntax of a variable declaration statement is given in Figure 3.1.

THE CHAR TYPE

The Pascal pre-defined identifier **char** describes variables which can take values corresponding to any character available on the computer. For example. a, A, %, >, + are all values which a variable of type **char** could take.

So, the statement, **ch: char;**, in the variable declaration section of our program tells the compiler to:

1) Allocate an area of memory large enough to store a character value.
2) Note the identifier **ch** as referring to the area of memory allocated.

MAKING CHOICES

In the previous program we were not interested in which character had been entered, but only in the fact that the user of the program had

variable declaration

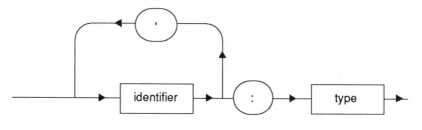

Figure 3.1

responded. Now let us look at a slightly more complex example. Suppose that we want to issue a question to which the response may be either 'y' (for yes) or 'n' (for no), and to print one of two replies, depending upon the response. In order to do this we need to be able to:

1) Determine which of the possible responses has been typed in.
2) Choose which message to print, according to which response is typed in.

In order to achieve this, we must first consider what are the possible responses. In this case we assume that what will be typed in will be either 'y' or 'n' (followed by 'enter'). So we need to compare the character typed in with 'y' (say) and then act accordingly. Here is how this can be done:

```
program choice (input,output);
var
  ch : char;
begin
writeln;
writeln ('Is it your birthday today?');
writeln ('Type "y" or "n"');
readln (ch);
if ch = 'y'  then writeln ('Happy Birthday')
             else writeln ('Goodbye');
end.
```

This program uses an **if** statement to choose between two courses of action. The **else** part of the statement is optional. Below are some examples of **if** statements:

- if ch = 'y' then writeln ('good');
- if ch = 'a' then writeln ('A')
             else if ch = 'b' then writeln ('B')
                          else writeln ('mistake');
- if ch = 'a' then writeln ('A')
             else if ch = 'b' then writeln ('B');

The syntax of an **if** statement is shown in Figure 3.2. Note the absence of a semi-colon at the end of the **if** part of the statement whenever the **else** part is included. You may be tempted to terminate the statement **writeln ('happy birthday')** in our example program, with a semi-colon, but this is incorrect, since what follows is still part of the same **if**

if statement

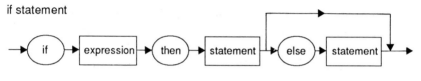

Figure 3.2

statement. If you do put one in inadvertently the compiler will assume that it marks the end of the **if** statement, and will report a syntax error when it reaches the delimiter **else**.

If the *expression* (see below) determining the choice is true (in our example, if the character 'y' is typed in) then the statement following the 'then' delimiter is executed. If the expression is false then the statement following the 'else' delimiter (if any) is executed. Try typing in the program and running it to see this happening.

Sometimes the statement following either the **if** or **else** delimiter is itself an **if** statement. When this happens we speak of the **if** statements being 'nested' (ie one inside the other).

To check that you have understood the syntax of **if** statements, look at the example below and decide which are correct and which contain syntax errors:

```
1) if ch = 'x'  then writeln;
2) if writeln  then readln (ch);
3) if ch = 'y'  then
                else writeln ('ch incorrect');
4) if ch = 'q'  then readln (ch);
                else writeln;
```

Now look back at our example program. What will happen if you replace the delimiter **else** with **;** and then run the new version? Edit the program and run it to see if you were right.

EXPRESSIONS

In general, an expression is some sort of calculation, involving any of a number of operators acting upon variables or sub-expressions. We will find out more about exactly what an expression consists of later.

Every expression has its own type, just as each variable has to be declared as being of a particular type. There are various rules about where the different types of expressions may be used. The expression which we are concerned with here is of the **boolean** type. This means that it can take one of two values: either **true** or **false**.

If we look at the expression, **ch** = **'y'**, in more detail we can see that it consists of a variable (**ch**) and a constant (**'y'**) operated on by a logical operator (=). As you might expect, this expression will take the value **true** if **ch** has the value of the character y, and **false** otherwise.

WHAT'S GONE WRONG?

Press down the 'CAPS LOCK' key on your keyboard. Then try running the 'Happy Birthday' example program. Does the computer still wish you a happy birthday? What has gone wrong?

If you have carried out this experiment then you will have realised that it would be helpful if the program could recognise both y and Y as 'yes' answers to our question. We can do this by replacing the condition **ch** = **'y'** in the **if** statement with (**ch** = **'y'**) **or** (**ch** = **'Y'**). This is a more complicated boolean expression involving a combination of operators.

This condition will be true if *either* y *or* Y is typed in in response to the question, 'Is it your birthday today?'. The brackets are used to ensure that the compiler knows in which order you intend the various parts of the expression to be evaluated. Sub-expressions (ie expressions which form part of a larger expression) which are in brackets are always evaluated first. So the brackets in our example ensure that the program will evaluate the two sub-expressions: **ch** = **'y'** and **ch** = **'Y'** and then apply the operator **or** to them. Now try running the modified program with and without 'CAPS LOCK' on.

ANOTHER INTERACTIVE PROGRAM

Now let's try a more complicated question-and-answer program. Suppose that you are an employer who wants to choose a shortlist of applicants to interview for a job. You want a simple program that will use information from the application forms to assess each candidate's suitability for the post, and print out a grading.

We will assume that only yes-and-no questions need be answered, and that each question will have a clear 'good' and 'bad' response. For the present, we will calculate the grading simply by adding an appropriate number to the candidate's score for each 'good' answer. Thus the higher the score, the more suitable the applicant. Let us suppose that our ideal applicant would:

1) Have at least 5 years' experience in Pascal programming.
2) Be under 35.
3) Drive a car.

And we will assume that these requirements have been listed in order of importance, and that it would be reasonable to score 3 for having quality 1, 2 for quality 2, and 1 for quality 3.

So, for example, a response of 'yes, yes, no' would give a score of 3 + 2 + 0 = 5, while a response of 'no, yes, yes' would give a score of 0 + 2 + 1 = 3.

In essence, this program will simply be a matter of 'glueing together' a number of **if** statements of the sort used in our previous example. Here is how we could ask and respond to question 1:

```
writeln ('At least 5 years' 'experience?');
readln (ch);
if (ch = 'y') or (ch = 'Y') then
```

In order to calculate the score, we will also need to declare a suitable variable in which we can store the total as we calculate it, and we will also need to know how to make this result appear on the screen. At the end of execution of the program, the screen display should look something like Figure 3.3.

THE INTEGER TYPE

In order to store the number of points scored by an applicant, we need to declare a variable in which we can store any value which this score could take. Since we calculate the score by adding together whole numbers, the score will also be a whole number. In Pascal we can allocate space to store whole numbers by declaring a variable of the type **integer**. We will use the statement **score : integer** under the **var** heading in the declaration part of our program.

THE ASSIGNMENT STATEMENT

It is all very well having a space reserved to keep the score, but we need a way of putting the score into that space, and of changing it as necessary. To do this we use an assignment statement, such as this:

```
score := 0;
```

```
Programming experience > 5yrs?
y
Under 35?
y
Car Driver?
y

Final score = 6
```

Figure 3.3

This particular assignment puts the value 0 into the space allocated for the variable score. We often read this statement as, 'score *becomes equal to* 0'.

Later in the program, we will want to increase the score whenever a 'good' answer is given. We use another assignment statement for this, such as:

score := score + 1;

This takes whatever value is in score, adds 1 to it, and puts the result back into score.

DESIGNING THE SHORTLISTING PROGRAM

Now that we have all the necessary 'building blocks' available, we can start to design our program.

In the declaration part of our program we will need to declare an integer variable to hold the score, and a character variable to hold the answer to the question currently being considered:

```
var
    score : integer;
    ch : char;
```

The main body of the program will include three **if** statements to deal with the three questions which we are considering. For example:

```
writeln ('Under 35?');
readln (ch);
if (ch = 'y') or (ch = 'Y') then score := score + 2;
```

You should now be able to write the other two program segments to deal with the remaining two questions and answers. Then type in an appropriate program heading, followed by the variable declaration section shown above, and finally the three question-and-answer segments. (Don't forget to put **begin** and **end.** to show where the main program instructions start and finish!)

(If you are confused, don't worry. The complete program is given later in the chapter.)

The program is now nearly complete, but it does not, as yet, output the result of its calculations. We need to add another **write** or **writeln** statement to give the final score. Integer variables can be output simply by putting the variable identifier inside the brackets in a **writeln** statement:

```
write (score)   or
writeln (score)
```

To make our output more intelligible, it is useful to include a message explaining what the number that is output represents. This can be done using a separate **write** statement, or we can include a number of different items in a single **write** statement, like this:

```
write ('The score is ',score,' points.');   or
writeln ('Score = ',score);
```

Note that, if we wish to include a space to separate the text from the number **score**, then we have to include it explicitly between the inverted commas in the **write** statement.

When you have added an appropriate output routine, your program will look something like:

```pascal
program shortlist (input,output);
var
  score:integer;
  ch:char;
begin
writeln;
writeln;
writeln ('Programming experience > 5yrs?');
readln (ch);
if (ch='y') or (ch='Y') then score := score + 3;
writeln;
writeln ('Under 35?');
readln (ch);
if (ch='y') or (ch='Y') then score := score + 2;
writeln;
writeln ('Car driver?');
readln (ch);
if (ch='y') or (ch='Y') then score := score + 1;
writeln;
writeln ('Final score = ',score);
end.
```

Try running this program, keeping a note of the answers which you have typed in and the score which you would expect. Is the final result correct? Now try running it again several times, checking the result each time.

If you are very lucky, you may get the correct result on every occasion. But it is quite likely that you will get something quite absurd on all but the first run, or even every time. This is because we have forgotten to initialise our variable, **score**. That is, to set its value at the start of our calculations. Some computer systems will set all variable values to zero at the start of a program run, but the majority will simply leave whatever rubbish happens to have been left in that storage location from previous use. So, it is very important to make sure that we never allow a variable to be used without first assigning an appropriate value to it. Now correct this mistake by adding this statement:

score := 0;

after **begin** and run the program again. It should now produce the correct answer each time.

MORE ADVANCED TOPICS

The Boolean Type

In our example programs we compared a character input at the keyboard with a specific value so as to establish whether or not they were the same. The result of this comparison could take one of two values: true or false. In other words, we used an expression of boolean type.

It is also possible to declare variables to be of boolean type. For example:

var
  yes : boolean;
  ok : boolean;
  found, stop, tryagain : boolean;

At this stage, variables which can only take two values may not appear to be very useful. However, we will find them valuable tools to improve the readability of more complex programs.

Boolean Expressions

We have met one sort of boolean expression. We have made a comparison between two items, testing whether or not they are equal. There are several other boolean operators, which can be used to establish more complex relationships between items. The boolean operators are:

NOT
AND
OR
= <> < > <= >=

We will look at each operator in turn:

NOT
Suppose that A has been declared as a boolean variable. Then the expression **NOT** A will be **true** whenever A is **false** and **false** whenever A is **true**.

AND
If A and B are boolean variables, then A **AND** B will take the value **true** if and only if A and B *both* have the value **true**. Otherwise A **AND** B will be **false**.

OR

If **A** and **B** are boolean variables then **A OR B** will be **true** if *either* **A** is true *or* **B** is true *or both* **A** *and* **B** are **true**. **A OR B** will be **false** only if **A** is **false** *and* **B** is **false**.

=

Unlike the operators **NOT, AND** and **OR**, the comparison operator = can operate on variables or expressions which are of types other than boolean. In fact, any of the types which we have met so far can be compared using =. The expression **A** = **B** will be **true** if **A** and **B** both have the same value. The expression will be **false** otherwise.

< >

< > can be read as 'is not equal to'. It too can be used to compare expressions of any of the types which we have met so far. A< >B will be **true** if A and B are *not* equal. It will be **false** otherwise. A< >B is exactly equivalent to the expression **NOT(A = B)**.

< >   <=   >=

These operators can only be used to compare expressions whose type has a definite *ordering*. In other words, we can only compare **A** with **B** using one of these operators if we have a definite idea of what it means to say 'A is greater than B'.

Of the types we have met so far, the integer, char and boolean types all satisfy this criterion. For the integers it is obvious what is means to say that one value is greater than another. The two boolean values are defined to be such that false is less than true. The characters will also have a definite order, but this may vary from one implementation to another.

Precedence of Boolean Operators

The operators have been listed above in order of *decreasing precedence*. Those grouped together on the lowest level have equal precedence. This means that, if a boolean expression containing more than one operator, is written without brackets, then the operation nearest the top of the list will be performed first.

Let us look at an example. If **A** and **B** are boolean variables then the expression **NOT A=B** will be evaluated by first evaluating **NOT A** and then comparing **NOT A** with **B**. If we wish to compare **A** with **B** *first*, then we must insert brackets: **NOT (A=B)**.

When comparing non-boolean expressions, an error may be registered at compile-time if the necessary brackets are not included. For example, if **A, B, C** and **D** are integers then the expression: **A=B AND C>=D** is wrong. The compiler will attempt to perform the operation **B AND C** *first*. Since **B** and **C** are integers, this does not make sense, and the compiler will register an error. The correct expression would be: **(A=B) AND (C>=D)**.

Write and Writeln

So far we have used **write** and **writeln** to output messages enclosed in inverted commas, and the values of integer variables. It is, however, possible to write more complex expressions *provided that they are of a suitable type*. Of the types which we have so far encountered, the char, boolean and integer types can be output using a **write** statement. It is not possible, however, to output the contents of a set.

Here are some examples of legal **write** and **writeln** statements:

```
write ('The price is : ', i, ' pounds and ',j, ' pence');
writeln ('Total expenditure = ',x=y=z);
writeln (i+4, j-3, k+7, i+j+k-24);
```

EXERCISES

1. Look at the following programs:

```
program sillymessage (input,output);
var
   choice:integer;
begin
writeln;
writeln ('Type in an integer from '0' to '3'.');
readln (choice);
if choice > 1
    then if choice <= 2
            then writeln ('Tea for two')
            else writeln ('Think Big!')
    else if choice < 1
            then writeln ('A nice round number!')
            else writeln ('Look after number 1!');
end.
```

What will be displayed on the screen in response to each of the inputs 0, 1, 2, 3? Now run the program and check your answer.

(Note the indentation of the program listing, which helps you to see which if, then and else delimiters go together. This does not make any difference to the compiler's interpretation of the program, but it makes the program much easier for mere human beings who want to know what is going on!)

2. Rewrite your shortlisting program to calculate scores according to the following rules:

   a) score 1 point for each year's programming experience, up to a maximum of 10.
   b) score 4 points for being under 35, or 2 points for being under 45.
   c) score a final total of zero for non-driver.

   Which question is it most sensible to ask first? Why?

*3. Add some further questions to your shortlisting program, so as to increase the number of possible scores. Then decide on a 'pass' score, which determines whether or not a candidate should be included in the shortlist. Modify your program to print out a message to say whether or not a particular candidate should be included.

(Hint: you will need to use a boolean expression involving the integer variable **score** and one of the operators > ('is greater than'), **>=** ('is greater than or equal to'), **<** ('is less than'), or **<=** ('is less than or equal to'). For example, you might use a condition such as: **score >= 15, score = 23**, or **score < 5** in an **if** statement.)

*4. Which of the following are correct boolean expressions, if **B1, B2, B3** are boolean variables, and **I1, I2, I3** are integer variables?
(i) **B1**   (ii) **B1 + B2**   (iii) **B1 AND I1 = 2**   (iv) **(I1 >= 4) OR (I1 < 1)**
(v) **(B1 = B2 AND (I1 = I2)** (vi) **(I1 <4) OR ((I2> = 6) AND (I3 < > 10)**
(vii) **NOT B3**

Evaluate each of the correct expressions when the variables concerned have the following values: **B1=true, B2=false, B3=false, I1=1, I2=6, I3=10**

4 Have Another Go

INTRODUCTION

In this chapter we will look at some shortcomings of the programs which
we wrote in Chapter 3, and amend them to make them more satisfactory
for the user. We will also discuss ways of improving the style of
programming so as to make the code more easy to understand.

NEW PASCAL FEATURES

1) **repeat...until**
2) Sets
3) Procedures

WHEN USERS DO THE WRONG THING

Let's have another look at the 'Happy Birthday' program from
Chapter 3:

```
program choice (input,output);
var
  ch : char;
begin
writeln;
writeln ('Is it your birthday today?');
writeln ('Type in "y" or "n"');
readln (ch);
if (ch = 'y') or (ch = 'Y')
  then writeln ('Happy Birthday')
  else writeln ('Goodbye')
end.
```

What happens if your finger slips when you are trying to type in y, and you enter u instead? Try it and see.

The fact that a program like this interprets any response other than 'yes' as a negative reply is even more of a problem in programs such as the shortlisting program (from Chapter 3), where it would be easy not to notice the mistake. Then a slip could result in an incorrect score being recorded, without the user being aware that anything was wrong.

This illustrates an important general point about writing any interactive program: you must always allow for users who attempt to use it incorrectly. Whenever a program asks for information to be entered, you should consider:

1) What constitutes the complete list of valid responses?
2) What other responses might the user enter? (Including unlikely or stupid responses. You must not assume that the user knows anything about computers or programming.)
3) What action do we want the program to take if an invalid response is entered?

Now let's look at the first two of these in the case of the 'Happy Birthday' program. It would be better if we had a definite 'no' answer to check the answer against, as well as checking for a 'yes' answer. You could then take appropriate action if an answer which is neither 'yes' nor 'no' is typed in. If we decide that the valid responses are: Y, y, N, and n, then the other possible responses comprise any other character whatever. So we can check the validity of a character by using the condition:

(ch = 'Y') or (ch = 'y') or (ch = 'N') or (ch = 'n')

This technique, of checking the validity of data before attempting to process it, is one which we shall want to use again and again.

It would be helpful to the user if we tell him what the complete list of valid responses is, by means of a message on the screen. He may also need to be reminded to press 'enter' after typing his response. So we will replace the statement:

writeln ('Type in "y" or "n"')   with:
writeln ('Type in "y"/"Y" or "n"/"N" then "enter"')

Now we will move on to our third consideration: *what should the program do* when an invalid character is typed in? In this, as in most interactive programs, it would be helpful if, after typing in an invalid character, we were given an opportunity to put right our mistake. It would be much better if the program returned to the point at which we had to type in our answer and allowed us to have another go ... and another ... and another ... until we type in something which the program can understand.

REPEAT ... UNTIL

We can instruct the computer to perform a sequence of statements *repeatedly until* a certain condition is satisfied by placing delimiters **repeat** and **until** before and after the sequence, and adding a boolean expression immediately after **until** to specify the required condition.

In our 'Happy Birthday' program, we want to repeat the sequence of statements concerned with asking for and receiving the answer to the question 'is it your birthday?' until the answer is one of: y, Y, n, N.

This is how it looks in Pascal:

```
repeat
  writeln ('Type in "y"/"Y" or "n"/"N" then "enter"');
  readln (ch);
until (ch = 'y') or (ch = 'Y') or (ch = 'n') or (ch ='N');
```

The syntax of the repeat loop is given in Figure 4.1.

This is an example of a *condition-controlled loop,* since the program 'loops' (ie performs a sequence of instructions over and over again) until a certain *condition* is satisfied.

Modify the 'Happy Birthday' program to include this loop, and then run it. Try typing in invalid characters and check that you are asked to enter a further character.

repeat...until construct

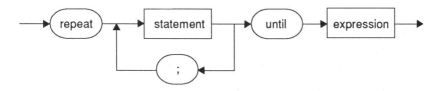

Figure 4.1

SIMPLIFYING THE CONDITION

We could modify the shortlisting program in a similar way, so as to allow each question to be repeated until a sensible answer is entered. But the condition

(ch = 'y') or (ch = 'Y') or (ch = 'n') or (ch = 'N')

would become very tedious to write out every time we wanted to ask a question. And what if we had a large number of 'sensible' answers to check for ? A condition such as:

(ch = 'a') or (ch = 'b') or (ch = 'c') or...or (ch = 'z')

would be very clumsy, and take a long time to type in.

In Pascal we can write exactly the same conditions like this:

ch in ['Y', 'y', 'N', 'n']   (for the former case) and
ch in ['a'.. 'z']   (for the latter case)

which are much shorter and neater.

Here we are checking whether the variable **ch** belongs to (is *in*) a particular *set* of characters. Don't worry if you came across sets in maths at school, and didn't understand them. All you need to know is that a set is a way of talking about a collection of items, all of the same type (the *base* type). So, a set of characters means a collection of characters, a set of integers means a collection of integers, and so on.

We are interested in a particular set of characters: the set consisting of the characters y, Y, n and N. In other words, the set of valid responses to our question. In Pascal we can express this set in the following way:

['y', 'Y', 'n', 'Y']

To find out whether the variable ch has the value of one of the members of this set, we need to find out whether the boolean expression:

ch in ['y', 'Y', 'n', 'N']

is **true** or **false.**

So, using sets whenever we wish to check the value of **ch**, we could change our 'Happy Birthday' program to:

program choice (input,output);
**   var ch : char;**

```
begin
writeln;
writeln ('Is it your birthday today?');
repeat
   writeln ('Type in "y"/"Y" or "n"/"N" then "enter"')
   readln (ch);                    N
until ch in ['y', 'Y', 'n', 'Y'];
if ch in ['y', 'Y']
   then writeln ('Happy Birthday')
   else writeln ('Goodbye')
end.
```

Try out this new version, and check that it does indeed behave in the same way as the previous one.

STRUCTURE DIAGRAMS

Although our 'Happy Birthday' program is very short and simple, we can now see that in writing it we have produced segments of code to perform three separate operations in turn:

1) Display question.
2) Accept answer.
3) Display reply.

The annotated listing below indicates which segment is which:

```
     program
     choice (input,output);
     var
           ch : char;
     begin
1)   writeln;
     writeln ('Is it your birthday today?');
     repeat
2)   writeln ('Type in "y"/"Y" or "n"/"N" then "enter"');
     readln (ch);
     until ch in ['y', 'Y', 'n', 'Y'];
3)   if ch in ['y', 'Y']   then writeln ('Happy Birthday')
                                else writeln ('Goodbye')
     end.
```

We can illustrate the three-part structure of this program using the diagram in Figure 4.2.

Structure diagram of happy birthday program

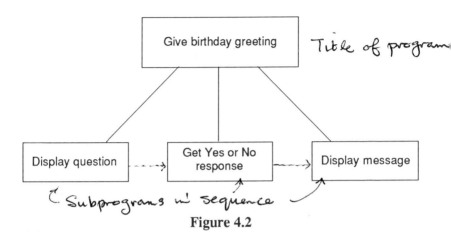

Figure 4.2

Diagrams of this kind are known as structure diagrams, because they describe the structure of a program. The lower line of boxes together give a more detailed description of the box to which they are linked above. Each box describes a sub-operation which forms part of the main operation described in the top box.

Note that the operations described in the boxes on the lower level are *not* operations which are to be performed *after* that described in the top box.

We will find it very useful, when considering more complex programming problems, to be able to divide an operation up into a number of more simple operations in this way. By refining a problem into a number of simpler sub-problems, it is possible to design a good overall structure for a program, before writing any code. We will, therefore, normally construct structure diagrams first, rather than making a diagram of a program which has already been written. Program design and the use of structure diagrams will be explored further in Chapter 5.

PROCEDURES

Section 2 of our program is illuminating, so we will now take a closer look at it:

```
repeat
  writeln ('Type in "y"/"Y" or "n"/"N" then "enter"');
  readln (ch);
until ch in ['y', 'Y', 'n', 'Y'];
```

This is a very useful piece of code. We can use it whenever we want to accept a 'yes' or 'no' answer to a question. We could use it lots of times, for example, in a program where we need to ask a number of such questions.

It is also an interesting piece of code, because it forms one of the three basic operations in our program design.

For reasons which will be discussed later, we will now use these lines of code to define a *procedure*. A procedure is like a smaller program within a main program. (We will not study procedures in depth at this stage. There will be more detailed discussion of them in later chapters.) In order to be able to use a procedure, it must be defined in the declaration section of our program. We can define this procedure using the following program segment:

```
procedure GetYesOrNo;
begin
repeat
  writeln ('Type in "y"/"Y" or "n"/"N" then "enter"');
  readln (ch);
until ch in ['y', 'Y', 'n', 'Y'];
end;
```

Once the procedure has been defined, we can execute this segment of code simply by *calling* the procedure **GetYesOrNo**. In order to call a procedure, we simply use its name (in this case 'GetYesOrNo') as a statement in the program. So our program can now be written:

```
program choice (input,output);
var
  ch : char;
procedure GetYesOrNo;
  begin
  repeat
    writeln ('Type in "y"/"Y" or "n"/"N" then "enter"');
    readln (ch);
  until ch in ['y', 'Y', 'n', 'Y'];
```

```
    end;
begin {main program}
writeln;
writeln ('Is it your birthday today?');
GetYesOrNo;
if ch in ['y', 'Y']then writeln ('Happy Birthday')
                  else writeln ('Goodbye')
end.
```

At first sight, introducing the procedure **GetYesOrNo** may appear to be making a perfectly simple and straightforward program unnecessarily complicated. However, there are a number of reasons why the use of procedures is desirable.

Remember the shortlisting program from Chapter 3? In that, we asked a number of questions, and each required a 'Yes' or 'No' answer. If we declare a procedure to accept the answer, we no longer need to repeat the same code many times. Try it for yourself. Define a procedure in the declaration section of your program. Then call the procedure each time you want to accept the answer to a question. The annotated listing below may help:

```
program shortlist (input,output);
var
  score : integer;
  ch : char;
  {Define a procedure to accept a 'Yes' or 'No' answer here}
begin
score := 0;
writeln;
writeln ('Programming experience > 5 yrs?');
readln (ch);
  {replace with call to your new procedure}
if (ch='y') or (ch='Y') then score := score + 3;
writeln;
writeln ('under 35?');
readln (ch);
  {replace with call to your new procedure}
if (ch='y') or (ch='Y') then score := + 2;
writeln;
writeln ('Car driver?');
```

```
readln (ch);
{replace with call to your new procedure}
if (ch='y') or (ch='Y') then score := score + 1;
writeln;
writeln ('Final score = ', score);
end.
```

(If you get stuck, there is a full listing of a suitable program in Appendix A, but try to do it yourself first.)

Now, suppose that at a later date we decide that we want to change the characters which we use for 'yes' and 'no' (to 'a' for 'affirmative' and 'n' for 'negative', say). We now no longer have to search through the whole program to find the parts which need to be changed. We can simply alter the procedure **GetYesOrNo**. And, however many times we may have called this procedure, once we have modified it the new version will be executed every time.

Another reason for using procedures concerns the 'readability' of programs. Computer programs, once written, often need to be modified to suit new requirements or to remove errors. Sometimes this will be done by someone other than the original writer, or after a long time interval. It may then be difficult for the person looking at the code to understand what is going on. A program listing is much easier to follow if the overall structure of the program is made clear in the way in which it is written.

In our 'Happy Birthday' example, the program will be more easily understood now that the three-part nature of its design is clearly evident. By choosing a meaningful name (GetYesOrNo – you may be able to think of a better one) for the procedure, we have made it easier for someone else to understand what the program does.

We could make the structure even more obvious (although, in a program as short and simple as this, it is hardly necessary) by defining separate procedures for *each* of the three sub-operations:

```
program choice (input,output);
var
  ch : char;
procedure GetYesOrNo;
  begin
  repeat
```

```
    writeln ('Type in "y"/"Y" or "n"/"N" then "enter"');
    readln (ch);
    until ch in ['y', 'Y', 'n', 'Y'];
    end;
  procedure AskQuestion;
    begin
    writeln;
    writeln ('Is it your birthday today?');
    end;
  procedure DisplayMessage;
    begin if ch in ['y', 'Y']  then writeln ('Happy Birthday')
                               else writeln ('Goodbye');
    end;
  begin  { main program }
  AskQuestion;
  GetYesOrNo;
  DisplayMessage;
  end.
```

The main body of the program now consists entirely of three procedure calls. And, as each procedure has a name which describes its job, it is very easy to understand what the program is designed to do.

Note

We could improve readability further by using a more meaningful name for the variable at present called **ch** (response, perhaps).

DOCUMENTATION

However readable a program may be, it is useful if additional documentation is made to accompany the source code. This should include details of what the program is designed to do and how this has been achieved. Any structure diagrams used in the design of the program should be retained, after the program has been written, for future reference. It would also be helpful to make a list of all the variable names, giving a brief explanation of what each variable is used for.

MORE ADVANCED TOPICS

More About Sets

Every set is a set of some base type. The *base* type may be any *ordinal type.* An ordinal type is one where it is possible to list all the values which a variable of that type could take.

The character type is ordinal, since the number of possible characters is typically 128 or 256.

The boolean type is also ordinal, as it takes only the two values 'true' and 'false'.

The integer type is also ordinal, since every Pascal implementation has some maximum value which an integer variable can take. (Pascal has a special name, *maxint,* for the largest integer which can be used.) In theory you could use a set containing any of the integers within the range available on your computer. In practice, however, there will almost certainly be some much smaller limit on the range of integers which can be used as elements of sets, and this will be imposed by your Pascal implementation. Turbo Pascal, for example, insists that any integers used as members of sets are from the range 0 to 255.

An example of a non-ordinal type is the standard type real. This type consists of all the 'real' numbers available on your particular computer system. Real numbers are simply any numbers which are not expressed as integers. Examples are: 1.5, −3.6, 10004.721. They are stored in different size memory spaces from those used for integers, so you must not attempt to copy real variables into integer variables or vice versa.

It is also possible to have variables which are sets, and these must be declared in the variable declaration section. At this stage we will only use sets whose elements are characters. They can be declared like this:

GoodChars: set of char;

To define the contents of a set we use a *set constructor*, which is a list of the elements of the set enclosed between square brackets. Here are some examples:

```
['y', 'Y', 'n', 'N']
[0, 1, 2, 3, 4, 5, 6, 7, 8, 9]   or, equivalently,
[0. .9]
['a'. .'z', 'A'. .'Z']
[]
```

As you can see, sets can be defined either by listing their elements, or by defining certain *subranges* of the base type. A subrange of integers is defined by giving the first and last numbers in the subrange. The set concerned then contains all the numbers between these two. In the case of characters, the only characters which are required by the ISO Pascal standard to appear in any particular order are the alphabetical and numerical characters. So we can only sensibly use subranges of characters from within one of the three subranges:

'a'. .'z'

'A''. .'Z'

'0'. .'9'   (Note that '0'. .'9' represents the *characters* '0' to '9', while 0. .9 would refer to their values as integers.)

There is also a special set, called the *empty set*, which has no elements. It is represented by empty square brackets: [].

The items within square brackets in a set constructor are not limited to numbers and characters. If x, y have been declared as integer variables, and c1,c2,c3 as char variables, then the following set constructors are valid:

[x,y] [c1] [x .. y] [x .. x+5] [y–x .. y] [c1,c2,c3] [c1,c2 .. c3] ['a'. . c2]

(Care must be taken, when using subranges, that the variables are listed in the correct order. If the value of x is *greater* than the value of y then the set [x .. y] will be empty. In this case, if you wish to include all the integers between x and y, you would need to use the set [y .. x].)

The general form of the set constructor is illustrated by the syntax diagram in Figure 4.3. Don't worry that you still do not know the general

set constructor

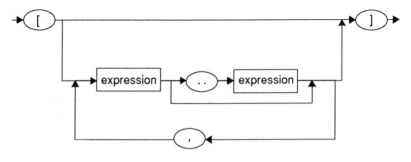

Figure 4.3

form of an *expression*, we will only be requiring extremely simple expressions at this stage.

We can assign a value to a variable of type **set of char** like this:

GoodChars := ['y', 'Y', 'N', 'n'];

We can use any set constructor, provided that all the elements of the set are characters.

EXERCISES

1. The structure diagram in Figure 4.4 describes the operations which need to be performed as part of a program for recording details of houses for an estate agency. We can further refine the operation 'Find how many bedrooms' as in Figure 4.5. Make similar diagrams to show how the other operations ('find how many reception rooms' and 'find how many bathrooms') can be refined.

2. The operation 'accept digit', from question 1, involves reading in a

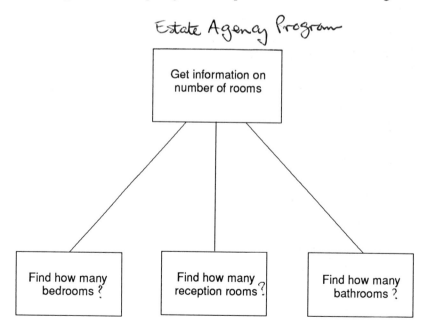

Figure 4.4

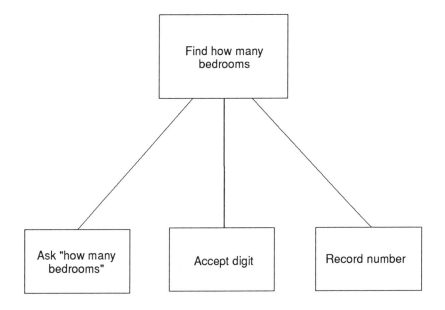

Figure 4.5

single character from the keyboard, and checking that it is a digit. Write a procedure to do this, using a repeat loop to allow invalid responses to be corrected.

*3. Consider the following program:

```
program OddOrEven (input,output);
var
  Digits,OddDigits: set of char;
  CharTypedIn:char;
procedure InitialiseSets;
  begin Digits := ['0'..'9'];
  OddDigits := ['1', '3', '5', '7', '9'];
  end;
procedure InputDigit;
  begin
  repeat
  writeln ('Type in a digit.');
  readln (CharTypedIn);
```

```
      until CharTypedIn in Digits;
      end;
   procedure CheckDigit;
      begin
      if CharTypedIn in OddDigits
        then writeln (CharTypedIn,' is odd')
        else writeln (CharTypedIn, ' is even')
      end;
   begin {main program}
   InitialiseSets;
   InputDigit;
   CheckDigit;
   end.
```

Look at each procedure in turn, and decide what it does. Make a list of the variables and explain what each is used for. Now look at the program as a whole. What will it do when you run it? Check your answer by typing in, compiling and running it.

*4. Using the program from exercise 3 to help you, write a program to determine whether a digit is larger or smaller than 5 and to display an appropriate message. (You will have to decide on an appropriate action to take when 5 is typed in.)

(Hint: use a set called GreaterThanFive)

5 What Would You Like To Do?

INTRODUCTION

In Chapter 3 we looked at a way of choosing between two courses of action, depending on information typed in at the keyboard. But suppose we need to be able to respond to something more complex than simple yes/no answers. In this chapter we will look at a way of making choices between more than two alternatives using a new construct, the case statement. We will then go on to discuss a particular class of interactive programs called 'menu-driven' programs, which require the ability to make such choices.

NEW PASCAL FEATURES

1) **case** statements
2) Compound statements

MAKING CHOICES IN PASCAL

Figure 5.1 represents an office block. Each suite of offices has a code-letter A,B,C, etc. Let us suppose that we are to write a program to help visitors to find the suite which they require, by giving the floor on which any particular suite can be found.

Our task can be split into two parts:

1) Input the code-letter of the suite required.
2) Determine which floor it is on, and print helpful directions accordingly.

Figure 5.2 shows how this can be represented as a structure diagram.

The process described in box 1 is a simple application of the methods

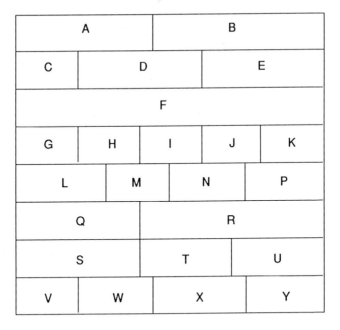

Figure 5.1

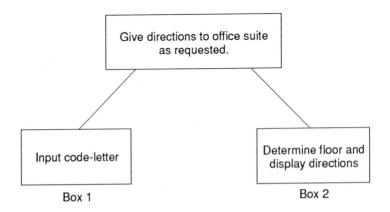

Figure 5.2

described in Chapter 4. We will need to declare a variable in which to store the code-letter which is typed in, and to define the set of valid letters. Box 2 is more interesting. We need a way of choosing between alternative courses of action, depending upon which code-letter has been entered.

Following this structure, we can begin to construct our program, leaving gaps to indicate procedures which have still to be completed:

```
program Directions (input,output);
var
   Code : char;
   ValidChars:set of char;
procedure GetCode;
   begin
   {need procedure to display options and read code-letter into variable
   Code}
   end;
procedure FindFloor;
   begin
   {need procedure to select a suitable message depending upon the
   value of Code}
   end;
begin
GetCode;
FindFloor;
end.
```

Try to fill in the missing lines in the procedure 'GetCode' for yourself. Remember to check that a valid code has been entered, and allow the user to try again if not. Try to compile the program with your procedure, and correct any syntax errors. Then try running it. It is often useful, when designing complex programs, to test portions of a program before completing the whole. Any mistakes which we may have made will be easier to find at this stage than it would be after the whole program has been completed.

Let us now look at the procedure 'FindFloor'. Our first problem is how to determine which floor a given suite of offices is on. This is simply a matter of inspecting the code-letter and comparing it with a list of code-letters for each floor. We then need to output a suitable message depending upon which list our code-letter belongs to.

Figure 5.3 shows how this choice can be represented in a structure diagram. The *selection* conditions are listed in boxes containing a circle. Each *selection* box is connected to a box below it, which gives details of the required operations. Later on we will meet examples where several boxes are connected beneath a selection box, in order to describe a more complex operation.

We could make this choice by using a series of **if** statements like this:

```
if code in ['A', 'B'] then ...
else if code in ['C', 'D', 'E'] then ...
    else if code = 'F' then ...
        else ...
```

However, this would be very tedious to write out. It would also be difficult to understand since it does not correspond well to the structure illustrated in Figure 5.3. Another drawback is concerned with the execution of the code generated by this construction. Suppose the user requires directions to suite Y. Before the required message can be displayed, no fewer than seven **if** statements must be executed! This means that it will take significantly longer to get directions to suites on the ground floor than on the seventh floor. And if the office block were higher, the delay in finding suites on the ground floor would be even greater.

We can avoid these problems by using a **case** statement:

```
case code of
    'A', 'B'                    :writeln ('Floor 7.');
    'C', 'D', 'E'               :writeln ('Floor 6.');
    'F'                         :writeln ('Floor 5.');
    'G', 'H', 'I', 'J', 'K'     :writeln ('Floor 4.');
    'L', 'M', 'N', 'P'          :writeln ('Floor 3.');
    'Q', 'R'                    :writeln ('Floor 2.');
    'S', 'T', 'U'               :writeln ('Floor 1.');
    'V', 'W', 'X', 'Y'          :writeln ('Ground Floor');
end;
```

When we use a **case** statement, we first identify an *expression* (in this case simply the variable **code**) whose value will determine which option we must take. We then list all the possible values which this expression *might* take, and group them according to which option each indicates. Then we define the action to be taken in each case using a single

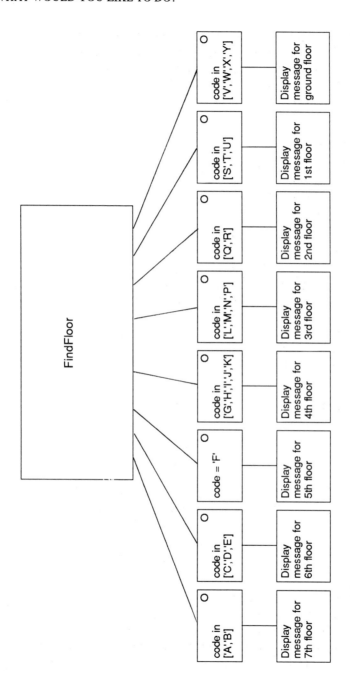

Figure 5.3

statement (in this case a **writeln** statement). This is easier to follow than a series of **if** statements, since the various alternatives are listed in a logical way, together with the appropriate responses. At run time, the code executed for each alternative in a **case** statement will be of equal length, so there will not be delays when certain options are chosen.

Here are some more examples of case statements:

i) **case DayNumber of**
```
    1: writeln ('Sunday');
    2: writeln ('Monday');
    3: writeln ('Tuesday');
    4: writeln ('Wednesday');
    5: writeln ('Thursday');
    6: writeln ('Friday');
    7: writeln ('Saturday');
end;
```
ii) **case DayNumber of**
```
    1, 7: writeln ('Weekend');
    2: writeln ('Monday');
    3: writeln ('Tuesday');
    4: writeln ('Wednesday');
    5: writeln ('Thursday');
    6: writeln ('Friday');
end;
```
iii) **case digit of**
```
    '1': int := 1;
    '2': int := 2;
    '3': int := 3;
    '4': int := 4;
    '5': int := 5;
    '6': int := 6;
    '7': int := 7;
    '8': int := 8;
    '9': int := 9;
    '0': int := 0;
end;
```

The general form of the **case** statement is shown in Figure 5.4.

We are now ready to fill in the gaps in our office directions program:

case statement

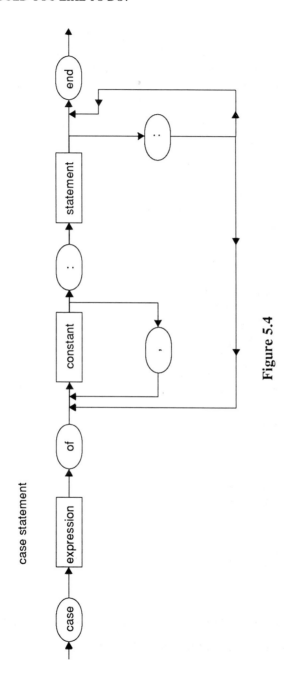

Figure 5.4

```
program Directions (input,output);
var
  Code : char;
  ValidChars:set of char;
procedure GetCode;
  begin
  ValidChars := ['A'. .'Y'];
  repeat
    writeln ('Please enter code letter.');
    readln (Code)
  until Code in ValidChars
  end;
procedure FindFloor;
  begin
  case code of
      'A', 'B'                 :writeln ('Floor 7.');
      'C', 'D', 'E'            :writeln ('Floor 6.');
      'F'                      :writeln ('Floor 5.');
      'G', 'H', 'I', 'J', 'K'  :writeln ('Floor 4.');
      'L', 'M', 'N', 'P'       :writeln ('Floor 3.');
      'Q', 'R'                 :writeln ('Floor 2.');
      'S', 'T', 'U'            :writeln ('Floor 1.');
      'V', 'W', 'X', 'Y'       :writeln ('Ground Floor');
  end;
  end;
begin
GetCode;
FindFloor;
end.
```

CHECKING FOR VALID EXPRESSIONS IN A CASE STATEMENT

Whenever a **case** statement is used it is important to make sure that we have listed all the values which our expression might take. If it happens that the expression takes a value which is not included then an error will occur when we run the program. In this particular example there is no danger that the variable 'code' will take any value other than those listed, since the procedure 'GetCode' only accepts valid code-letters. If no such checking has been done, it is often advisable to include a check before a **case** statement. For example:

```
if DayNumber in [1..7] then
  case DayNumber of
    1,7: writeln ('Weekend');
    2:   writeln ('Monday');
    3:   writeln ('Tuesday');
    4:   writeln ('Wednesday');
    5:   writeln ('Thursday');
    6:   writeln ('Friday');
  end
else writeln ('Error in DayNumber');
```

Note

Some Pascal implementations include a very convenient addition to the ISO standard, which enables programmers to avoid this problem by including a final category covering all unlisted values. For example, in Turbo Pascal we could write:

```
case DayNumber of
  1,7: writeln ('Weekend');
  2: writeln ('Monday');
  3: writeln ('Tuesday');
  4: writeln ('Wednesday');
  5: writeln ('Thursday');
  6: writeln ('Friday');
  else writeln ('Error in DayNumber');
end;
```

THE COMPOUND STATEMENT

Now let us get back to our office-directions program. We said in our plan that we should give 'helpful directions'. So far, our response is informative, but perhaps a little brief. Suppose that we wish to produce a message such as:

The office you require is on the seventh floor.
You are recommended to take the lift.
Take the corridor on your left, and continue
through the fire doors. The lift is located
on the left.

This can be done using a series of **writeln** statements; but in a **case** statement we are only allowed one statement to describe each alternative course of action. One possible solution would be to define a separate procedure for each message, and to replace the single **writeln** statements with procedure calls, like this:

```
case code of
  'A', 'B'                 : Message7;
  'C', 'D', 'E'            : Message6;
  'F'                      : Message5;
  'G', 'H', 'I', 'J', 'K'  : Message4;
  'L', 'M', 'N', 'P'       : Message3;
  'Q', 'R'                 : Message2;
  'S', 'T', 'U'            : Message1;
  'V', 'W', 'X', 'Y'       : MessageGround;
end;
```

However, this will increase the size of our source program significantly. So are these additional procedures really desirable? Let's look back for a moment at the reasons for using procedures, which we discussed in Chapter 4. They were:

1) In order to re-use segments of code.
2) In order to improve the readability of our program.

In this instance each procedure will be called only once, and the use of the **case** statement for selecting alternative messages already makes the program easy to follow.

So, instead of a procedure call, we will use a compound statement. This is simply a way of grouping a number of statements together, in place of a single statement. To do this we put the reserved word begin before the first statement, and end after the last statement. Here are some examples:

```
i)   if ch in ['y', 'Y'] then
       begin
       score := score + 1;
       writeln ('score so far = ', score);
       end;
ii)  case DayNumber of
     1: writeln ('There are no trains on Sundays');
     2, 3, 4, 5, 6: begin
                    writeln ('Trains on weekdays are at');
                    writeln ('06   15   42');
                    writeln ('minutes past the hour,');
```

```
            writeln ('commencing at 0706');
            writeln ('and finishing at 2315');
            end;
7:    begin
      writeln ('Trains on Saturdays are as for weekdays');
      writeln ('but commencing at 0742');
      writeln ('and finishing at 2242');
      end;
```

Figure 5.5 shows the syntax of a compound statement.

While compound statements are very useful, we should be wary of using them indiscriminately. It is always worth considering whether or not a procedure call would be more appropriate. Defining a procedure to perform a task is more time-consuming in the short term, but may be very worthwhile in the long run, particularly if the same task has to be performed more than once in a program. Compound statements containing more than a few statements within them can make a program difficult to follow, especially if they contain structures such as if statements repeat loops etc, perhaps themselves containing compound statements!

So, before using a compound statement, ask yourself: am I going to want to use this code again? Would my program be more easy to understand if I used a procedure with a meaningful name? If the answer to either of these questions is 'yes' then a procedure is preferable.

You should now be able to modify the office-directions program to give full instructions for reaching each floor of the building. Use your imagination to supply helpful suggestions. Perhaps it would be useful to define two procedures, one giving instructions for finding the lift, and

Compound statement

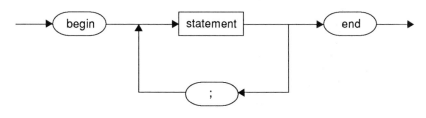

Figure 5.5

the other giving directions to the stairs. These instructions could then easily be displayed whenever the required office is situated upstairs.

MENU-DRIVEN PROGRAMS

These are a particular class of interactive programs, which allow the user to make choices as to which of the facilities provided he wishes to use. A 'menu' of choices is displayed on the screen together with instructions for choosing each option.

For example, when we use an ATM computer terminal to get information about our bank account we are given a menu to choose from, such as:

REQUEST CURRENT BALANCE
REQUEST STATEMENT
WITHDRAW CASH
DEPOSIT CASH
RETURN CARD

After selecting an option from the menu, the user may be given further choices until he has completed the tasks which he requires. The fact that all the alternative courses of action are displayed on the screen at each stage make these programs particularly easy to use. For this reason they are becoming increasingly widely used, since they do not require trained operators.

Now let us look at the design of a simple menu-driven program. Suppose we want the user to be able to find the address or telephone number of one of his friends from a list. We could display the list of names on the screen. When a name has been chosen, he could be offered the choice of either address or telephone number.

We can, therefore, split up our program into three parts:

1) Input name.
2) Input choice of address/telephone number.
3) Determine the result and display this information.

This is illustrated as a structure diagram in Figure 5.6.

For simplicity, we will limit ourselves at this stage to a list of only three names:

A. N. Other of 1, Somewhere Street, Anytown, tel. 12345;

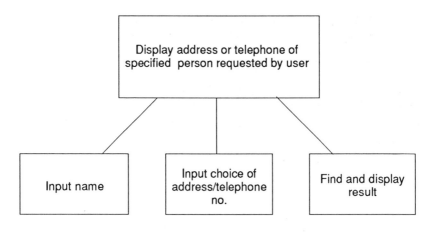

Figure 5.6

N. O. One of 144, NoWhere Avenue, Nothingville, tel. 54321;
and Y. E. T. Another of 73 Elsewhere Lane, tel. 24680.

The first two parts are simple applications of the techniques which we explored in previous chapters. You should be able to write procedures corresponding to boxes 1 and 2 in Figure 5.6. They could, for example, be called **NameMenu** and **AorTMenu**.

NameMenu would:

1) Produce the following screen display:

> **Which name do you require?**
> **(1) A. N. Other**
> **(2) N. O. One**
> **(3) Y. E. T. Another**
> **Enter the number of the name you require.**

2) Input the result of this enquiry and store the result in a **char** variable.

AorTMenu would:

1) Produce the following screen display:

> **Do you require the address or telephone number?**
> **Enter 'A' for address or 'T' for telephone.**

2) Input this result and store it in another **char** variable.

The task of finding and displaying the correct result is a little more complex. We need to select the correct response depending upon the information input by procedures **NameMenu** and **AorTMenu**. It will be easiest to do this in two stages:

first select according to name
then select according to whether the address or telephone number is required.

Figure 5.7 shows how the selection process can be described using a structure diagram.

The choice of name can best be done using a **case** statement. When it comes to the choice between address or telephone number, however, we could equally well use an **if** statement. Usually when we have a choice between only two alternatives it is appropriate to use an **if** rather than a **case** statement. But in this instance it is possible that we may want to widen the choice later to allow the selection of other personal details. If we use a **case** statement it will be easy to amend the menu to include other items.

Assuming that the choices are stored in variables called **NameCode** and **AorT**, the following procedure could be used:

```
procedure ShowResult;
begin
case NameCode of
    '1' : case AorT of
        'A' : begin
                writeln ('1, Somewhere Street');
                writeln ('Anytown');
                end;
        'T' : writeln ('12345');
        end;
    '2' : case AorT of
        'A' : begin
                writeln ('144, Nowhere Avenue');
                writeln ('Nothingville');
                end;
        'T' : writeln ('54321');
        end;
```

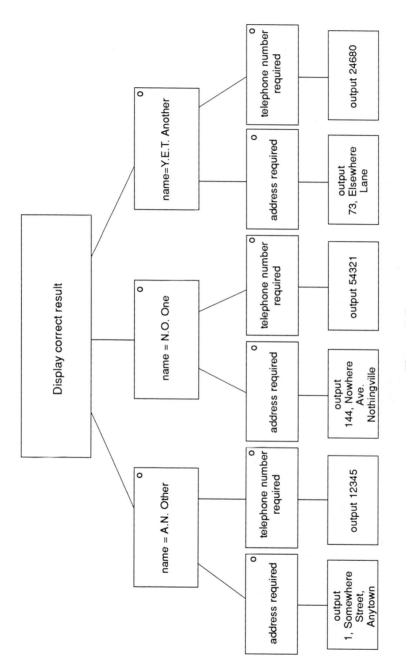

Figure 5.7

```
        '3' : case AorT of
                'A' : writeln ('73, Elsewhere Lane');
                'T' : writeln ('24680');
                    end;
    end;
    end;
```

Note the optional indentation of the statements within each **case** statement, which helps us to see easily where each **case** begins and ends.

Try to complete the program using this procedure in conjunction with your own procedures for displaying the choices and inputting the results. (Take care that you do not allow incorrect values of **NameCode** or **AorT** to be used in the **case** statements.) When you have a working version, find a friend (preferably one who is unfamiliar with computers) to try it out for you. Does he find it easy to know what to do? – and hard to produce run-time errors? Perhaps the procedure **ShowResult** should be modified to allow lower-case as well as capital A and T to be input?

A working version of this program is included in Appendix A.

EXERCISES

1. Amend the office-directions program to allow both upper- and lower-case letters to be accepted.

2. Write a program which inputs alphabetic characters (upper- or lower-case) and outputs the equivalent upper-case character.

3. Write a procedure to convert a single digit typed in at the keyboard (read in as a character) into its integer equivalent, and stores the result in an integer variable. Use this procedure to write a program which will add two digits and display the result.

4. Look at the following program. Try to decide what it is designed to do. Test your answer by compiling and running it.

```
    program Calculator (input,output);
    var
        DigChar, OpChar : char;
        Digits,Operations : Set of char;
        ThisInt,Total : integer;
        Finished : boolean;
    procedure InitSets;
```

```
  {initialises set of valid character}
    begin
    Digits := ['1'..'9', '='];
    Operations := ['+', '−', '*', '='];
    end;
procedure GetDigit;
  {reads in a digit}
    begin
    repeat
      readln (DigChar)
    until DigChar in Digits;
    case DigChar of
      '0': ThisInt := 0;
      '1': ThisInt := 1;
      '2': ThisInt := 2;
      '3': ThisInt := 3;
      '4': ThisInt := 4;
      '5': ThisInt := 5;
      '6': ThisInt := 6;
      '7': ThisInt := 7;
      '8': ThisInt := 8;
      '9': ThisInt := 9;
      '=': Finished := true;
  end;
  end;
procedure GetOp;
  {reads in an arithmetic operation}
    begin
    repeat
      readln (Opchar);
    until OpChar in Operations;
    if OpChar = '=' then Finished := true;
    end;
procedure Calc;
  {performs calculations until '=' entered}
    begin
      {initialise variables}
    finished := false;
    Total := 0;
    OpChar := '+';
```

```
        {read in characters until "="}
      repeat
        GetDigit;
        If not finished then
          begin
          case OpChar of
            '+':Total := Total + ThisInt;
            '-':Total := Total - ThisInt;
            '*':Total := Total * ThisInt;
          end;
          writeln ('Total so far = ', Total);
          GetOp;
          end;
    until finished; {"=" has been entered}
    writeln;
    writeln;
    writeln ('Final total = ', Total);
    end;
  begin
  InitSets;
  Calc;
  end.
```

5. An estate agent requires a program which will allow him to keep records of each of the houses which he is selling, giving details of the accommodation provided. He needs to be able to:

i)   add new houses to the list;
ii) remove houses from the list;
iii) get a list of all the houses which satisfy certain criteria entered from the keyboard.

Draw a structure diagram illustrating how this could be implemented as a menu-driven program with three options on the main menu.

Using this structure, write a program with dummy procedures (ie just the name and **begin** and **end**) corresponding to the boxes on the lower level of your diagram. (Don't worry that you do not yet know how to fill in all the procedures.)

Complete the procedure which displays the main menu and inputs the user's choice of operations.

6 Making the Grade

INTRODUCTION

So far we have only been able to deal with single characters or numbers. It is often convenient to group characters together, in order to manipulate whole words or sentences easily. We may also wish to make lists or tables of numbers, such as the examination scores of a group of students or the prices of items in a shop.

In this chapter we will write a program to store a list of examination marks and to calculate the grade which corresponds to each mark.

NEW PASCAL FEATURES

1) Array types
2) Local variables
3) The **succ** and **pred** operators.

STORING TABLES OF INTEGERS

Suppose that we wish to be able to type in a list of the examination scores of candidates (up to a maximum of 30 candidates), which will then be converted to a grade for each candidate and the result displayed on the screen, with the highest grades listed first and lowest grades last.

This task can be described using the structure diagram in Figure 6.1. Using this structure, we can make a tentative start on our program, leaving gaps where we need to fill in code:

```
program ListGrade (input,output);
var
   {declare variables to hold the marks and grades}
```

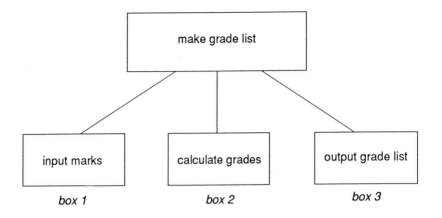

Figure 6.1

```
procedure Inmarks;
   begin
   {input the marks}
   end;
procedure CalcGrades;
   begin
   {calculate grades according to marks attained}
   end;
procedure OutGrades;
   begin
   {output candidate numbers and grades in grade order}
   end;
begin {main program}
Inmarks;
CalcGrades;
OutGrades;
end.
```

Let us look first at the process described in box 1 of Figure 6.1. We need to input each mark and store it in an appropriate variable, ready to be processed. This technique of performing a task repeatedly is known as *iteration*. Figure 6.2 shows the structure diagram for the iteration required to input the marks. The box with a star in the corner contains

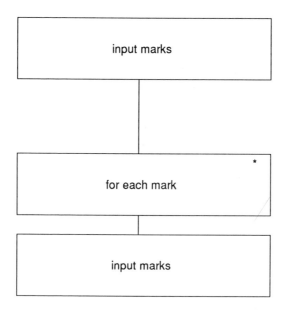

Figure 6.2

instructions concerning how many times the iteration is to be performed. The box below it gives details of the process which is to be iterated.

Now we can start to fill in the code for the procedure **InMarks**. We will assume that each candidate can be identified by an integer between 1 and 30. It will help the user if he is prompted for each mark by a message such as:

Enter mark for candidate 1.

We already know how to display such a message on the screen.

Pascal allows integers to be read in using a **readln** statement, such as:

readln (mark);

where **mark** has been declared as a variable of type integer. It is important that the user enters a valid combination of characters (ie a combination which is recognisable to the compiler as an integer). Otherwise a run-time error will occur and the program will be aborted.

So now we can write code to input a single mark and store it in an integer variable. We need to be able to repeat this operation for each candidate. Our first problem is where to store the marks. We could declare 30 separate integer variables and use 30 separate **readln** statements to read a mark into each of them; but this would be very tedious. And suppose we had a list not of 30 but of a 1000 candidates? To get round this difficulty, we need to declare a variable of an array type.

ARRAY TYPE VARIABLES

We will declare a single *array* variable to hold the examination marks of all 30 candidates. We will use the following declaration in the variable declaration section of our program:

> **MarkList: array [1..30] of integer;**

The compiler will then allocate enough space in the memory to store 30 integers. The individual integers (known as the *elements* of the array) are associated with the *index* numbers from 1 to 30. We can access a single element of the array by using its index enclosed in square brackets after the name of the array. For example:

MarkList [1] := 0;	puts the value 0 into the first element of **MarkList**
readln (MarkList [24]);	inputs an integer from the keyboard and puts its value into the 24th element of **MarkList**
MarkList [i] := j;	inputs the value of the integer variable **j** into the ith element of **MarkList**

Here is a working version of **InMarks**. It illustrates a number of points concerning the handling of array variables, which are discussed below.

```
procedure InMarks;
  var
    i : integer;
  begin
  writeln ('Enter the marks for each candidate.');
  writeln ('Enter -1 to end.');
  writeln;
  i := 1;
  repeat
    writeln ('enter the mark for candidate ',i,
             ' or -1 to end');
```

```
    readln (MarkList [i]);
    i := i+1;
until (i=31) or (MarkList [i]=-1);
end;
```

INDEXING ARRAYS

We need to be able to select each element of **MarkList** in turn, starting with the first and going on until the user indicates that the last candidate's number has been reached. To do this we use the integer variable **i** to *index* the array. This means that to select a particular element of **MarkList**, we make **i** equal to the number of the element we require, and then select the ith element.

In this case, we set **i** equal to 1 before we start to read in the list of marks. After each mark is entered, **i** is incremented by 1. The process of reading in a mark and then incrementing **i** is repeated until the end of the list is reached.

Arrays do not have to be indexed by integers. The following array declarations illustrate how arrays with char or boolean indices could be declared:

Cypher : array ['a'..'z'] of char;
AddOn : array [false..true] of integer;

Care must be taken to ensure that the subrange which determines the size of the array is defined correctly. The 'lower' or 'earlier' of the two bounds must be listed first. For example, **array [false..true]** or **array [1..5]** are correct since the boolean value false is defined to have a lower 'ordinal value' than true. An attempt to declare a variable of type **array [true..false] of integer** or **array [5..1] of integer**, would produce an error at compile-time.

LOCAL VARIABLES

You will have noticed that the *index* variable, **i**, was declared not in the declarative section at the top of the *program*, but in a variable declaration within the procedure **Inmarks** itself. Variables which are declared *within* a procedure are referred to as being *local* to that procedure. Such variables can only be referred to in statements within the procedure in which they are declared. For example, if we were to attempt to use **i** in the main body of this program, the compiler would report an error indicating that an undeclared identifier was being used.

There are three main reasons for using local rather than global (ie declared in the main declarative section at the head of the program) variables:

1) Space-saving

At run time global variables occupy space in the memory for the entire time that the program is running. Local variables, however, have space allocated to them only when the procedure in which they are declared is entered. On leaving a procedure, the space allocated to local variables is released. So the use of local variables can significantly reduce the amount of memory used in running a program.

2) Safety

When a variable is required for a specific purpose in a particular procedure, it is advantageous to declare it within that procedure. This helps to avoid mistakes which occur when the same variable is re-used for a variety of different tasks in different procedures. It is difficult to trace a problem involving a global variable whose value may be altered in a number of different procedures during the course of execution of a program.

3) Readability

Locally declared identifiers help to make a program more easily understood. It is easier to see what a variable is used for if it is declared within the procedure in which it will be used. And if modifications to the program are necessary at a later stage, there is no danger that changing the value of a local variable will cause unexpected side-effects on other sections of the program.

USING 'ROGUE' VALUES TO TERMINATE A LIST

We want to know when the list of marks is complete. To do this we ask the user to type in a value which we know cannot possibly be a correct mark – a 'rogue' value. This is a standard technique, which we will often find useful.

CHECKING THE RANGE OF AN ARRAY INDEX

In this case, we have been told that the maximum number of marks will be 30. However, it would be unwise to rely on this. The users of computer programs frequently fail to follow their own rules! So, when we check for the end of the list at the end of the repeat loop, we also check to see whether the number of marks entered has reached 30 (ie whether we are preparing to read in mark number 31).

This is important, since we have only allocated enough space to hold an array of 30 marks. If we try to assign a value to element 31 of **MarkList** we will either (if we are lucky) produce a run time error, or (if we are unlucky) alter the value of whatever item has been allocated the next memory space beyond **MarkList**. This would have totally unpredictable consequences! Whether we are lucky or unlucky here depends on the sophistication of our compiler error checking at run time.

So, whenever we use a variable to index an array, we must take care never to allow that variable to take a value outside the range stated in the array declaration. In our program, this means keeping i with the range 1...30 whenever it is to be used to index **MarkList**.

TESTING AN INDIVIDUAL PROCEDURE

We can now test **InMarks** by running the program, leaving the other procedures as dummies. Try entering different values and different numbers of marks. In particular, test the extreme cases of an empty list and a list of a full 30 marks. Test that the repeat loop does indeed terminate if more than 30 marks are entered. Thorough testing of each part of the program as it is written will help to avoid errors later on.

IMPROVING THE DESIGN OF OUR PROGRAM

When we look at the processes described in boxes 2 and 3 of Figure 6.1, we discover that they each require a task to be iterated (see Figure 6.3).

Now let us look carefully at the boxes describing the process for inputting the marks and the boxes for calculating the grades. In both cases we have an iteration which must be performed *for each mark entered*. This means that, if we follow our present plan, we will go through the list of marks twice during the execution of our program. Once to input the marks, and then again to calculate the corresponding grade for each mark. It would be more efficient if we were to input each mark and calculate the corresponding grade at the same time.

In view of this, it would be sensible to combine the processes of inputting marks and calculating grades so as to perform the iteration only

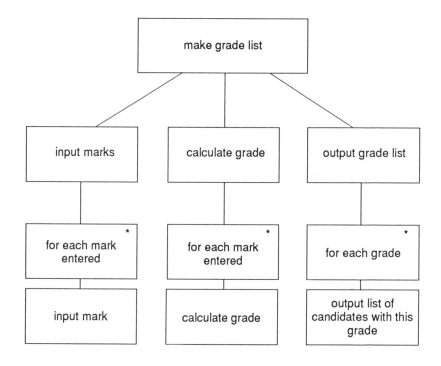

Figure 6.3

once. Figure 6.4 shows the modified structure diagram. This illustrates an important point concerning program design. It is sometimes the case that our initial refinement of a task does not lead to the best way of performing that task. In this case, we *separated* two processes which are better done together. We were alerted to this problem by seeing the two *iteration* boxes which contained *the same instructions*. Had we not decided to alter our plan, our program would have contained code which was duplicated in the procedures **InMarks** and **CalcGrades**.

Using our revised design, our program looks like this:

```
program ListGrade (input,output);
var                 {declare variables to hold the grades}
  MarkList : array [1..30] of integer;
procedure CalcGrades;
  var
    i : integer;
```

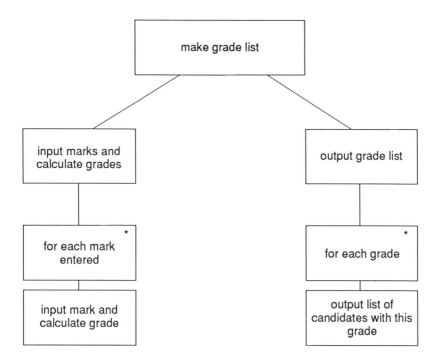

Figure 6.4

```
  begin
  writeln ('Enter the marks for each candidate.');
  writeln ('Enter –1 to end.');
  writeln;
  i := 1;
  repeat
     writeln ('enter the mark for candidate ',i, ' or –1 to end');
     readln (MarkList [i]);
  {calculate grade according to mark attained}
     i := i+1;
  until (i=31) or (MarkList [i–1]=–1);
  end;
procedure OutGrades;
  begin
  {output candidate numbers and grades in grade order}
  end;
```

```
begin
CalcGrades;
OutGrades;
end.
```

CALCULATING THE GRADES

We will use the following rules for calculating grades (assuming whole numbers only are allowed:

grade 'A' for marks above 80%,
grade 'B' above 55% and below 81%,
grade 'C' above 40% and below 56%,
grade 'D' above 25% and below 41%,
grade 'E' below 26%.

We will need to store the grade for each candidate, once it has been calculated. The most satisfactory way of doing this is to declare an array of characters indexed by the candidate numbers. The grades will be put into this array by **CalcGrades**. The array will also be used by **OutGrades** to find the list of candidates having each grade. So we will declare a global variable, **GradeList**, of type **array [1..30] of char**.

The simplest way to determine the grade for each candidate will be to use a series of **if** statements:

if MarkList [i] >80 then GradeList [i] := 'A'
else if MarkList [i] >55 then GradeList [i] := 'B'
else if MarkList [i] >40 then GradeList [i] := 'C'
else if MarkList [i] >25 then GradeList [i] := 'D'
else GradeList [i] := 'E';

You should now be able to complete the procedure **CalcMarks**.

NESTING ITERATED PROCESSES

We will now look at the process described in box 3 of Figure 6.1. We have already refined it (see Figure 6.3) into an iteration, repeating, *for each grade,* the process of outputting the list of candidates with that grade. But how do we go about making each list? A simple way of doing this is to look through the list of candidates checking each to see if he has scored the required grade. In other words, we are performing *another* iteration, this time *for each candidate.* Figure 6.5 shows how this can be

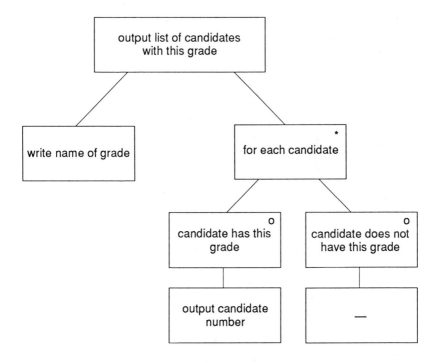

Figure 6.5

represented in a structure diagram. Note the empty box beneath the selection box containing 'candidate does not have this grade'. This is to show that no action is to be taken in this case.

We can now complete our program:

```
program ListGrade (input,output);
var
   MarkList : array [1..30] of integer;
   GradeList : array [1..30] of char;
   Lastcand : integer;
procedure CalcGrades;
   {reads in marks and determines grades}
      var
        i : integer;
      begin
```

```
writeln ('Enter the marks for each candidate.');
writeln ('Enter –1 to end.');
writeln;
i := 1;
repeat
  writeln ('Enter the mark for candidate ',i,' or –1 to end');
  readln (MarkList [i]);
  if MarkList [i] >80 then GradeList [i] := 'A'
  else if MarkList [i] >55 then GradeList [i] := 'B'
        else if MarkList [i] >40 then GradeList [i] := 'C'
              else if MarkList [i] >25 then GradeList [i] := 'D'
                    else GradeList [i] := 'E';
  i := i+1;
until (i=31) or (MarkList [i–1]=–1);
LastCand := i–1;
end;
procedure OutGrades;
{outputs candidates with each grade}
  var
    Grade : char;
    Cand : integer;
  begin
  Grade := 'A';
  repeat
    writeln;
    writeln ('Grade ', Grade);
    writeln;
    Cand := 1;
    repeat
      if GradeList [Cand] = Grade then writeln ('candidate ',
      cand);
      Cand := Cand + 1;
    until Cand > LastCand;
    Grade := Succ(Grade);
  until Grade > 'E'
  end;
begin
CalcGrades;
OutGrades;
end.
```

THE SUCC AND PRED OPERATORS

In order to look at each grade in turn, we have made use of the operator **succ**. This is an operator which can be used on any *ordinal* type (such as char, integer, boolean). **Succ (grade)** simply means 'the next character after grade'. Similarly, if we wished to find the character *preceding* **grade**, we could use the operator **pred**. In the case of integers, **succ (i)** is equivalent to **i+1**, and **pred (i)** is equivalent to **i–1**.

KEEPING INFORMATION FOR USE IN A LATER PROCEDURE

Note the global variable **LastCand**, which we have declared to store the index to the final mark entered (ie the actual number of candidates). This is necessary, since we need to know how many entries in the array of grades must be checked. **LastCand** is assigned a value in procedure **CalcGrades**. Think carefully about why it is given the value **i–1** and not **i**. If you are unsure then work through an example on a scrap of paper. In Chapters 9 and 10 we will look at other ways of passing information from one procedure to another.

MORE ADVANCED TOPICS

Array Indices

The index to an array can be of *any* ordinal type. (Ordinal types are described in the "more advanced" section of Chapter 4.) An array *cannot* be indexed by any non-ordinal type, since each value which the index can take corresponds to an element of the array. So it must be possible to list the values which an array index could take. This is only possible if the index is of ordinal type. For example, the type declaration

   RealIndexArray : array [1.5 .. 2.4]

is illegal, since the real numbers between 1.5 and 2.4 cannot be listed.

Arrays of Arrays

Suppose that the candidates in our previous example had taken a number (three, say) of separate examinations, each of which must be taken into account when determining their final grade. The marks might be recorded in a table, such as in Figure 6.6.

candidate number	paper 1	paper 2	paper 3
1	80%	67%	43%
2	56%	32%	77%
3	42%	74%	19%
4	95%	89%	78%
5	2%	15%	11%
6	64%	35%	71%

Figure 6.6

We could store the marks for each candidate in an array of integers, such as this:

var
    CandMark : array [1..3] of integer;

We can represent this array by the diagram in Figure 6.7. Each small box represents the space to store an integer value. The numbers above the boxes are their indices.

In order to deal with the marks scored by the whole group of candidates, we can declare an array, each of whose elements is an array such as that declared above:

var
    MarkList : array [1..30] of array [1..3] of integer;

array[1..3] of integer

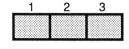

Figure 6.7

This array can be represented by Figure 6.8. The array **MarkList** is then made up of 30 elements, represented by rectangular boxes. Each of these elements is itself made up of three integer elements, represented by square boxes.

array[1..30] of array[1..30] of integer

Figure 6.8

Let us suppose that the grades are to be allocated according to the following rules:

1) For each candidate the average score over the three papers must be calculated, and then this will be used to determine the grade.
2) No candidate may gain a grade higher than 'C' if he has scored below 20% on any paper, regardless of his scores on other papers.

To find the average score we need to find the total of the scores on all three papers and then divide by 3. It will be sensible to keep a running total for each candidate as his marks are entered. We can then perform the division before calculating the grade as before. A new portion of code must be added to check whether or not the grade must be reduced because of poor performance on a single paper. Here is a modified version of **CalcGrades**:

```
procedure CalcGrades;
    var
```

```
    i, j, AverageMark, TotalMark : integer;
   begin
   writeln ('Enter the marks for each candidate.');
   writeln ('Enter –1 to end.');
   writeln;
   i := 1;
 {read in marks for each candidate}
   repeat
     j := 1;
     TotalMark := 0;
   {read in marks for each paper and calculate total}
     repeat
       writeln ('Enter the mark for candidate ',i,' in paper ',j);
       if j = 1 then writeln (' or –1 to end');
       readln (MarkList [i,j]);
       TotalMark := TotalMark + MarkList [i,j];
       if MarkList [i,j] < 20 then TooLow := true;
       j := j+1;
     until (j > 3) or (MarkList [i,1]=–1);
     AverageMark := TotalMark div 3;
     if AverageMark > 80 then GradeList [i] := 'A'
     else if AverageMark > 55 then GradeList [i] := 'B'
         else if AverageMark > 40 then GradeList [i] := 'C'
             else if AverageMark > 25 then GradeList [i] := 'D'
                 else GradeList [i] := 'E';
     if (MarkList [i,1] < 20) or (MarkList [i,2] < 20) or (MarkList
       [i,3] < 20) then
       if GradeList [i] < 'C' then GradeList [i] := 'C';
     i := i+1;
   until (i=31) or (MarkList [i–1,1] =–1);
   LastCand := i–1;
   end;
```

Indexing an Array of Arrays

In order to select a simple element from our array of arrays we need two indices. The first index selects an array of 3 integers from our array of arrays. The second index selects a single integer from this array of 3. Look back at Figure 6.8 to see how this works. Thus:

– **MarkList [1]** denotes the top row, an array of 3 integers, while

– **MarkList [1,1]** denotes the top left, an integer element of the array.

Since **MarkList [1]** is itself an array, we could refer to its first element as **MarkList [1] [1]**. This is exactly equivalent to **MarkList [1,1]**. Usually we will use the method with indices separated by commas, unless there is a particular reason for wishing to emphasise the fact that we are dealing with an array of elements, each of which is itself an array.

Another name for an array of arrays is a *2-dimensional* array. We can picture a 2-dimensional array as being like a table of values. We could, for example, write down a table of examination marks for the candidates in our problem by making a list of names down the side of the page, with the numbers of the papers across the top.

In Pascal we are not limited to 2-dimensional arrays. We can declare arrays with 3, 4, 5 or more dimensions. The limit will depend on the computer system and the sizes of the arrays. For example, if the examination candidates in our previous example were divided into two groups, A and B, we might use a 3-dimensional array to store the marks of candidates in both groups:

MarkList : array ['A'..'B'] of array [1..30] of array [1..3] of integer

An equivalent, but shorter, way of making this declaration is:

MarkList : array ['A'..'B', 1..30, 1..3] of integer

Note that the first index of this array is not an integer, but a character.

Division of Integers

In order to find the average mark for a candidate we need to add up the marks for each of the three papers and then divide by 3. However, the result of dividing an integer by 3 *exactly* will not always be an integer. This can cause problems. We cannot store the result of an *exact* division in an integer variable, since the integer variables can only be used to store integer values. For this reason, Pascal has two distinct division operators. The following two assignment statements illustrate how they can be used:

IntVar2 := IntVar1 div 5   {integer division}
RealVar := IntVar1/5   {real division}

In the first example, the value which will be stored in **IntVar2** corresponds to the (integer) number of times which 5 can be divided into

IntVar1, leaving a remainder if necessary.

In the second example, **RealVar** will be given the real value of the exact division of **IntVar1** by 5.

Detecting the End of the Candidate List

When we had only one mark to be entered for each candidate it was a simple matter to ask the user to enter the *rogue value* –1 to indicate that the last candidate's mark had been entered. Now that each candidate will have three marks to be entered we need to decide how to end the list.

Since our calculations require a full three marks in order to select a grade, we do not wish to give the user the option of ending the list after entering only one or two marks for a particular candidate. This is why the writeln statement asking for each mark has been modified, so that the user is given the option of entering –1 only when the *first* mark is requested.

Once –1 has been entered, no more marks should be requested. The condition:

until (j > 3) or (MarkList [i,1]=–1)

at the end of the loop concerned with reading in the marks for each paper, ensures that both loops will be terminated when the end of the list is reached.

Deciding When to Alter the Grade

Normally the grade calculated using the average marks gained will be the correct final grade. We will only need to alter the grade if both of the following are true:

1) The candidate has scored below 20% on one or more papers.
2) The candidate's overall grade is better than grade 'C'.

A little thought is required to determine what 'better than' grade 'C' means in Pascal terms. What we mean is that the candidate has scored grade 'A' or grade 'B'. In other words, his grade character is a letter occurring *before* 'C'. When we are dealing with any ordinal type, *before* can be translated as *less than*, since we can think of an ordinal type as a list of values starting with the smallest and increasing as we go through the list.

Improvements to the Program

Although this program performs the tasks required, it has a number of
shortcomings. These can be categorised under two headings: those
concerned with efficiency of execution and those concerned with
readability of the source code. With a short program, these problems
might not seem very important, however, we will look at possible ways
of improving the code, since these will be applicable to more complex
programs where such considerations are of great importance.

Improvements to Increase Efficiency

Look at the source code of the procedure **CalcGrads**. Count how many
times the array **MarkList** is used. Notice how the *same* element of the
array is referred to several times on each pass through the **repeat** loops.

Every time an element of an array is accessed its address has to be
calculated. The compiler will give instructions which will add an
appropriate number to the address of the start of the array. So the
compiled code to access an array element will be longer than that to
access a single variable of the same type as the element. This means that,
if an element of an array is to be used a number of times, it may be more
efficient to *copy* its value into a separate variable and then refer to that
variable *instead* of to the array element.

Below is a modified version of **CalcGrades**, which makes significantly fewer references to elements of the array **MarkList**:

```
procedure CalcGrades;
  var
    i, j, AverageMark, TotalMark, Mark : integer;
    TooLow : boolean;
  begin
  writeln ('Enter the marks for each candidate.');
  writeln ('Enter –1 to end.');
  writeln;
  i := 1;
{read in marks for each candidate}
  repeat
    j := 1;
    TotalMark := 0; {initialise total}
    TooLow := false; {initialise flag}
```

```
{read in marks for each paper and calculate total}
    repeat
        writeln ('Enter the mark for candidate ',i, 'in paper ',j);
        if j = 1 then writeln (' or –1 to end');
        readln (Mark);
        if mark < > –1 then begin
                        MarkList [i,j] := Mark;
                        TotalMark := TotalMark + Mark;
                        If Mark < 20 then TooLow := true; {set flag}
                        j := j+1;
                        end;
    until ( j > 3) or (Mark=–1);
    if Mark < > –1
    then begin
        AverageMark := TotalMark div 3;
        if AverageMark > 80 then GradeList [i] := 'A'
        else if AverageMark > 55 then GradeList [i] := 'B'
            else if AverageMark > 40 then GradeList [i] := 'C'
                else if AverageMark > 25 then GradeList [i] := 'D'
                    else GradeList [i] := 'E';
        end;
    if TooLow
        then if GradeList [i] < 'C' then GradeList [i] := 'C'; i := i+1;
    until (i=31) or (Mark=–1);
    LastCand := i–1;
    end;
```

The procedure has been improved in three ways:

(1) Using a Temporary Variable

The local variable **Mark** has been declared to store the value of the most recently entered mark. This reduces the number of times when it is necessary to refer to **MarkList [i, j]**, by replacing such references with references to **Mark**.

Using the variable **Mark** has the added advantage that we can read the number entered by the user into this variable *without* altering the array containing the list of marks. This would be useful if, for example, we wished to carry out some check on the validity of the mark before adding it to the list.

(2) Using a Boolean Variable as a 'Flag'

The boolean variable, **TooLow** has been introduced in order to avoid the cumbersome condition,

if (MarkList [i, 1] < 20) or (MarkList [i, 2] < 20) or (MarkList [i, 3] < 20)

This enables us to make the same check by comparing each mark with 20 *as it is entered*. We can record whether or not a candidate has scored below 20% in any of his papers by altering the value of **TooLow** from **false** to **true** if a mark of below 20% is encountered.

This technique is known as 'setting a flag', because we are using the boolean variable (or flag) **TooLow** to signal whether or not a certain condition has been satisfied. This method is often useful.

It is important to make sure that the flag is correctly initialised before it is used.

(3) By-passing Unnecessary Code

A check has now been introduced so that, once a −1 has been entered, no more calculations are performed. Previously the program continued through the grade allocation process, regardless of the fact that the current mark was, in fact, not a true mark but a rogue value entered for the purpose of terminating the list of candidates.

Improvements to Increase Readability

The two modifications described above do in fact improve the readability as well as the efficiency of the procedure **CalcGrades**. This is because it is not always easy, when reading a program listing, to work out which element of an array is referred to when a reference such as **MarkList [i, j]** is encountered. By using the temporary variable, **Mark**, and the flag, **TooLow**, we make it clear that it is the marks of the *current* candidate with which we are concerned.

The listing below includes additional improvements to readability. Again, they are not strictly necessary in so short and simple a program.

```
program ListGrades (input,output);
type
   Papers = 1..3;
```

```pascal
    Candidates = 1..30;
    CandMarks = array [Papers] of integer;
    MarkListType = array [Candidates] of CandMarks;
    GradeListType = array [Candidates] of char;
var
    MarkList : MarkListType;
    GradeList : GradeListType;
    Lastcand : integer;
procedure CalcGrades;
    var
      i, j, AverageMark, TotalMark, Mark : integer;
      TooLow, ListFinished : boolean;
    begin
    writeln ('Enter the marks for each candidate.');
    writeln ('Enter -1 to end.');
    writeln;
    i := 1;
    ListFinished := false;
{read in marks for each candidate}
    repeat
      j := 1;
      TotalMark := 0;
      TooLow := false;
{read in marks for each paper and calculate total}
    repeat
      writeln ('Enter the mark for candidate ',i, ' in paper ', j);
      if j = 1 then writeln (' or –1 to end');
      readln (Mark);
      if Mark = –1 then ListFinished := true
      else begin
        MarkList [i, j] := Mark;
        TotalMark := TotalMark + Mark;
        If Mark < 20 then TooLow := true;
        j := j+1;
        end;
    until ( j > 3) or ListFinished;
    if not ListFinished
      then begin
        Averagemark := TotalMark div 3;
        if AverageMark > 80 then GradeList [i] := 'A'
```

```
      else if AverageMark > 55 then GradeList [i] := 'B'
        else if AverageMark > 40 then GradeList [i] := 'C'
          else if AverageMark > 25 then GradeList [i] := 'D'
            else GradeList [i] := 'E';
      end;
    if TooLow then
      if GradeList [i] < 'C' then GradeList [i] := 'C';
    i := i+1;
    until (i=31) or ListFinished;
    LastCand := i-1;
    end; {CalcGrades}
  procedure OutGrades;
    var
      Grade : char;
      Cand : integer;
    begin
    Grade := 'A';
    repeat
      writeln;
      writeln ('Grade ',Grade);
      writeln;
      Cand := 1;
      repeat
        if GradeList [Cand] = Grade then writeln ('candidate ',cand);
        Cand := Cand + 1;
      until Cand > LastCand;
      Grade := Succ(Grade);
    until Grade > 'E'
    end; {OutGrades}
  begin {main program}
  CalcGrades;
  OutGrades;
  end.
```

Using Boolean Variables

To the uninitiated, the conditions **until (j>3) or (MarkList [i,1]=–1)**
and **until (i=31) or (MarkList [i–1] =–1)** appear rather cryptic. It would
certainly be desirable to include comments explaining their purpose.

We have already made improvements by replacing **MarkList [i-1]**

with **Mark**. This avoids any difficulty concerning which element of
MarkList we are referring to. We could, in addition, declare a boolean
variable, which is made to become true as soon as the end of the list of
candidates is reached.

A suitable name for this variable is **ListFinished**. We must take care
to *initialise* **ListFinished** to **false** before starting to read in the list. When
−1 is entered **ListFinished** must be assigned the value **true**. We can then
change our loop conditions to read **until (j>3) or ListFinished** and **until
(i=31) or ListFinished**.

Type Definition

Our variable declaration **MarkList : array [1..30] of array [1..3] of
integer** is rather cumbersome. It is also not immediately obvious what
the two indices into the array correspond to. We could make it easier for
another programmer to understand the structure of **MarkList** by using
a *type* definition. A type definition section may be included in the
declaration section of a Pascal program. This section consists of the
reserved word **type** followed by a number of type definitions.

We have already seen how we can declare variables which have a type
other than one of the pre-defined Pascal types (integer, real, boolean,
char). In developing our exam grades program we made use of three
different array types. A type definition is a way of giving a *name* to a new
type, which we can then use when declaring variables of that type. We
could, for example, have used the following type definitions to describe
our three array types:

> **MarkListType = array [1..30] of integer;**
> **GradeListType = array [1..30] of char;**
> **MarkListType = array [1..30] of array [1..3] of integer;**

or, equivalently,

> **MarkListType = array [1..30, 1..3] of integer;**

Our 2-dimensional array might be more easily understood if we
defined it in two stages like this:

> **CandMarks = array [1..3] of integer;**
> **MarkListType = array [1..30] of CandMarks;**

This makes it clear that we are dealing with an array of 30 candidates,
each with an array of three integer marks.

The syntax of the type definition section is given in Figure 6.9. We have not, as yet, met all the possible kinds of 'type description'. The syntax for each individual kind will be included at the point in the text where it is described.

Subrange Types

When defining an array type, we give a type to which each of the elements of the array will belong, and we also give a *subrange* of some ordinal type which will be used to index the array. For example 1..30 is a subrange of the integer type, while 'A'..'D' is a *subrange* of the character type.

It is possible to define a new type to be a subrange of an already-defined type. For example:

Grades = 'A'..'D';
Candidates = 1..30;
MarkRange = 0..100;
Papers = 1..3;

If we include these definitions *before* the definitions of our array types in the type definition section, we could define the array types like this:

CandMarks = array [Papers] of MarkRange;
MarkListType = array [Candidates] of CandMarks;
GradeListType = array [Candidates] of Grades;

This produces an obvious improvement in readability. There is, however, an additional reason for using the subrange types **Grades** and **MarkRange**. This is concerned with run-time range checking.

If it is known that a particular variable can never legally be assigned a value outside a particular range, it can be useful to know if this rule is ever violated. If a variable has been defined as being within a particular subrange, then the compiler should produce code to check that it is never given a value outside this range. Since it significantly increases the amount of code produced, most compilers only include range checking when it is specifically requested at compile-time. Each implementation will have its own way of allowing this option to be selected. Normally range checking should only be turned on when a program is being developed or debugged in order to detect mistakes in the source code.

Sometimes variables declared as belonging to some subrange of the

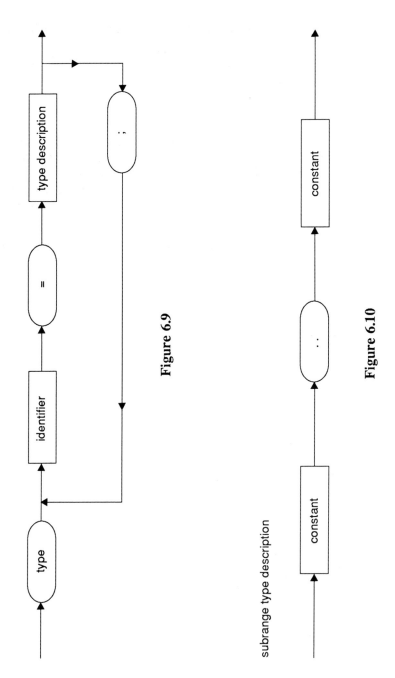

type definition section

Figure 6.9

subrange type description

Figure 6.10

integer type will occupy less memory than those declared as integers.

Figures 6.10 and 6.11 give the syntax of subrange and array type definitions. Figure 6.12 gives the syntax of a constant. We will discuss constant identifiers later.

Scope of Identifiers

As we have seen, it is possible to declare variable identifiers which are *local* to a particular procedure. This means that they cannot be used *outside* the procedure in which they are declared. *Global* identifiers (ie those declared in the declaration section at the beginning of the main program), however, may be referred to from within any procedure as well as in the main program.

It is also possible to declare *procedures* within other procedures. For example:

```
program Nest (input,output);
var
  Global : integer;
procedure level1;
  var
    var1 : integer;
  procedure level2;
    var
      var2 : integer;
    begin {level2}
    var2 := 2;
    var1 := var1 + var2;
    global := global + var2;
    end; {level2}
  begin {level1}
  var1 := 1;
  level2;
  Global := Global + var1;
  end; {level1}
begin {main program}
global := 0;
level1;
writeln (global);
end. {main program}
```

array type description

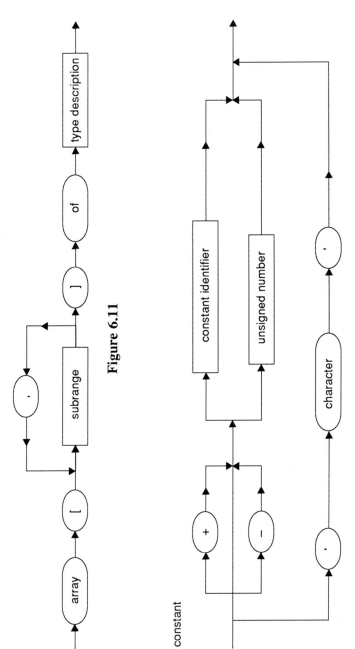

Figure 6.11

constant

Figure 6.12

This is known as *nesting* of procedures. Here, the procedure **level2** is contained within **level1**. This means that variables declared in procedure **level1** can be accessed from within **level2**. However, variables declared in **level2** can be accessed *only* from within **level2** itself.

It sometimes happens that two procedures each have local variables which perform very similar functions. In this case, it may be that we may choose to use the same name for both variables.

Provided that the two procedures concerned are *disjoint* (ie neither is defined within the other), this will cause no problems. The two variables, although having the same name, will be treated as completely different entities. Each will be available only within the procedure in which it is declared.

However, if two *nested* procedures use identical identifiers, great care must be taken. Let us look at an example:

```
program Nest (input,output);
var
  Global : integer;
procedure level1;
  var
    i : integer;
  procedure level2;
    var
      i : integer;
    begin
    i := 2;
    global := global + i;
    end; {level2}
  begin {level1}
  i := 1;
  level2;
  Global := Global + i;
  end; {level1}
begin {main program}
global := 0;
level1;
writeln (global);
end.
```

Which variable is referred to, when the identifier i is used within **level2**? Is it the variable declared in **level2**, or that declared in **level1**? According to the rules which we have seen so far, both variables are available within **level2**.

To answer questions such as this, there is a concept known as the 'scope' of an identifier. This means the area of the program within which an identifier is valid. The scope of an identifier is defined to be the *block* (ie procedure or program) in which it is defined, and any enclosed block which does not re-define it. Figure 6.13 may help.

program	identifiers which may be used
program nest(input,output); var global : integer procedure level1;	

var
    i,j:integer
  procedure level2;	

var
      i ,k: integer
    begin
    i:=2;
    global:= global+i;
    end
	i
	k (declared in level2)
	
	j (declared in level1)
	
	global (declared in main program)

begin
  i := 1;
  level2:
  global :=global+i;
  end;
	i
	j (declared in level1)
	
	global (declared in main program)

begin
global := 0;
level1;
writelin(global);
end.
	global (declared in main program)

Figure 6.13

Whenever the identifier **i** occurs within **level2**, it is the variable local to **level2** which is accessed. It is now impossible to refer to the identifier i declared in **level1** from within **level2**.

Look at each of these example programs carefully. Use pencil and paper to work out what values you expect the variables to take as the program is running. Then type each program into the computer and run it. If the final value of **global** which is displayed is not what you predicted, you may find it useful to add writeln statements to give the values of other variables at different stages.

Don't worry if these rules seem complicated. They are not really as difficult as they appear at first sight. There is an easy way to avoid problems. That is: *never* use the same identifier to refer to more than one item within a program.

EXERCISES

1. Make suitable variable declarations to store:
   a) The ages of a class of 35 children;
   b) The prices of 150 items;
   c) A name of up to 20 characters;
   d) A four-digit PIN-number.

2. Write a program which will:
   i) Ask for a four-digit code number to be entered;
   ii) Check the number against a specified code;
   iii) Display a "welcome" message if the number was entered correctly;
   iv) Display a warning if the number was incorrect.

3. Modify your program from question 3 to allow the user four attempts at entering the correct code, before displaying the warning.

4. Write a program to decode messages typed in using the following cypher: each letter of the message is entered as an integer with 1 corresponding to 'a', 2 to 'b' etc, using an array of characters indexed by the subrange 1..26 to enable you to perform the necessary conversion from numbers to letters. Modify your program to make the output more intelligible by defining the code-number 0 to correspond to a space between words.

*5. Which of the following are correct type definitions?
   i) Name = array [1.20] of char;

ii) Dimensions = array [1..2] of integer;
iii) RoomSizes = array [1..6] of Dimensions;
iv) Ages = array [34..10] of real;
v)   RoomSizes = array [1..6,1..2] of integer;
vi) ThreeD = array ['a'..'z',1..4, false..true] of 0..10;

*6. An estate agent wishes to store information about houses on computer. Write a procedure which will input the length and width of each bedroom and store them in an array. Estate agents and their clients are not generally conversant with metric measures, so the dimensions of each room are to be entered as an integer number of feet, followed by a second integer giving the inches. Your array should store these two values separately so that the information can be displayed later in the same form. You will need to decide on a maximum number of bedrooms allowed, and on a way of indicating when the list is complete.

*7. The following (pointless) Pascal program has an error reported at compile-time, as indicated. Why?

```
program silly (input,output);
procedure AddOne;
  var
    i : integer;
  begin
  i := i + 1;
  end;
begin
readln (i);
        ^
     unknown variable
AddOne;
writeln ('The answer is ',i);
end.
```

*8. What number will be output when this program is run?

```
program Careless (input,output);
var
  oops : integer;
procedure Level1;
  var
    oops : integer;
  procedure Level2
```

```
      begin
      oops := 2;
      end;
      begin
      oops := 1;
      Level2;
      end;
    begin
    oops := 3;
    Level1;
    writeln (oops);
    end.
```

What number will be output if the variable declaration section of procedure **Level1** is removed?

*9. Modify the grade-calculating program so that the user is given the option of altering one or more of the marks after the complete list has been entered. He should be allowed to select a candidate by entering the candidate number. The candidate's mark in each paper should then be displayed in turn, and the user given the choice of amending each mark or leaving it as it is. Once the user is satisfied with a candidate's mark, the new grade should be calculated.

7 Words and Sentences

INTRODUCTION

In this chapter we will design a program which will store a short letter. The user will be able to add a name and other details. He will then be able to instruct the program to print out the whole letter.

NEW PASCAL FEATURES

1) Character strings
2) **read**

COME TO A PARTY

Let us suppose that we have been asked to write a program to print out personalised party invitations. Each invitation will consist of the following message:

Dear <name1>
Please come to a party <time> ↙ *at*
on <date>
  best wishes
  <name2>

The items enclosed in < > are to be filled in with characters entered by the user.

STRINGS

Let us look first at how we will input and store the items <name1>, <time>, <date> and <name2>. They will each consist of a number of characters (possibly including spaces). So we could input each character in turn and store them in an array of char. However, ordinary arrays have the disadvantage that they can only be output by outputting each element separately.

For example, if **MarkList** has been declared as an array of integer (as in Chapter 6), then the statement **write (MarkList)** is illegal. In order to output the elements of **MarkList**, we would have to list each element separately in one or more write statements, such as:

write (MarkList [1], MarkList [2], MarkList [3])

Fortunately, arrays of characters are so universally useful that there is special provision within the Pascal language to make it easier to use them. There is a special type of array of char (usually known as a *string*) which can be output as a whole, rather than only as single characters. Here are some examples:

Line : Packed array [1..60] of char;
name : Packed array [1..20] of char;
message : Packed array [1..50] of char;

The significance of the word **Packed** is not of any importance at this stage. However, it is important to remember that arrays of characters can *only* be treated as strings if they are declared as **packed** arrays. Notice that a string *must* be indexed by a subrange of the integers starting with 1. So, the following arrays of char are *not* valid strings:

NotPacked : array [1..30] of char;
WrongIndex : packed array [5..10] of char;
CharIndex : packed array ['a'..'z'] of char;

It is important to remember that the length of a string is set permanently when it is declared in the variable declaration section of a program or procedure. Whenever we use a string variable we must ensure that it has enough elements to hold at least as many characters as will be needed at any stage during the execution of the program.

If the word we want to store in it at any time is shorter than its declared length, then we must consider what value we want to have in the remaining elements. Usually it will be acceptable to 'pad out' the string with spaces in all the elements beyond those actually in use. Sometimes, however, other characters might be appropriate.

DESIGNING THE PROGRAM STRUCTURE

Presumably a number of guests will be invited to any party, so it will be necessary to print out several invitations each with the same entries for <time>, <date> and <name2>; but with different values of <name1>. This makes it sensible for us to split the program into two operations:

    1) Input <time>, <date> and <name2>.
    2) For each <name1>, input <name1> and print out invitation.

Figure 7.1 illustrates this design in a structure diagram. The two main operations can be further refined to produce the diagram featured in Figure 7.2.

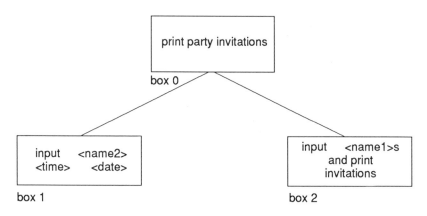

Figure 7.1

We can now make a tentative outline for our program:

```
program party (input,output); {box 0}
{prints party invitations}
procedure GetName2; {box 1a}
begin
{input name of sender}
end;
procedure GetTime; {box 1b}
begin
{input time of party}
end;
```

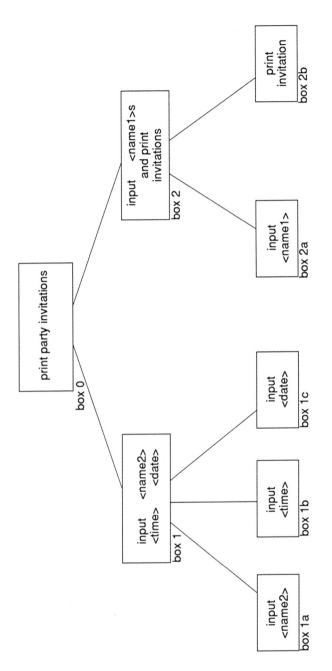

Figure 7.2

```
procedure GetDate; {box 1c}
begin
{input date of party}
end;
procedure GetPartyInfo; {box 1}
begin
{inputs information about party}
GetName2;
GetTime;
GetDate;
end;
procedure GetName1; {box 2a}
begin
{input name of guest}
end;
procedure Invitation; {box 2b}
begin
{print personalised invitation}
end;
procedure MakeInvitations; {box 2}
begin
{make invitation for each guest}
repeat
GetName1;
Invitation;
until {last guest entered}
end;
begin {main program body} {box 0}
GetPartyInfo;
MakeInvitations;
end.
```

It is instructive to study the order in which the procedures have been defined. Compare this with the positions of the corresponding boxes in Figure 7.2. Notice that a procedure which performs a task described in a box at the *lowest* level of our structure diagram must be defined before the procedure corresponding to the box to which it is joined above. For example, **GetName2** (box 1a) is defined *before* **GetPartyInfo** (box 1). This is because the code defining a procedure must occur earlier than any code which calls on that procedure.

VARIABLE DECLARATIONS

We will need to declare string variables to hold each of <name2>, <time>, <date> and <name1>. For the moment we will declare strings of length 20 for each. Since they will be used by a number of different procedures, we will declare them as global variables in the variable declaration section of the main program:

```
var
  Name2, time, date, name1: packed array [1..20] of char;
```

OUTPUTTING THE INVITATION

Now we will look at the procedure **Invitation**, which prints out the finished invitation. We will discuss later how to send the output to a printer. For the moment we will simply produce a display on the screen.

Let us suppose, for the present, that the necessary information has already been input into the variables **name2, time, date** and **name1**. We can display the invitation using **writeln** statements:

```
procedure Invitation;
{print personalised invitation}
writeln;writeln;
begin
writeln ('Dear ', name1);
writeln ('Please come to a party at ', time);
writeln ('on ', date);
writeln ('          Best wishes, ');
writeln ('          ', name2);
end;
```

We can test this procedure by adding statements within procedures **GetName2, GetTime, GetDate** and **GetName1** to assign values to the string variables. We will then be able to run the program. Try running the following amended version to check that the invitation is displayed correctly:

```
program party (input,output); {box 0}
{prints party invitations}
var
   Name2, time, name1: packed array [1..20] of char;
   procedure GetName2; {box 1a}
```

```
begin
name2 := 'Fred              ';
{temporary assignment for testing purposes}
{input name of sender}
end;
procedure GetTime; {box 1b}
begin
Time := '7.30 p.m.             ';
{temporary assignment for testing purposes}
{input time of party}
end;
procedure GetDate; {box 1c}
begin
date := '1st May              ';
{temporary assignment for testing purposes}
{input date of party}
end;
procedure GetPartyInfo; {box 1}
begin
{inputs information about party}
GetName2;
GetTime;
GetDate;
end;
procedure GetName1; {box 2a}
begin
name1 := 'Charlie             ';
{temporary assignment for testing purposes}
{input name of guest}
end;
procedure Invitation;
{print personalised invitation}
begin
writeln ('Dear ', name1);
writeln ('Please come to a party at ', time);
writeln ('on ', date);
writeln ('            Best wishes, ');
writeln ('            ', name2);
end;
procedure MakeInvitations; {box 2}
```

```
begin
{make invitation for each guest}
{repeat}
GetName1;
Invitation;
{until last guest entered}
end;
begin {main program body} {box 0}
GetPartyInfo;
MakeInvitations;
end.
```

It is important to remember that whenever we assign to a string variable using a 'literal string' (ie characters enclosed with single inverted commas), we must ensure that the literal string is the correct length. This is why the names, time and date in the program above have had spaces added to 'pad them out' to 20 characters.

INPUTTING STRINGS

Now we will write the procedure **GetName2**, which will input the name of the sender of the invitations. Many Pascal implementations (including Turbo Pascal) have some facility which allows a whole string to be input as a single item. However, ISO standard Pascal does not include this. So we will read in the strings which we require one character at a time.

To do this we will use a repeat loop. We will repeatedly read in a character *until* the <enter> key is pressed. Up until now we have always used readln to input data from the keyboard. Now we will need another pre-defined procedure: **read**.

If **ch** has been declared as a **char** variable then the statement **read (ch)** inputs a character and stores it in **ch**. There is a special way of finding out when the <enter> key has been pressed. The standard function, **eoln**, can take either of the boolean values **true** and **false**. **Eoln** is *true* when all the characters up to <enter> have been read in. It is *false* if there are still characters available to be read from the current input line.

Here is how we can use read and eoln to complete the procedure **GetName2**:

```
procedure GetName2;
{input name of sender}
```

```
var
  i : integer;
begin
writeln ('Enter name of sender. ');
i := 1;
repeat
  read (Name2[i]);
  i := i+1;
until eoln;
end;
```

Notice that, after the repeat loop has been executed, our array index, **i**, is the index to the *next* element *beyond* the end of the actual name typed in. Also, the last character to be read in is the last letter of the name, *not* an end-of-line character. This is because **eoln** becomes true *immediately* after the last character on a line has been read in.

Try amending your program to include this version of **GetName2**. Run the program several times and see what results you get. You may well produce a very pretty display of hieroglyphics on your screen! This is because we have forgotten to 'pad out' the string variable **Name2** with suitable characters. This means that the characters beyond the last one which you typed in will be whatever values happen to have been left in that storage location from previous use.

We could use the following repeat loop to pad out the string with spaces:

```
repeat
  Name2[i] := ' ';
  i := i+1;
until i > 20;
```

We need to consider what will happen if a name of *more* than 20 characters is entered. At the moment the procedure will simply carry on reading characters and attempting to put them into elements of the array **name2** regardless of whether or not we have already filled all the available elements. This may cause a run time error – or worse! (as we discussed in Chapter 6). We can easily add a check at the end of our repeat loop to ensure that no more than 20 characters are read in:

```
procedure GetName2;
{input name of sender}
var
```

```
  i : integer;
begin
writeln ('Enter name of sender. ');
i := 1;
repeat
  read (Name2[i]);
  i := i+1;
until eoln or (i>20);
if i <= 20 then
  repeat
    Name2[i] := ' ';
    i := i+1;
  until i > 20;
end;
```

We can make versions of **GetTime, GetDate, GetName1** in a very similar way. However, we need to make sure that whenever we read in characters from the keyboard they are the ones which we intended to input, and not part of some previous user response. If we simply stop reading after 20 characters have been read in, then, when we come to read in the next piece of information, the remaining characters of the current line will still be in the input buffer. So, for example, instead of reading in the time, we might read in the final letters of the sender's name!

To see this happening try including the following version of **GetTime** in your program, together with the version of **GetName2** listed above. If you enter a name longer than 20 characters you should get some interesting invitations displayed!

```
procedure GetTime;
{input time of party]
var
  i : integer;
begin
writeln ('Enter time of party. ');
i := 1;
repeat
  read (Time[i]);
  i := i+1;
until eoln or (i>20);
if i <= 20 then
```

```
repeat
  Time [i] := ' ';
  i := i+1;
until i > 20;
end;
```

USING READLN TO SKIP UNWANTED CHARACTERS

We can solve this problem by using the procedure **readln**. Used alone, without any identifiers enclosed in brackets following it, **readln** has the effect of moving on to the next line of input without reading in any more characters from the present line. So we can 'throw away' any surplus characters by adding a **readln** statement after the loop which reads in the characters of **name2**:

```
repeat
  read (name2[i]);
  i := i+1;
until eoln or (i>20);
readln;
```

We should also insert a **readln** statement at the corresponding place in **GetTime**. Check that these procedures are now correct by running your program with these amendments.

You should now be able to complete procedures **GetDate** and **Get-Name1**, by adapting the code for **GetName2**.

TERMINATING THE LIST OF NAMES

To complete our program we need to decide on a way of the user indicating when the list of guests is complete. We can use a 'rogue value' to terminate the list, as we have done before. We must choose a suitable rogue value for the first character of **name1**, ie a character which will *never* be entered in an actual name. There are a number of possibilities, but we will use *.

Here is a new version of **MakeInvitations**, including a **repeat** . . . . **until** the rogue value is entered:

```
procedure MakeInvitations;
begin
{make invitation for each guest}
repeat
```

GetName1;
if Name1[1] < > '*' then Invitation;
until Name1[1] = '*';
end;

Notice the if statement which ensures that no invitation is made for a guest with the name '*'.

Modify your program to include this procedure and test that the correct invitations are displayed on the screen. Don't forget to include a message to the user telling him how to terminate the list of names.

SENDING OUTPUT TO A PRINTER

The ISO standard for Pascal does not specify any way of directing output to a printer. However, there is sure to be a way of doing so on your system. You should consult the manual for your system or ask for advice about how to do this. Below is a discussion of one way in which you *may* be able to send output to a device other than the screen.

ISO Pascal allows output to be sent to a device other than the standard output device (usually the screen) by declaring a *file* type variable. Files can be of many types, but at this stage we will only be concerned with files of characters (or *text* files).

We can declare a file variable to represent our printer in the variable declaration section of our program:

printer : file of char;   or, equivalently:
printer : text;

We also need to list the identifier **printer** in the program heading:

program party (input,output,printer);

this tells the compiler that, as well as the standard input and output files, we also require another *external* file to be available. (*External* simply means that data output to this file will be sent to some external device, such as a disk, printer or magnetic tape. Similarly, data read in from an external file, will be read from an external device.)

If we wish to write output to a file variable, then we must prepare it first by using a **rewrite** command. The statement **rewrite (printer)** must be executed before any attempt is made to send output to the file variable **printer**. We can output characters or strings to our new file by adding the identifier **printer** as the first identifier after the open bracket in our **writeln** statements:

```
procedure Invitation;
{print personalised invitation}
begin
writeln (printer); writeln (printer);
writeln (printer, 'Dear ', name1);
writeln (printer, 'Please come to a party at ', time);
writeln (printer, 'on ', date);
writeln (printer, '          Best wishes,');
writeln (printer, '                      ', name2);
end;
```

Notice that, where we had a statement consisting of **writeln** alone, we now need to add brackets containing the identifier **printer**.

There are several ways in which it may be possible on your system to use an external file to send output to the printer on your computer system. Perhaps there will be a special pre-defined identifier, which you can use as the name of the printer file. It may be that you will need an extra statement in your program to tell the compiler that your file variable is to represent the printer. For example, using Turbo Pascal on a PC, the following version of the main program would cause the invitations to be printed:

```
begin {main program body} {box 0}
GetPartyInfo;
Assign (printer, 'prn');
Rewrite (printer);
MakeInvitations;
close (printer);
end.
```

The **assign** and **close** commands are not standard Pascal. They are peculiar to Turbo Pascal. However, you may find that your Pascal implementation uses something similar. The statement **close (printer)** terminates output to **printer** and ensures that all the text is sent out. If this was omitted, part of our invitation might be left in a output buffer.

Find out how to send output to your printer. Then print out some party invitations using this program.

Note to Turbo Pascal users

Turbo Pascal does not recognise the file type 'file of char' as being the special text file type. So you will find it necessary to declare your printer file using the Pascal pre-defined identifier **text** as the type: printer : text;

MORE ADVANCED TOPICS

Packed and Unpacked Arrays

When Pascal was invented, computers had relatively little storage space for program variables. It was, therefore, important to use the memory economically. However, it is sometimes more easy for the processor to access array elements if they are stored in a way which leaves unused memory space between the array elements.

Thus, it was necessary to be able to choose whether to store arrays so as to take up as little space as possible, or to store them so as to use as little processor time as possible. Pascal provided this facility by allowing two sorts of array type: packed and unpacked.

If it was necessary to move the elements of a packed array into an unpacked array of the same base type, this could be done using the **unpack** command. Similarly an unpacked array could be copied into a packed array using **pack**. Here are some examples of array declarations and use of **pack** and **unpack**:

```
var
    string : packed array[1..10] of char;
    chararray : array[1..10] of char;
    table : array[0..10] of integer;
    packedtable : packed array[0..10] of integer;
    realtable : array[0..12] of real;
    Packreal : packed array[0..24] of real;
```

unpack (string,chararray,0);
        {copies the elements of string into **chararray**, putting **string[1]**
        into **chararray[1]**, **string[2]** into **chararray[2]** etc.}
pack (table,packedtable,0);
        {copies the elements of **table** into **packedtable**, putting **table[0]**
        into **packedtable[0]** etc.}
pack (realtable,packreal,5);
        {copies the elements of **realtable** into **packreal**, putting

realtable[0] into **packreal[5]**, **realtable[1]** into **packreal[6]** etc. }

Don't worry if you find this difficult to follow. It is unlikely that you will ever need to use packed arrays other than for strings. And it is extremely unlikely that you will need to use **pack** or **unpack**.

Figure 7.3 gives the syntax for an array type definition, including the option of declaring an array to be packed.

Compatibility of Array Types

It is possible to copy all the elements of one array into another array in a single assignment provided that the arrays are 'compatible'. Two arrays are compatible if either:

1) they were declared in the same variable declaration, for example:

thisarray,thatarray: array[1..5] of integer;

or
2) they were declared using the same type identifier *and* that identifier has not been re-defined between the two variable declarations, for example:

type
  arraytype = array[0..9] of real;
var
  first : arraytype;
  index : integer;
  second : arraytype;

With the above declarations, the following assignments are legal:

first := second;
thatarray := this array;

However, arrays which have been declared in an identical way, but not in the same declaration statement are not compatible. For example, the array variables **one** and **two**, declared below, are not compatible:

var
  one : array[1..6] of char;
  two : array[1..6] of char;

Your Pascal compiler should register an error if an assignment such as **one := two** is attempted.

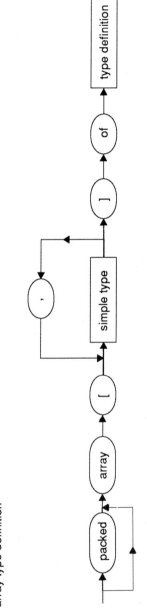

Figure 7.3

array type definition

Compatibility of Strings

As we have seen in our party invitation program, it is possible to assign a value to a string by putting it equal to a 'literal string' or 'string constant'. For example, the statement, **name1 := 'Fred   '**, puts the characters 'F', 'r', 'e', 'd' into the first 4 elements of **name1**, and puts spaces in the remaining 16 elements.

It was necessary for us to include the extra spaces after the name 'Fred', not only in order to ensure that **name1** did not include any unwanted characters, but also because the constant 'Fred' would not have been *compatible* with **name1**. A string constant is only compatible with a string variable if the variable has been declared to have exactly the same number of elements as the characters in the constant string.

Comparison of Arrays

Two compatible arrays can be compared using the operators = and < >. **array1 = array2** will be **true** if and only if *all* the elements of **array1** are identical to the corresponding elements of **array2**.

In addition, compatible strings (ie strings of equal length) may be compared using the operators <, >, <= and >=. The ordering of the strings is according to the usual rules for establishing the alphabetic order of words. For example, the following are **true**:

'ABCD' < 'ABCE'
'baaa' > 'abcd'
'zz' > 'xy'

The ordering of strings involving characters other than alphabetic characters depends on the ordering of the values of the type char. This ordering is determined by your Pascal implementation.

Printing on a Fresh Page

In order to produce each party invitation on a separate sheet of paper, it would be convenient to instruct the printer to move to the top of a new sheet before printing. This can be done by using the pre-defined Pascal procedure **page**. However, some Pascal implementations (including Turbo Pascal) do not include this procedure. In this case, you can move to the top of a new sheet by writing a formfeed character to the printer file. Usually **writeln (printer,chr(12))** will do this.

EXERCISES

1. Which of the following type definitions are valid strings?
   i)   packed array[0..6] of char
   ii) array[1..10] of char
   iii) packed array[1..20] of char
   iv) packed array[1..15] of boolean
   v)   packed array[1..2000] of char
   vi) packed array[3..7] of char

2. Modify the party invitation program to allow the user to enter the address of the venue of the party. Don't forget to allow sufficient space to store all the characters of the address!

3. Write a program which will input information from the keyboard, and then print out a railway ticket in the following format. Examples of the information to be typed in are in **bold** type.

PASCAL USERS RAILWAY COMPANY PLC

from	**Warrington**	to	**Oxford**
class	**2nd**	single/return	**return**
child/adult	**adult**	price	**£23.64**

---

4. (More difficult.) Modify your program from question 3 to allow the user to alter one or more of the entries on the ticket before it is finally printed out. You will need to display the information on the screen in the form in which it will be printed. You could then offer a menu of code letters to allow him to choose an item to alter or to elect to print out the ticket. Use a repeat loop to enable him to change a number of items. A case statement would be appropriate for selecting between options.

8 Dear Mr Smith ...

INTRODUCTION

In Chapter 7 we wrote a program which allows the user to type in character strings (names, dates etc), which are then included as part of a standard letter. The main text of the letter was defined by literal strings contained in the program itself. This means that if we wish to alter the letter, we must alter the *source code* of the program. It would be more convenient if our program allowed the *user* to type in the text. This would allow him to use the same program to print a number of different standard letters.

In this chapter we will write a program which will allow the user to type in a standard letter, which will be stored in memory. He will then be able to enter a list of names. The program will print out a personalised letter addressed to each name on the list.

NEW PASCAL FEATURES

1) Arrays of strings
2) **while** loops
3) **for** loops

DEFINING THE PROBLEM

The first thing to do when designing a program, is to make a clear plan of what the program is required to do. Let us suppose that we have been asked to write a program which will:

1) Input a short letter, typed in from the keyboard.
2) Input a list of names.
3) For each name in the list, insert the name at an appropriate place

in the letter, so as to produce a letter beginning 'Dear <name> ...'.
4) For each name on the list, print out the personalised letter.

THE OVERALL DESIGN OF THE PROGRAM

We can now start to design our program. Let us look back at requirements 1–4, listed above. The first thing to notice is that requirement 1 is concerned with an operation which will be performed only *once* during the execution of the program, while requirements 2, 3 and 4 all involve operations which are to be performed for *each* name. So it makes sense to group together 2, 3 and 4. We can then perform an *iteration* of this group of operations.

Figure 8.1 is a structure diagram illustrating how this can be done.

CHOOSING SUITABLE 'DATA STRUCTURES'

We can also decide on how we are going to store the information which we will need. We will need to store:

1) The text of the letter
2) Each name
3) Information about where to insert the name.

If a real client were to give us this specification, we would need to ask for more information before we could proceed. For example:

– What exactly does he mean by a 'short' letter? We will need to

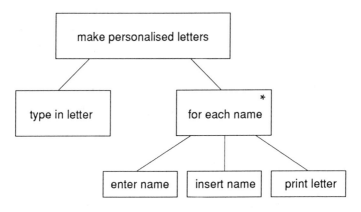

Figure 8.1

allocate memory space to store the letter, so we need to know how much space to allow.

- How is the program to know where to insert the name? Would it, for example, be satisfactory for the user to type in a particular combination of characters (eg '$' at the end of the line where the name is to appear) at the point in the letter where the name is required?

- Is there a limit on the number of names which may be entered? If so, what is the largest number of names which we must allow for? If only a few names will be required, we could store all the names at once. If the number of names is large, we may have to deal with a few at a time.

- Is it necessary for the letters to be all printed together after the complete list has been entered, or could a letter be printed immediately after each name has been entered?

For the moment we will assume that our client does not mind what method is used to determine where the name should be inserted, or when each letter is printed. We will set the maximum length of the letter at 20 lines, each of up to 50 characters. However, the number of names required may vary from two up to several thousand. We will also assume that the name will always be added as the last word appearing on a line of text.

The text of the letter and the names both consist of groups of characters. An obvious way of storing them is to use strings.

The text of the letter is limited to 20 lines, each of up to 50 characters, so we could store the entire text using 20 strings, each of length 50. This can be done by defining an array of strings, like this:

LetterText : array[1..20] of packed array[1..50] of char

Our program will be more readable if we first define a string **type, line,** to describe a line of text:

type
    line = packed array[1..50] of char;
var
    LetterText : array[1..20] of line;

Figure 8.2 illustrates this data structure.

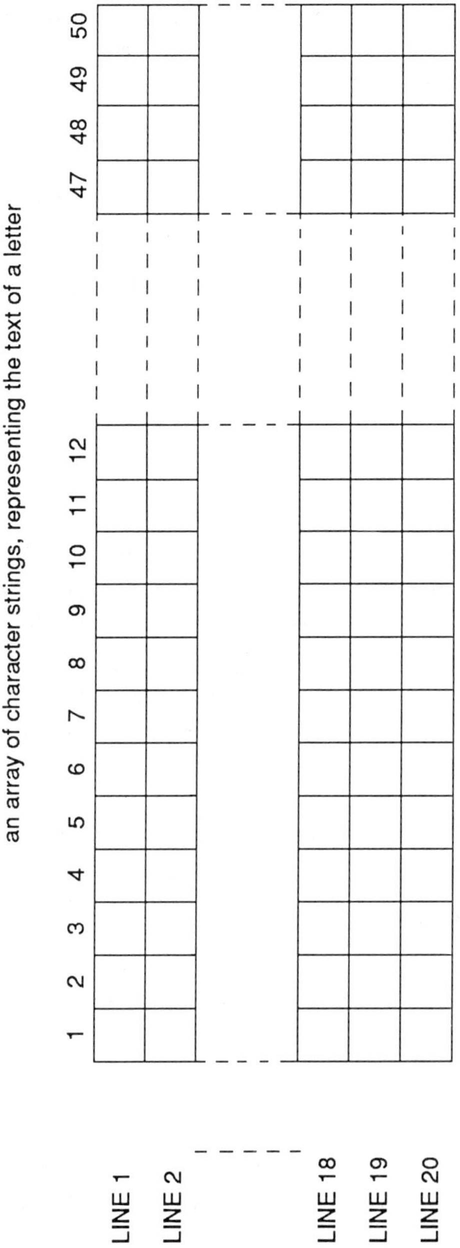

an array of character strings, representing the text of a letter

Figure 8.2

We can perform operations on individual string elements of **LetterText** by enclosing the number of the element required in square brackets after the identifier **LetterText**. For example **LetterText[14]** refers to the 14th string element of **LetterText**.

We can also manipulate individual characters of this array by adding the number of the element *within* the string. For example, **LetterText [1,5]** refers to the 5th character of the 1st string element of **LetterText**.

An example may help to make this clearer. Suppose that the following letter is stored in **LetterText**:

Dear Sir
Thank you for your recent enquiry, which
is now receiving our urgent attention.
I hope to be able to give you more
details shortly.

Then **LetterText [3]** would be a string of length 50 containing the *entire* string 'is now receiving our urgent attention. ', while **LetterText [1,6]** would refer to the single character 'S' (at the beginning of 'Sir').

For the present, we will print each letter out immediately after the corresponding name has been entered (as we did with our party invitations in Chapter 7). So we need only store one name (the name currently being processed) at a time. We can, therefore, use a single string variable for this purpose. We will need to decide on a suitable length for this string. It must be long enough to cope with any name which may be entered. As in Chapter 7 we will use a string of 20 characters:

name : packed array[1..20] of char;

We now need to consider how we are going to store information about where we are to insert the name. We can identify any point in our letter if we know which line it is on *and* which character within the line. So we could use two integers, such as:

lineno, charno: integer;

If, for example, the name was required starting at the 20th character on the 5th line then the program could record this by setting **lineno** equal to 5 and **charno** equal to 20.

BEGINNING ON THE PROGRAM

We are now ready to make a tentative start on writing the source code of our program. Using the data structures described above, and the program design of Figure 8.1, we can write the following 'skeleton' program:

```
program Letter (input,output);
type
  line = packed array[1..50] of char;
var
  LetterText : array[1..20] of line;
  name : packed array[1..20] of char;
  LineNo,CharNo : integer;
procedure EnterLetter;
begin
{Allow user to type in main text}
end;
procedure Entername;
begin
{Allow user to type in name}
end;
procedure Insertname;
begin
{Insert name into main text}
end;
procedure PrintLetter;
begin
{Print out letter}
end;
procedure MakeLetters;
begin
Repeat
  Entername;
  Insertname;
  PrintLetter;
until {end of list}
end;
begin
EnterLetter;
MakeLetters;
end.
```

INPUTTING THE MAIN TEXT

The main text of the letter is to be typed in, at run time, as lines of text terminated by pressing the <enter> key. Our program must read in the characters on each line in turn and store them in the array **LetterText**. We must not forget to 'pad out' any unfilled elements of each line with spaces. Figure 8.3 is a structure diagram illustrating this process.

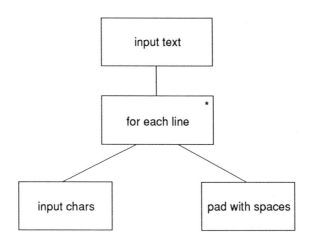

Figure 8.3

When inputting the characters of each line, we must check for the marker which will tell us that a name is to be inserted. If the name marker occurs, the position in the text must be recorded so that each name may be added at this point. Figure 8.4 shows how the process of inputting a line of text can be refined. We will choose to mark the position where a name is to be inserted by a dollar sign ($) followed by a new line character. This is a suitable choice, since it is unlikely that '$' would occur naturally as the last character on a line.

We are now ready to start writing the procedure **EnterLetter**. Here is a 'skeleton' version:

procedure EnterLetter;
　　procedure GetChar;

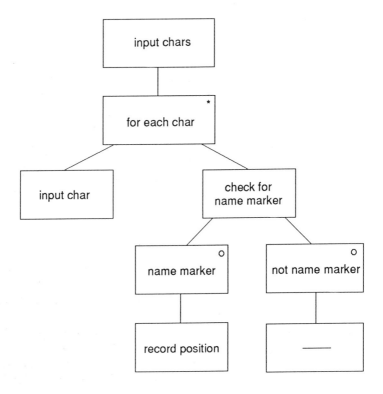

Figure 8.4

```
{inputs a character and checks for marker}
begin
{input next character}
if {character = name marker}
   then {record position}
end;
procedure GetLine;
{inputs a line of text}
begin
{for each character}
   GetChar;
{pad line with spaces}
end;
begin
```

```
{for each line of text}
  GetLine;
end;
```

The procedures **GetChar** and **GetLine** are *local* to **EnterLetter**. This means that they may only be called from within **EnterLetter**. We could not, for example, issue a call to **GetLine** from the main body of our program, or from **EnterName**. We can, however, call **GetChar** from within **GetLine**, because they are both defined locally within the same procedure (**EnterLetter**). There is further discussion of *locally defined identifiers* in the 'more advanced topics' section of Chapter 6. You may find it helpful to refer to that now, but do not worry if you find it a little confusing at this stage.

PROCESSING A CHARACTER OF TEXT

We can input a character using a read statement. Unless the character is the name marker we will wish to store it in the next available element of the current line. To do this we need to know which line is being processed and which is the next element of this line. This information can be made available to the procedure **GetChar** by storing it in global variables. We will declare two integer variables **CurLine** and **CurChar** to hold the number of the current line and the current position within the line. We must take care to initialise these variables before calling **GetChar** for the first time, as well as to increment them whenever we move on to a new character or new line.

We will declare a local variable within **GetChar** to hold the character which has just been read in. This character will then be copied into the appropriate element of **LetterText** unless it turns out to be the name marker character. We can recognise the name marker by checking for a '$' character occurring at the same time as eoln being true. We can now complete **GetChar**:

```
      procedure GetChar;
{0} {inputs a character and checks for marker}
      var
      ch : char;
      begin
{1} read (ch);
{2} if (ch = '$') and eoln
        then begin
```

```
{3}        LineNo   := CurLine;
{4}        CharNo   := CurChar
           end
       else begin
{5}        LetterText [CurLine,CurChar] := ch;
{6}        CurChar := CurChar + 1 {move on to next element}
           end;
    end;
```

(The numbers in curly brackets will be used for reference later in the chapter.)

INPUTTING A LINE OF TEXT

To input a line of text we need to perform an iteration. We must process one character of text *for each character on the current line*. In other words, we must keep on reading in characters and processing them *until* we reach the end of the current line. We can do this using a **repeat** loop:

```
    procedure GetLine;
{0} {inputs a line of text}
    begin
{1} CurChar := 1; {note initialisation of CurChar}
    repeat
{2}    GetChar;
{3} until eoln;
    readln;
    CurLine := CurLine+1; {move on to next element}
{pad line with spaces}
    end;
```

The **readln** statement completes the process of reading in a line of text by skipping past any end-of-line marker characters which may be produced by pressing the <enter> key. This makes sure that the next character read in will be the first character on the next line of text.

DRY RUNS

When writing a segment of a program, it is often helpful to test that the code is correct by performing a 'dry run'. This means choosing some sample data for the program to process, and then going through the program line by line, writing down what will happen when each statement is executed.

Let us test the procedures **GetLine** and **GetChar** by doing this. We will make a table, showing the values of each of the variables which are altered by these procedures at each line within the procedures (see Figure 8.5).

First we will try using a short, simple line of text. Suppose that the user typed in the following as the 15th line of text:

Yours sincerely,

At the start of execution of **GetLine** for this particular line, the variable **CurLine** will have been set to 15. We do not know what the values of **CharNo** or **LineNo** are. **Eoln** is false. The value of **LetterText [CurLine]** is undefined. We can start our 'dry run' by filling in these values on the top line of our table for procedure **GetLine**.

The first 'executable' statement (ie statement which produces code to be executed at run time) of this procedure is the statement labelled {1}. This statement assigns the value 1 to **CurChar**. So we can put in this value on the next line of our table (Figure 8.6).

The statement labelled {2} is a call to **GetChar**, so we now need to start filling in our second table. On entering **GetChar**, the global variables will have the same values as they had immediately before **GetChar** was called. So we can copy their values from the table for **GetLine**. **Ch** is undefined. Statement {1} reads in the first character of text. Using our chosen text data, this gives **Ch** the value 'Y'. Figure 8.7 shows the table for **GetChar** so far.

Continuing in this way will produce the tables shown in Figure 8.8 after one character has been processed.

Make a copy of the blank tables in Figure 8.5. Fill these in with the values obtained when the next character is read in. Are the values of the variables after each character is read in what we were expecting them to be?

Once we are confident that the procedure is dealing correctly with 'ordinary' characters, we need to check that it can also cope with special characters. Suppose that we have reached the point where the last character of our test data (ie the ',' at the end of 'Yours sincerely,') is about to be read in. This means that we are at statement {2} in **GetLine**. **CurChar** will have the value 16, since we are about to read in the 16th character. Figure 8.9 shows the tables produced by continuing the dry run.

InLine

	CurLine	CurChar	LineNo	CharNo	eoln	text[CurLine]
{0}						
{1}						
{2}						
{3}						

InChar

	Ch	CurChar	LineNo	CharNo	eoln	text[CurLine]
{0}						
{1}						
{2}						
{3}						
{4}						
{5}						
{6}						

Figure 8.5

InLine

	CurLine	CurChar	LineNo	CharNo	eoln	text[CurLine]
{0}	15	-	-	-	false	undef
{1}	15	1	-	-	false	undef
{2}						
{3}						

Figure 8.6

InChar

	Ch	CurChar	LineNo	CharNo	eoln	text[CurLine]
{0}	undef	1	-	-	false	undef
{1}	'Y'	1	-	-	false	undef
{2}						
{3}						
{4}						
{5}						
{6}						

Figure 8.7

InLine

	CurLine	CurChar	LineNo	CharNo	eoln	text[CurLine]
{0}	15	-	-	-	false	undef
{1}	15	1	-	-	false	undef
{2}	15	2	-	-	false	['Y'][undef][undef]......[undef]
{3}	15	2	-	-	false	['Y'][undef][undef]......[undef]

InChar

	Ch	CurChar	LineNo	CharNo	eoln	text[CurLine]
{0}	undef	1	-	-	false	undef
{1}	'Y'	1	-	-	false	undef
{2}	'Y'	1	-	-	false	undef
{3}						
{4}						
{5}	'Y'	1	-	-	false	['Y'][undef][undef].......[undef]
{6}	'Y'	2	-	-	false	['Y'][undef][undef].......[undef]

Figure 8.8

InLine

	CurLine	CurChar	LineNo	CharNo	eoln	text[CurLine]
{0}						
{1}						
{2}		15	16	-	false	['Y']['o']['u']['r']['s'][''][''] [n']['c']['e']['r']['e']['l']['l']['y'][undef]... ...[undef]
{3}						

InChar

	Ch	CurChar	LineNo	CharNo	eoln	text[CurLine]
{0}	undef	16	-	-	false	['Y']['o']['u']['r']['s'][''][''][''] [n']['c']['e']['r']['e']['l']['l']['y'][undef]... ...[undef]
{1}	';'	16	-	-	true	['Y']['o']['u']['r']['s'][''][''][''] [n']['c']['e']['r']['e']['l']['l']['y'][undef]... ...[undef]
{2}	';'	16	-	-	true	['Y']['o']['u']['r']['s'][''][''][''] [n']['c']['e']['r']['e']['l']['l']['y'][undef]... ...[undef]
{3}						
{4}						
{5}	';'	16	-	-	true	['Y']['o']['u']['r']['s'][''][''][''] [n']['c']['e']['r']['e']['l']['l']['y'][undef]... ...[undef]
{6}	';'	17	-	-	true	['Y']['o']['u']['r']['s'][''][''][''] [n']['c']['e']['r']['e']['l']['l']['y'][undef]... ...[undef]

Figure 8.9

This looks very satisfactory. The repeat loop will terminate correctly as soon as the last character on the line has been processed. However, we have not yet tested these procedures thoroughly. We need to check that they can also deal correctly with a line which includes the name marker character. Let us now perform a second dry run assuming that the user has typed in the following as the first line of text:

 $

This means that he requires the first line of the letter to consist simply of the personalised name. Figure 8.10 shows the result of this dry run. Again, our program appears to be behaving correctly.

Finally, let us suppose that the user wishes to insert a blank line in his letter. To do this, he will press the 'enter' key as the first character of a line (the 14th line, say). Try to fill in the tables for yourself. You will probably have some difficulty in deciding what character will be read in at statement {1} of **GetChar**. In this case we are attempting to read in a character when we have already reached the end of the current line. So what value will be put into **ch**? The ISO standard for Pascal requires that a space character will be obtained whenever a **read** is performed when **eoln** is true. However, some implementations do not adhere to this. In particular, Turbo Pascal will give the value 13 (ie the ASCII code 'carriage return').

We need to modify our program to take account of blank lines in the text. We need to check whether or not **eoln** is true *before* executing the statements within the **repeat** loop in **GetLine**. If **eoln** is true, the program needs to pad out the entire current line of **LetterText** with spaces and skip on to the next line of input immediately.

We could do this by inserting an if statement:

```
      procedure GetLine;
{0} {inputs a line of text}
      begin
{1} CurChar := 1;
      if not eoln then
            repeat
{2}              GetChar;
{3}        until eoln;
      readln;
      CurLine := CurLine+1;
```

InLine

	CurLine	CurChar	LineNo	CharNo	eoln	text[CurLine]
{0}	1	-	-	-	false	undef
{1}	1	1	-	-	false	undef
{2}	1	1	1	1	true	undef
{3}	1	1	1	1	true	undef

InChar

	Ch	CurChar	LineNo	CharNo	eoln	text[CurLine]
{0}	undef	1	-	-	false	undef
{1}	'$'	1	-	-	true	undef
{2}	'$'	1	-	-	true	undef
{3}	'$'	1	-	1	true	undef
{4}	'$'	1	1	1	true	undef
{5}						
{6}						

Figure 8.10

{pad line with spaces}
end;

However, Pascal has a less cumbersome way of performing this task. There is a second kind of condition-controlled loop – the **while** loop – which allows the iteration condition to be checked at the start of the loop, rather than after the loop has been executed for the first time.

WHILE LOOPS

Here is a modified version of **GetLine**, using a **while** loop to control the iteration:

```
      procedure GetLine;
{0} {inputs a line of text}
      begin
{1} CurChar := 1;
      while not eoln do
{2}    GetChar;
      readln;
      CurLine := CurLine+1;
      {pad line with spaces}
      end;
```

A **while** statement consists of the reserved words **while** and **do** separated by a boolean expression giving the conditions under which the statement immediately following (the 'body' of the loop) is to be executed:

while <boolean expression> **do** <statement>

In the example above, the statement **GetChar** will be performed while **eoln** is false. Here are some more examples:

i)   while x < y do x := x + z;
ii) while ch < > ' ! ' do
      begin
      name [i] := ch;
      read (ch);
      i := i+1;
      end;

Figure 8.11 gives the syntax of a **while** loop.

while statement

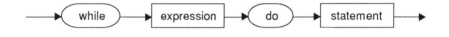

Figure 8.11

Whether a **repeat** or a **while** loop should be used depends upon whether the process concerned is to be performed *at least once* regardless (use **repeat**), or whether it is only to be performed *at all* if the iteration conditions are satisfied initially (use **while**).

PADDING A STRING WITH SPACES

There are two alternative ways of padding out a string with spaces. The first is to copy the characters which we want into the elements at the beginning of the string and then to fill the remaining elements with a space character (as we did in Chapter 7). The second method is to fill all the elements of the string with spaces *before* copying any characters into the string.

An advantage of using the second method is that the 'padding' can be done using a single assignment statement. For example:

Text [1] :=
'   ';

would put a space character into every element of the string **Text [1]**.

We are now ready to complete the procedure **GetLine**:

```
    procedure GetLine;
{0} {inputs a line of text}
    begin
{1} CurChar := 1;
    LetterText [CurLine] :=
    '                                        ';
    while not eoln do
{2}     GetChar;
    readln;
    CurLine := CurLine+1;
    end;
```

RECOGNISING THE END OF THE LETTER

We need to give the user a way of indicating that he has finished typing in the main text of his letter. We will choose to use a per cent character (%) alone on a line as a marker to indicate this. We must now devise a way of checking when this marker has been entered.

Setting a Flag

The procedure **GetChar** deals with processing characters as they are read in. So we will need to amend this to take into account our new condition. But it is the outer procedure **EnterLetter** which contains the iteration which is to be performed *until* the end of the letter is reached. So we need to be able to communicate this fact from one procedure to another. To do this we must use a variable which is available to both procedures. We will declare a boolean variable, **EndReached**, within **EnterLetter**. This variable can be used by **GetChar**, since **GetChar** is also defined within **EnterLetter**. We will initialise **EndReached** to false before starting to process the text. It will then be set to true within **GetChar** when the end-of-text marker is reached. Using a variable in this way is known as 'setting a flag'. This is because it is a 'signal' which indicates when a particular set of circumstances exists.

The use of boolean flags is discussed further in the 'more advanced topics' section of Chapter 6.

We can now complete **EnterLetter**:

```
procedure EnterLetter;
var EndReached : boolean;
  procedure GetChar;
  {inputs a character and checks for marker}
  var
    ch : char;
  begin
  read (ch);
  if eoln
    then if (ch = '%') and (CurChar = 1)
            then EndReached := true {note no ;}
            else if (ch = '$')
                    then begin
                            LineNo := CurLine;
```

```
                        CharNo := CurChar
                        end {note no ;}
                     else LetterText [CurLine,CurChar]
                                         := ch
         else begin
             LetterText [CurLine,CurChar] := ch;
             CurChar := CurChar + 1
             end;
         end;
         procedure GetLine;
         {inputs a line of text}
         begin
         CurChar := 1;
         LetterText [CurChar] :=
            '                                    ';
         while not eoln do GetChar;
         readln;
         CurLine := CurLine+1;
         end;
      begin
      EndReached := false;
      CurLine := 1; {note initialisation of CurLine}
      writeln ('Type in text of letter');
      writeln ('Put $ to insert name');
      writeln ('Enter % to end');
      repeat
         GetLine;
      until EndReached;
      end;
```

Read this procedure through carefully. It uses three different 'control constructs' (ie statements that determine which course of action is to be followed): if ... else, while ... do and repeat ... until. Think about why each has been chosen. Look particularly carefully at the nest of if statements. (You may like to refer back to Chapter 3 to remind yourself of how to use nested if statements.)

Now test the procedure by typing in and running the program so far:

```
program Letter (input,output);
type
```

```
    line = packed array [1..50] of char;
var
    LetterText : array [1..20] of line;
    name : packed array [1..20] of char;
    LineNo, CharNo, CurLine, CurChar : integer;
procedure EnterLetter;
var EndReached : boolean;
    procedure GetChar;
    {inputs a character and checks for marker}
    var
      ch : char;
    begin
    read (ch);
    if eoln
      then if (ch = '%') and (CurChar = 1)
            then EndReached := true
            else if (ch = '$')
                    then begin
                         LineNo := CurLine;
                         CharNo := CurChar;
                         end
                    else LetterText [CurLine,CurChar]
                                              := ch
        else begin
            LetterText [CurLine,CurChar] := ch;
            CurChar := CurChar + 1
            end;
    end;
    procedure GetLine;
    {inputs a line of text}
    begin
    CurChar := 1;
    LetterText [CurLine] :=
      '                                            ';
    while not eoln do GetChar;
    readln;
    end;
begin
EndReached := false;
CurLine := 1;
```

```
writeln ('Type in text of letter');
writeln ('Put $ to insert name');
writeln ('Enter % to end');
Repeat
  GetLine;
  CurLine := CurLine = 1;
until EndReached;
end;
procedure Entername;
begin
{Allow user to type in a name}
end;
procedure InsertName;
begin
{Insert name into main text}
end;
procedure PrintLetter;
begin
{Print out letter}
end;
procedure MakeLetters;
begin
{Repeat
  Entername;
  Insertname;
  PrintLetter;
Until end of list}
end;
    {main program}
begin
EnterLetter;
MakeLetters;
end.
```

PROCESSING THE LIST OF NAMES

The procedure **MakeLetters** performs a very similar task to that of the procedure **MakeInvitations** in the party invitation program of Chapter 7. We can, therefore, use similar code. If we again use '*' to terminate the list of names, we can complete the procedure like this:

```
procedure MakeLetters;
begin
Repeat
  Entername;
  if name [1] < > '*' then
    begin
    Insertname;
    PrintLetter;
    end;
until name [1] = '*';
end;
```

We can also make use of the code for reading in a name, which we wrote in Chapter 7. So we can easily complete **EnterName**:

```
procedure Entername;
begin
{Allow user to enter name}
var
  i : integer;
begin
writeln ('Enter name or * to end.');
i := 1;
repeat
  read (Name[i]);
  i := i+1;
Until eoln or (i>=20);
readln;
if i <= 20 then
  repeat
    Name[i] := ' ';
  until i > 20;
end;
```

Using the new technique introduced in this chapter for padding out with spaces, we can improve this procedure:

```
procedure Entername;
begin
{Allow user to enter name}
var
  i : integer;
```

```
begin
writeln ('enter name or * to end.');
name := ' ';
i := 1;
repeat
  read (Name[i]);
  i := i+1;
until eoln or (i >=20);
Readln;
end;
```

INSERTING A NAME INTO THE TEXT

Since it was stipulated that a name will only be added as the *last* item on
a line of text, it will be fairly straightforward to insert each name into the
text of the letter. We must simply replace the padding spaces on the
appropriate line with the characters of the current name. We will assume,
for the present, that there are always *at least 20* spaces available to hold
the name.

We clearly need to perform an iteration. We must copy each element
of **name** into an appropriate element of **LetterText**. **LineNo** and
CharNo hold values giving the element of **LetterText** into which we
must copy the first element of **name**, and so we could use the following
assignment statement to copy one element:

LetterText [LineNo,CharNo] := name[1]

The next element of name must be copied into the next element of

LetterText [LineNo]:
LetterText [LineNo,CharNo+1] := name[2]

and so on:

LetterText [LineNo,CharNo+2] := name[3]
LetterText [LineNo,CharNo+3] := name[4]
.
.
.
LetterText [LineNo,CharNo+19] := name[20]

In other words, *for each integer*, **i**, *from* 1 *to* 20 we need to perform the
assignment:

LetterText [LineNo,CharNo+i–1] := name[i]

We can write this in Pascal like this:

for i := 1 to 20 do
LetterText [LineNo,CharNo+i–1] := name[i]

FOR LOOPS

A **for** loop is known as a *count-controlled* loop. We need to use a 'control-variable'. The *control-variable* is given a starting value, which is assigned to it before execution of the loop for the first time. Each time the body of the loop is executed the control-variable is incremented by 1. The body is executed repeatedly until the control-variable reaches the stated terminating value.

In our example above, the control variable, i, is given the starting value of 1. The terminating value is set to be 20. So, the statement:

LetterText [LineNo,CharNo+i–1] :=name[i]

will be executed 20 times (once for each value of i from 1 to 20).

The above **for** statement has exactly the same effect as the following **while** statement:

i := 1;
while i <= 20 do
  begin
  LetterText [LineNo,CharNo+i–1] :=name[i];
  i := i+1
  end;

Here are some more examples of **for** loops:

i)   **for index := 1 to EndIndex do**
          table [index] := 0;
ii)   **for ch := 'a' to 'z' do**
          write (ch);
iii)   **for i := j to k+4 do**
          begin
          writeln ('i = ',i);
          writeln (LetterText[i])
          end;

Sometimes it is useful to use the control-variable to count downwards instead of upwards. We can do this by using the reserved word **downto** in place of **to**. Here is an example:

iv)   **for i := 10 downto 1 do**
        writeln ('In ',i, 'th place was ', Entrant [i]);

The syntax of a **for** loop is given in Figure 8.12.

The control-variable of a **for** loop must be of *ordinal type*. Ordinal types are discussed in the more advanced topics section of Chapter 4. For the present, the only ordinal types which we will use are: **integer, char** and **boolean**.

In order to prevent the possibility of a control-variable having its value inadvertently altered during the execution of the **for** loop, Pascal imposes some rules governing the use of control-variables:

1)   A variable can only be used as the control-variable of a for loop if it has been declared *locally* within the procedure immediately containing the loop. It would not, for example, be admissible to use the global variable **CurChar** as the control-variable of a **for** loop within **GetChar**.

2)   It is *not* permitted to assign a value to a control-variable *within the loop which it controls*. This means that the following loop is not acceptable:

for i := 1 to 10 do
  begin
  writeln (i);
  i := j;
  end;

However, the following assignment *outside* the loop *is* permitted:

for i := 1 to 10 do
  begin
  writeln (i);
  end;
i := j;

The value of the control-variable once the loop has been completed is *undefined*. This means that it could take *any* value. It can *not*, for example, be assumed to have the terminating value of the loop (although this *may* be the case in a particular implementation).

for statment

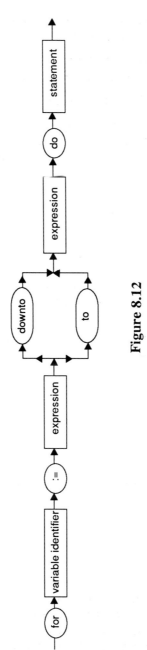

Figure 8.12

If, when a **for ... to** loop is about to be executed, the starting value is *greater* than the terminating value then the loop will not be executed *at all*. Consider, for example, the following:

for i := j to k do write (i); (where **i**, **j** and **k** are all integer variables)

With the initial values j=1 and **k**=4, the loop will be executed 4 times.

With **j**=1 and **k**=1, it will be executed once.

With **j**=4 and **k**=3, it will not be executed. The program will skip directly to the statement immediately following.

Pascal also imposes restrictions to prevent the starting or finishing values of a **for** loop being re-defined within the loop. It is not allowed to alter the values of *any* variables which form part of the expressions which determine the starting or finishing values of the control-variable, within the loop. For example, the following **for** loop contains the *illegal* assignment statement **k := k–1**:

```
for i := j to k do
  begin
  write (i);
  k := k–1;
  end;
```

COMPLETING OUR PROGRAM

We can now complete **InsertName** by declaring a local integer variable, **i**, as the control-variable of the following loop:

for i := 1 to 20 do
LetterText [LineNo,CharNo+i–1] := name [i]

Our only other remaining procedure, **PrintLetter**, requires a **writeln** statement of the following form:

writeln (LetterText [i])

for each line of text, *from* the first *to* the *last* line.

The number of the current line (**CurLine**) is incremented each time **GetLine** is executed. On the last time through **GetLine**, **CurLine** will start out with a value *1 greater* than the number of the last line of the letter (since the end-marker is entered on a line *beyond* the end of the letter). **CurLine** will then be incremented as **GetLine** is executed for the last

time. So, after the letter has been entered, the value of **CurLine** will be
2 greater than the number of the last line of the letter. (If you cannot
follow this, try a few 'dry-runs'. Or you could add a **write** statement to
display the value of **CurLine** and then run the program.)

So we need to write out **LetterText** [i] for each value of i *from* 1 to
CurLine–2:

```
for i := 1 to CurLine–1 do
  writeln (LetterText [i]);
```

Our completed program looks like this:

```
program Letter (input,output);
type
  line = packed array [1..50] of char;
var
  LetterText : array [1..20] of line;
  name : packed array [1..20] of char;
  LineNo,CharNo,CurLine,CurChar : integer;
procedure EnterLetter;
var EndReached : boolean;
  procedure GetChar;
  {inputs a character and checks for marker}
  var
    ch : char;
  begin
  read (ch);
  if eoln
    then if (ch = '%') and (CurChar = 1)
            then EndReached := true
            else if (ch = '$')
                    then begin
                      LineNo := CurLine;
                      CharNo := CurChar
                      end
                    else LetterText [CurLine,CurChar]
                                              := ch
    else begin
      LetterText [CurLine,CurChar] := ch;
      CurChar := CurChar + 1
      end;
  end;
```

```pascal
procedure GetLine;
{inputs a line of text}
begin
CurChar := 1;
LetterText [CurLine] :=
  '                                        ';
while not eoln do GetChar;
readln;
end;
begin
EndReached := false;
CurLine := 1;
writeln ('Type in text of letter');
writeln ('Put $ to insert name');
writeln ('Enter % to end');
repeat
  GetLine;
  CurLine := CurLine+1;
until EndReached;
end;
procedure Entername;
{Allow user to enter name}
var
  i : integer;
begin
writeln ('Enter name or * to end.');
name := '                        ';
i := 1;
repeat
  read (Name[i]);
  i := i+1;
until eoln or (i >=20);
readln;
end;
procedure InsertName;
var
  i : integer;
begin
{Insert name into main text}
for i := 1 to 20 do
```

```
    Text [LineNo,CharNo+i-1] := name[i];
end;
procedure PrintLetter;
var
  i : integer;
begin
{Print out letter}
for i := 1 to CurLine-2 do
  writeln (LetterText [i]);
end;
procedure MakeLetters;
begin
Repeat
  Entername;
  if name[1] < > '*' then
    begin
    Insertname;
    PrintLetter;
    end;
until name[1] = '*';
end;
  {main program}
begin
EnterLetter;
MakeLetters;
end.
```

(This program displays each letter on the screen. You will have to modify **PrintLetter** in order to send the output to your printer.)

MORE ADVANCED TOPICS

Changing the Size of an Array

Suppose that our client decides that he would like to be able to include names of up to 30 characters in his letters. We can modify our program to cope with this by changing the size of the string which holds the name. However, we must also change *any other* references to the size of this string. For example, the **for** loop in **InsertName** copies each of the 20 elements of **Name** into the appropriate elements of **LetterText**.

Of course, we can change this **for** loop so that it is executed 30 times simply by replacing the 20 with 30 in our source code. But it is not always easy to tell whether a particular number in the source code arises because it is the size of an array, or for some other reason. (We might, for example, be required to print out 20 copies of each letter. This would result in the number 20 occurring in our program quite independently of the size of any array.)

To make such changes easier, we could declare a *constant identifier* to describe the length of our name string. We can define a constant by including a constant declaration section in our program immediately after the program header. We can then use this constant when declaring **Name**, and again whenever we wish to refer to the length of **Name**. Here is the declaration section of our program, with these alterations:

```
program Letter (input,output);
const
  NameLength = 20;
type
  line = packed array [1..50] of char;
var
  LetterText : array [1..20] of line;
  name : packed array [1..NameLength] of char;
  LineNo,CharNo,CurLine,CurChar : integer;
```

This enables us to alter the length of **Name** simply by altering the value of **NameLength** defined in the constant declaration section.

It is always sensible to declare a constant identifier to describe any fixed value which may be referred to a number of times during a program. This improves readability, as well as making alterations easier. It is sometimes extremely difficult to work out why a particular number is included in the source code of the program. It is much easier to understand its significance if a constant identifier is used.

Constants need not be integers. It is possible to declare constants belonging to any of the standard Pascal types. Here are some examples:

```
const
  IntConst = 10;
  RealConst = 4.3;
  CharConst = 'a';
  BoolConst = true;
```

Figure 8.13 gives the syntax of the constant declaration section.

constant declaration

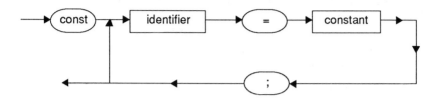

Figure 8.13

EXERCISES

1. Look at the following program. Which of the loops (marked {1}, {2} etc) are correct Pascal? What is the program intended to do? Correct it and run it.

```pascal
program MakePattern (input,output);
type
   LineType = packed array [1..80] of char;
   PageType = array [1..20] of LineType;
   PatType = packed array [1..5] of char;
var
   Page : PageType;
   Pats : array [1..10] of PatType;
   index,CurPat,CurLine,LastPat : integer;
procedure ReadPats;
{Reads up to 5 patterns into Pats}
var i : integer;
   procedure readPat;
   begin
   writeln ('enter a 5-character pattern');
{1} for i := 1 to 5 do
      begin
{2}   while eoln do readln;
      read (Pats[CurPat,i]);
      end;
   readln;
   Curpat := Curpat+1;
   end; {ReadPat}
```

```
begin {ReadPats}
writeln ('How many patterns do you wish to use?');
writeln ('Enter a number from 1 to 5');
{3} repeat
       readln (LastPat);
   until LastPat in [1..5];
CurPat := 1;
{4} for i := 1 to LastPat do ReadPat;
end; {ReadPats}
Procedure Copypats;
{Copies patterns into Page}
var ThisLine : integer;
Procedure CopyLine;
   var j : integer;
   begin
   index := 0;
{5} while index <= 76 do {Think. Why 76?}
       begin
{6}     for j := 1 to 5 do
           begin
           index := index + 1;
           Page [ThisLine,index] := Pats[CurPat,j];
           j := j + 1;
           end; {for}
       if CurPat = lastPat
           then CurPat := 1
           else CurPat := CurPat + 1;
       end; {while}
   end; {CopyLine}
begin {CopyPats}
CurPat := 1;
{7} For ThisLine := 1 to 20 do CopyLine;
end; {CopyPats}
Procedure ShowPage;
{Displays page of patterns}
begin
{8} for index := 1 to 20 do
       writeln (page[index]);
end; {ShowPage}
begin {main program}
```

```
    ReadPats;
    CopyPats;
    ShowPage;
    end.
```

2. Modify the standard-letter program to prevent too many characters being entered on any single line of the text. (You may simply throw away any extra characters entered.)

Make a similar modification to prevent the user typing in more lines of text than the program can cope with. Add a warning message to alert the user if he attempts to enter too many lines.

3. Modify the standard-letter program to give a warning message if the name-marker occurs more than once. Further modify it to give a warning if the name-marker character does not occur at all.

4. Modify the standard-letter program to allow up to five name-markers, so that the same name may be inserted up to five times in each letter.

*5. Change all the numbers giving the size of arrays in the standard-letter program into constant identifiers. Check that your new version is correct by running it. Then alter the size of names to 40 characters and the number of lines on the page to 60.

9 I've Got a Little List

INTRODUCTION

In this chapter we will make further improvements to the standard-letter program which we wrote in Chapter 8. This will include storing letters and lists of names on disk, so that they may be re-used. We will then write a very simple word processor program which will allow text to be entered, edited and saved to disk.

NEW PASCAL FEATURES

1) Parameters
2) Text files

REVIEW OF THE STANDARD-LETTER PROGRAM

If you have completed the exercises in Chapter 8, you should now have a program which will:

1) Allow the user to enter a letter of up to 20 lines of text, each line being up to 50 characters long. Extra lines or characters will be discarded.
2) Allow the user to include up to five 'name markers' in this text.
3) Allow the user to enter a name of up to 20 characters, which will then be inserted into the text whenever one of the name markers occurs. The completed letter will then be printed.
4) Allow the process of entering a name and printing a letter to be repeated as many times as the user chooses.

Here is a working version of the program so far. Do not worry if it is not identical to your version.

```pascal
program Letter (input,output);
type
  line = packed array [1..50] of char;
var
  LetterText : array [1..20] of line;
  Name : packed array [1..20] of char;
  CurLine,CurChar,MarkerIndex : integer;
  LineNos,CharNos : array [1..5] of integer;

procedure EnterLetter;
var EndReached : boolean;
  procedure MarkName;
  begin
  MarkerIndex := MarkerIndex+1;
if MarkerIndex <= 5
  then begin
      LineNos [MarkerIndex] := CurLine;
      CharNos [MarkerIndex] := CurChar
      end
  else begin
      writeln ('Only 5 name markers allowed.');
      MarkerIndex := 5
      end;
end;
procedure GetChar;
{inputs a character and checks for marker}
var
  ch : char;
begin
read (ch);
if eoln
  then if (ch = '%') and (CurChar =1)
        then EndReached := true
        else if (ch = '$')
              then MarkName
              else LetterText [CurLine,CurChar]:= ch
  else if CurChar > 50
        then begin
              writeln ('Line too long.');
```

```
                    while not eoln do read (ch);
                    end
              else begin
                    LetterText [CurLine,CurChar] := ch;
                    CurChar := CurChar + 1
                    end;
end;
procedure GetLine;
{inputs a line of text}
begin
CurChar := 1;
LetterText [CurLine] :=
'                                        ';
while not eoln do GetChar;
  readln;
  end;
begin
MarkerIndex := 0; {no name markers so far}
EndReached := false;
CurLine := 1;
writeln ('Type in text of letter');
writeln ('Put $ to insert name');
writeln ('Enter % to end');
repeat
  GetLine;
  CurLine := CurLine+1;
until EndReached or (CurLine > 20);
if CurLine > 20
  then writeln ('Text too long.');
if MarkerIndex = 0
  then writeln ('Warning. No name marker used.');
end;
procedure Entername;
{Allow user to enter name}
var
  i : integer;
begin
writeln ('Enter name or * to end.');
Name:= '                            ';
i :=1;
```

```
    repeat
      read (Name[i]);
      i := i+1;
    until eoln or (i >=20);
    readln;
    end;

    procedure InsertName;
    var
      i, j : integer;
    begin
    {Insert name into main text}
      for j := 1 to MarkerIndex do
    for i := 1 to 20 do
        Text [LineNos[j],CharNos[j]+i–1] := Name[i];
    end;
    procedure PrintLetter;
    var
      i : integer;
    begin
    {Print out letter}
    for i := 1 to CurLine–2 do
      writeln (LetterText[i]);
    end;
    procedure MakeLetters;
    begin
    repeat
      Entername;
      if name[1] < > '*' then
          begin
          InsertName;
          PrintLetter;
          end;
    until Name[1] = '*';
    end;
        {main program}
    begin
    EnterLetter;
    MakeLetters;
    end.
```

DEALING WITH LINES WHICH ARE TOO LONG

At present, if the user enters a line of text longer than 50 characters then the extra characters are simply thrown away. This will be extremely annoying for him, since the resulting letter is likely to be totally incomprehensible. We can make our program more 'user-friendly' by giving him the chance to correct his mistake.

We will alter our program so that the user is asked to re-type the whole of the offending line, using 50 characters or fewer. This can be done by altering the part of procedure **GetChar** which checks for lines which are too long:

```
if CurChar > 50
    then begin
            writeln ('Line too long.');
            writeln ('Please re-enter last line.');
            readln; {skip to next line of input}
            LetterText [CurLine] :=
        '                                        ';
            {reset current line to spaces}
            CurChar := 1; {Reset index}
        end
    else begin
            LetterText [CurLine,CurChar] := ch;
            CurChar := CurChar + 1
        end;
```

Notice that the index giving the current line (**CurLine**) remains unchanged, while **CurChar** is reset to 1. This ensures that next time a character is read in it will be copied into the first character of the current line. Perform a dry run to make sure that this new version will perform correctly. Then test it by running it.

PRINTING SEVERAL LETTERS AT ONCE

At present, the user of our program has to wait for each letter to be printed before he can enter the next name on his list. This is not very convenient. It would be better if he could enter the *entire* list of names at once, and then leave the program to print out all the letters together.

To do this we will need to define a suitable data-structure to store the list of names. An array of strings is an obvious choice. Each string will be of length 20, as before. But how many such strings should we allow? Looking back at the original program specification (see Chapter 8), we discover that 'several thousand' names may be required. We could use an enormous array, such as:

NameList : array [1..10000] of packed array [1..20] of char

But this will take up an inordinate amount of memory space. It is also unlikely that the user will want to type in as many as 10,000 names at one go.

We will choose a 'sensible' list size (large enough for the user's convenience, but not unmanageably big), and then process the letters in batches of this size. 50 letters is probably a suitable number.

To store our list of 50 names we will make the following declarations:

type
    NameType = packed array [1..20] of char;
var
    NameList: array [1..50] of NameType;

We will need an index for **NameList**, to give the number of the current name being read in. We could declare this as:

CurName : integer

Previously, the current name was stored in the variable **Name** (which is no longer needed). So, we must now change all references to **name** into references to **NameList [CurName]**. (Your editor will probably have a way of doing this quite easily – look for instructions such as 'search and replace' or 'find'.)

Now, all we have to do is to adjust MakeLetters, so that it reads in up to 50 names before printing. The following loop will read in the list of names:

```
CurName := 1;
repeat
  Entername;
  Curname := CurName+1;
until (NameList [Curname–1,1] = '*') or (CurName > 50);
```

We can then print out the letters using the following:

CurName := 1;

```
while (NameList [CurName, 1] < > '*') and (Curname < = 50) do
   begin
   InsertName;
   PrintLetter;
   Curname := CurName + 1
   end;
```
(i is an integer variable which must be declared in **MakeLetters**.)

To allow more than one batch of 50 letters to be processed, we must incorporate yet another loop into **MakeLetters**:

```
procedure MakeLetters;
begin
repeat
   CurName := 1;
   repeat
     Entername;
     CurName := CurName+1;
   until (NameList [CurName-1,1] = '*') or (CurName > 50);
   CurName := 1;
   while (NameList [CurName,1] < > '*')
              and (CurName < = 50) do
     begin
     InsertName;
     PrintLetter;
     CurName := CurName + 1;
     end;
until NameList [CurName,1] = '*';
end;
```

To test the program it will be more convenient to use a smaller batch size (three, say). Try it out using a variety of different list sizes. In particular, test that sizes smaller than, greater than, and equal to the batch size are all processed correctly.

PARAMETERS

Look at our new version of **MakeLetters**. There is a rather complicated **while** loop which steps through the list of names inserting them into the text and printing out each letter. In order to 'tell' **InsertName** which name is to be inserted, the global variable **CurName** must be set to the appropriate value before **InsertName** is executed. **InsertName** then 'finds' the appropriate name out of the array **NameList** and inserts it into the text.

A better way of 'handing' information from one procedure to another is to use *parameters*. In order to use a parameter in a procedure, it must be declared in the procedure heading. For example:

```
procedure table (i : integer);
var j : integer
begin
writeln (i, ' times table');
for j := 1 to 12 do
   writeln ( j, '   ', j*i);
end;
```

This declares that the procedure table has a parameter of integer type. Whenever **table** is called, a value for the parameter **i** must also be given. This is done by enclosing an *expression* of the correct type (in this case, integer) within round brackets after the procedure name. For example, to call **table** with the parameter value 2, we could write:

table (2);

This gives **i** the initial value 2 when the procedure **table** starts execution. The statements within **table** will then be executed exactly as if **i** had been declared as a local variable. Once table has been executed, **i** ceases to exist. If **table** is called *again*, a new initial value of **i** must be specified.

Parameters of this kind are called *value parameters*, because they are given a *value* on entry to the procedure. For the present, these will be the only kind of parameters which we will use.

Here are some more examples of parameter declarations and corresponding procedure calls:

1) **procedure OutName (name : packed array [1..10] of char);**
   OutName (FirstName);
   OutName ('Fred ');

2) **procedure Add (i, j : integer);**
   Add (1, 5);
   Add (m,n);
   Add (q,6);
   Add (p–q,r+s);

3)   **procedure PrintChars (c:char;number:integer);**
     printChars ('a',14);
     printchars (ch,n);
     printchars (name [i],53);

As you can see, procedures may have a number of different parameters. And these parameters may be of the same or different types. Figure 9.1 gives the syntax of a procedure heading including value parameters.

In our present program, we would like to be able to 'hand over' the value of a string of 20 characters to the procedure **InsertName**. We can do this by declaring a parameter in the heading of **InsertName**. We can then use this parameter within **InsertName** whenever we are referring to the name which we are inserting:

```
procedure InsertName (name:NameType);
var
  i,j : integer;
begin
{Insert name into main text}
for j := 1 to markerIndex do
  for i := 1 to 20 do
    Text [LineNos[j], CharNos[j]+i-1] := name[i];
end;
```

We must also modify **MakeLetters** so that an appropriate value is given to the parameter when **InsertName** is called:

```
procedure MakeLetters;
begin
repeat
  CurName := 1;
  repeat
    Entername;
    CurName := CurName+1;
  until (NameList [CurName-1,1] = '*') or (CurName > 50);
  CurName := 1;
  while (NameList [CurName,1] < > '*') and (CurName < = 50) do
    begin
    InsertName (NameList [CurName]);
    PrintLetter;
    CurName := CurName + 1
    end;
```

procedure header

parameter list – value parameters only

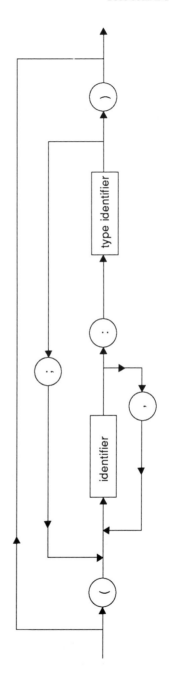

Figure 9.1

```
    until NameList [CurName,1] = '*';
  end;
```

And, now that we are no longer tied to using **CurName** to specify which name is to be inserted, we can simplify our source code. We will take advantage of the fact that, after the list of names has been read in, the value of **CurName** is exactly 1 greater than the index to the last name entered.

```
procedure MakeLetters;
var i : integer;
begin
repeat
  CurName := 1;
  repeat
    Entername;
    CurName := CurName+1;
  until (NameList [CurName-1,1] = '*') or (CurName > 50);
  if NameList [CurName-1,1] = '*' then Curname := Curname-1;
  for i := 1 to CurName-1 do
    begin
    InsertName (NameList [i]);
    PrintLetter;
    end;
until NameList [CurName,1] = '*';
end;
```

SAVING THE CONTENTS OF A LETTER FOR FUTURE USE

It would be useful if the user's letter were not lost once the program has finished running. We will now alter our program to allow him to 'save' the text of a letter for later use. We will also give him the option of retrieving a previously saved letter instead of typing in a new letter each time the program is run.

TEXT FILES

We can store lines of text in a *text file*. We met text files briefly in Chapter 7, when we discussed sending output to a printer. File handling is an area of Pascal where there are often variations in implementation. We will use standard ISO Pascal. You may need to make slight alterations in order to fit in with your particular system.

Before we can use a file we must declare it in the declaration section of our program. For example:

var
    LetterFile: file of char;

Turbo Pascal does not recognise the type **file of char** as being a text file. Turbo Pascal users *must* use the pre-defined type identifier **text** when declaring text files. Most other implementations allow either **text** or **file of char** to be used interchangeably.

At this stage we will only use files of char (or 'text files'). We can think of a text file as being a long list of characters arranged in order. This list may be subdivided into individual lines of text, or may be simply a continuous list of characters.

At any one time during execution of a program, the file may be *closed* (ie not available to the program) or *open* for *writing* (ie characters may be added to the file by the program) or *open* for *reading* (ie characters may be read from the file). But it is not possible to switch between *reading from* and *writing to* a file without closing the file in between these operations.

To open a file for writing, we use the **rewrite** command:

    rewrite (LetterFile);

This has the effect of 'throwing away' any characters which may previously have been written into **LetterFile**, and preparing an 'empty' file to be written to. It is not possible to add to the contents of an existing file.

To open a file for reading, we use the **reset** command:

    reset (LetterFile);

This closes **LetterFile**, if it has previously been opened, and makes it ready for the characters in it to be read. The contents of a file can only be read *in the order in which they were written to the file*. After a file has been reset, the first character to be read will be the character which was the first to be written to the file. In order to read a later character, characters must be read from the file in turn until the required character is reached.

It may help to think of a file as being like a train entering a tunnel. Each carriage (or character) enters the tunnel at one end. They emerge from the other end *in the same order* as they went in, and any particular carriage can only come out of the tunnel once all the carriages ahead of it have emerged.

When a file is open for reading or writing, a 'pointer' keeps track of the current position in the file. After **rewrite** the pointer will point to an empty storage space at the start of an empty file. As characters are written to the file, so the pointer moves to indicate the next available storage space in the file. After **reset**, the pointer points to the first storage space in the file. As characters are read from the file, so the pointer moves to indicate the next character which will be read in.

Each line of text within a text file is separated from the next by a special character (the end-of-line marker). When the file pointer reaches an end-of-line marker, **eoln** becomes true for that file. So we could, for example, read a line of text from **LetterFile** into an array, **Line**, of characters using the following loop:

```
while not eoln (LetterFile) do
  begin
  read (LetterFile,Line[i]);
  i:=1
  end;
```

Another pre-defined Pascal identifier **eof** simply gives information about whether or not the end of a file has been reached. **Eof (LetterFile)** will take the value false whenever there are still characters remaining to be read in **LetterFile**, and the value true when the last character has been read. It is important always to check whether the end of a file has been reached before attempting to read from it. Trying to read beyond the end of a file will produce a run-time error.

Figure 9.2 illustrates the way in which lines of text are stored in a file, and the way in which the file pointer moves and the values of **eoln** and **eof** vary as characters are read in from the file.

SAVING A LETTER IN A TEXT FILE

Here is a simple program using a text file. It allows the user to type in a short letter, which is copied into a text file and stored for future use.

```
program copy (input, output, LetterFile);
var
  LetterFile : text;
  ch : char;
begin
rewrite (LetterFile);
writeln ('Enter letter. Enter % to end.');
repeat
while not eoln do
  begin
  read (ch);
  if not ((ch='%') and eoln)
    then write (LetterFile,ch);
```

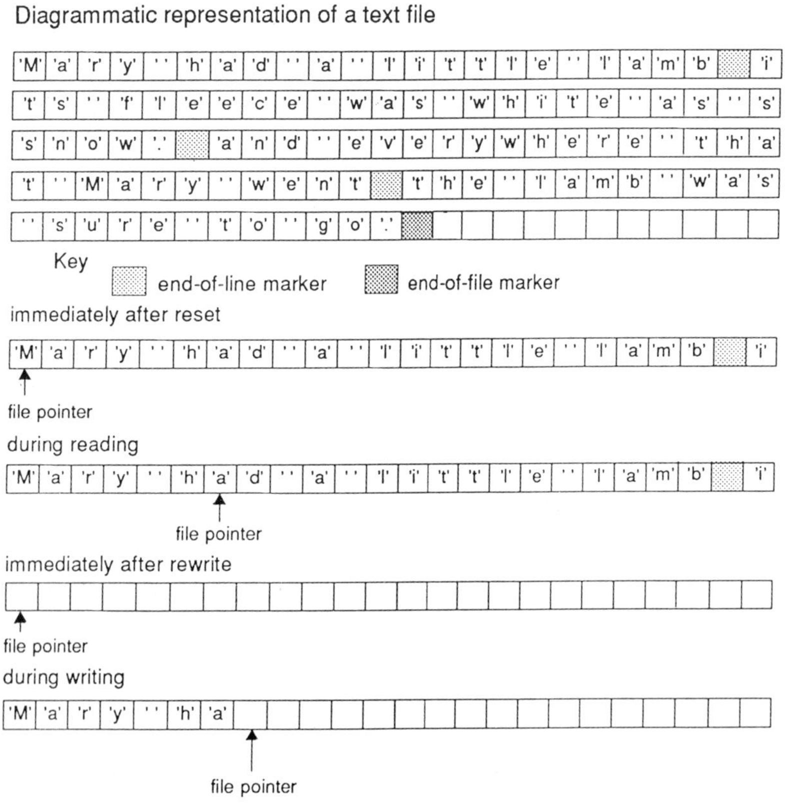
Diagrammatic representation of a text file
Key
end-of-line marker
end-of-file marker
immediately after reset
file pointer
during reading
file pointer
immediately after rewrite
file pointer
during writing
file pointer

Figure 9.2

```
   end;
 readln;
 writeln (LetterFile);
 until ch = '%';
 end.
```

The identifier of the text file is included in the program header to indicate to the compiler that the file we are using is to be stored *externally* (ie on disk, magnetic tape, etc).

The 'rogue value', '%', at the end of a line has been used to signify that the letter is complete.

After each line of text is read in, a **readln** command is used to skip on to the next line of input. This prevents any spurious characters (such as 'carriage return' or 'linefeed') being read.

The file **LetterFile** is opened for writing by the command **rewrite (LetterFile)**. Characters can then be added to the file by using a **write** statement with the file identifier as the first parameter, for example:

write (LetterFile,ch)

The text stored in **LetterFile** is separated into lines by using **writeln (LetterFile)** at the end of each line. This inserts a marker into the file to indicate where a new line begins.

Try running this program. You may need to make some alterations to suit your implementation. You may, for example, need to include an instruction to *close* the file at the end of the program. You may, perhaps, have to give the file a second *external* name to fit in with your computer system. Consult a manual or ask for advice.

Note to Turbo Pascal Users

You will need an **assign** command to give your file an external name. You can then give it any name you choose, including specifying a disk drive or directory to be used. Here are some examples:

1) **Assign (LetterFile,'letter');**
2) **assign (LetterFile,'B:letter');**
3) **Assign (LetterFile,'A:paslet.doc');**

To ensure that the file is written to disk at the end of execution, you should include a **close** command before the final **end**. Here is the complete program modified for use with Turbo Pascal:

```pascal
program copy (input, output, LetterFile);
var
  LetterFile : text;
  ch : char;
begin
assign (LetterFile,'letter');
rewrite (LetterFile);
writeln ('Enter letter. Enter % to end.');
repeat
while not eoln do
  begin
  read (ch);
  if not ((ch='%') and eoln)
    then write (LetterFile,ch);
  end;
readln;
writeln (LetterFile);
until ch = '%';
close (LetterFile);
end.
```

DISPLAYING A TEXT FILE ON SCREEN

Here is a program which reads in lines of text from the file created by the previous program and displays them on the screen:

```pascal
program ShowFile (input,output,LetterFile);
type
  LineType = packed array [1..50] of char;
var
  LetterFile : text;
  Letter : array [1..20] of LineType;
  LineIndex,CharIndex,i : integer;
begin
reset (LetterFile);
LineIndex := 1;
while not eof (LetterFile) do
  begin
  CharIndex := 1;
  while not eoln (LetterFile) do
    begin
    read (LetterFile,Letter[LineIndex,CharIndex]);
```

```
    CharIndex := CharIndex+1;
    end;
  readln (LetterFile);
  LineIndex := LineIndex+1;
  end;
for i := 1 to LineIndex do
  writeln (Letter[i]);
end.
```

As in the previous example, the file identifier, **LetterFile** is included in the program header to indicate that it represents an *external* file.

The file is opened for reading by the command, **reset (LetterFile)**. The contents of **LetterFile** can then be read character by character using **read** statements, such as **read (LetterFile,ch)**. At the end of each line (ie when **Eoln (LetterFile)** becomes true) **readln (LetterFile)** is used to skip on to the first character on the next line of text.

The characters contained in **LetterFile** are stored in an array of strings (like the one used in our standard letter program). Each string of 50 characters is used to store one line of text.

Read through this program carefully and make sure that you understand what each statement is for. Then try running it. You will have to make sure that a suitable file is available for the program to read from. The file created by the program **copy** (listed earlier) will do.

Note to Turbo Pascal Users

You will need to make slight alterations to the program listed above in order to run it:

1) Insert an **assign** command, such as that following, immediately before the statement **reset (LetterFile)**:

   assign (LetterFile,'Letter');

2) Insert the following statement before the final **end**:
   close (LetterFile);

MODIFYING THE STANDARD LETTER PROGRAM

We can now proceed to make alterations to our standard letter program in order to allow letters to be stored for future use.

We will introduce a *menu* (see Chapter 5), which will allow the user to choose between three options:

1) To run the program as before, without storing his letter.
2) To type in a letter from the keyboard and store it on disk.
3) To retrieve a previously stored letter and print out letters using names input from the keyboard.

Figure 9.3 shows the processes required for each of these options. Look at the boxes on the lowest level of this structure diagram. We have already written procedures to perform the processes described by boxes A, B, C and F. So, we can complete our program by writing code for boxes D and E as well as a menu-selection procedure.

We will use a text file variable, **LetterFile**, to store a letter on disk. We can then write each line of the letter to this file using **writeln** statements, just as we did when writing to the screen or printer:

```
procedure StoreLetter;
var
  i : integer;
begin
rewrite (LetterFile);
for i := 1 to CurLine–2 do
   writeln (LetterFile,LetterText[i]);
end;
```

We can read the letter from the disk, character by character using readln statements, somewhat as we did when reading in the letter from the keyboard. However, there are some differences.

When reading from the keyboard we had to check that the user did not attempt to type in too many letters on a line, or too many lines of text. If he did, then a warning message was produced and he was given the opportunity of correcting his mistake. When reading from disk there is no point in issuing warning messages, since the contents of the disk file cannot be altered. So our program must be capable of coping satisfactorily with whatever is input from the file.

Provided that the file which is to be read in has been created by the procedure **StoreLetter**, there will be no problem. This procedure stores only the contents of **text** (ie up to 20 lines of exactly 50 characters, padded out with spaces). The following procedure inputs a letter from a file of this kind, and stores it in **text**:

```
procedure ReadLetter;
var
```

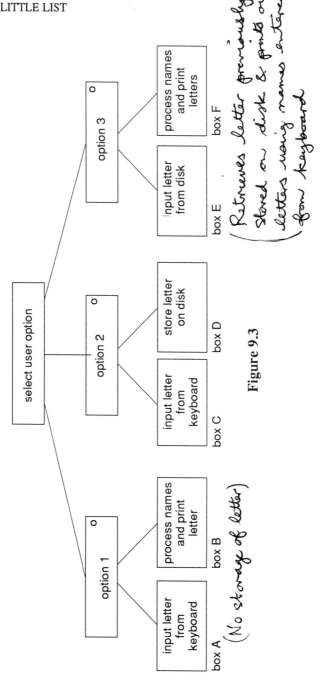

Figure 9.3

```
  i : integer;
begin
  CurLine := 1;
  reset (LetterFile);
  while not eof (LetterFile) do
    for i := 1 to 50 do
      read (LetterFile,LetterText[CurLine, j]);
  readln (LetterFile);
end;
```

However, there is one thing which we have not yet taken into account. As well as the text of the letter, we also need to store the information about *where* the name is to be inserted. At present this information is kept in two arrays, **LineNos** and **CharNos**. The values stored in these locations will be lost when the program finishes executing, so we must find a way of storing them on disk as well.

It will be most convenient if we can use *the same* file to store all the information required for a particular letter. So we will allocate an extra line of characters *at the beginning* of **LetterFile** to hold the name marker information.

STORING NUMBERS IN A FILE OF CHAR

It is possible to write numbers (in this case integers) to a text file, and to read them from a text file. For example, the statement, **write (LetterFile,23)** would send the characters '2', '3' (preceded by a number of space characters, which will vary from one system to another) to **LetterFile**.

Numbers can also be read from a file of char, but care must be taken to ensure that the sequence of characters read in does form a valid number, and that at least one space separates each number from the next. Otherwise a run time error will occur. When a number is read from a text file, the program skips past any spaces or end-of-line characters and then attempts to interpret all the characters up to the next space or end-of-line as a number.

Here are new versions of **StoreLetter** and **ReadLetter**, which incorporate storing and retrieving the name marker information:

procedure StoreLetter;
var

```
    i : integer;
  begin
  rewrite (LetterFile);
  for i := 1 to MarkerIndex do
    write (LetterFile, ' ', LineNos[i], ' ', CharNos[i]);
  writeln (LetterFile);
  for i := 1 to CurLine-2 do
    writeln (LetterFile,LetterText [i]);
  end;
  procedure ReadLetter;
  var
    i : integer;
  begin
  CurLine := 1;
  MarkerIndex := 0;
  reset (LetterFile);
  while not eoln (LetterFile) do
    begin
    MarkerIndex := MarkerIndex+1;
    read (LetterFile,LineNos[MarkerIndex],
                       CharNos[MarkerIndex]);
    end;
    readln (LetterFile);
  while not eof (LetterFile) do
    begin
    for i := 1 to 50 do
      read (LetterFile,LetterText[CurLine, j]);
    readln (LetterFile);
    CurLine := CurLine+1;
    end;
  end;
```

Take careful note of the **write** statement in **StoreLetter**, which outputs the contents of **LineNos** and **CharNos**. It is important to output the numbers in such a way as to enable them to be read in again by **ReadLetter**.

Space characters are written to the file *before* each integer so as to ensure that the numbers are separated by at least one space. It is important *not* to write a space *after* the last number on the line. This is because, when a number is read in from a text file, trailing spaces (ie spaces *after* the number) are not skipped. This means that, if a space were added after the last number, **eoln** would *not* become true after the last number on the line was read (since there would still be a space character on the current line).

THE MAIN MENU PROCEDURE

Using the methods of Chapter 5, we can write a procedure to display a menu and to allow the user to choose an option. Try to design such a procedure for yourself before looking at the one listed below. You will find the structure diagram in Figure 9.3 helpful.

```
procedure MainMenu;
var
  code : char;
  procedure DisplayOptions;
  begin
  writeln;writeln;
  writeln ('Which option do you require?');
  writeln;
  writeln ('1: enter letter and print');
  writeln ('2: enter letter and store');
  writeln ('3: retrieve letter from disk and print');
  writeln;
  end; {DisplayOptions}
  procedure GetCode;
  var
    validchars : set of char;
  begin
  validchars := ['1','2','3'];
  repeat
    writeln ('enter code number to select option');
    readln (code);
  until code in validchars;
  end; {GetCode}
begin {MainMenu}
DisplayOptions;
GetCode;
case code of
  '1':    begin
          EnterLetter;
```

```
            MakeLetters;
            end;
    '2':    begin
            EnterLetter;
            StoreLetter;
            end;
    '3':    begin
            ReadLetter;
            MakeLetters;
            end
        end; {case}
    end; {MainMenu}
```

Incorporate these three new procedures into your program (remember to alter the main body so as to call the main menu), and test it. Try out all the different options using a variety of lengths of letters and numbers of names.

A SIMPLE WORD-PROCESSOR

We will now use our knowledge of text files to write a very simple word-processor program. Our program will allow the user to specify left- and right-margins. The program will then read in an unformatted document from a text file (ie end-of-line markers occur only at the end of paragraphs), and format it as up to 100 lines of left-justified text. It will display it on the screen within the chosen margins, and the document can then either be stored on disk or printed out.

Figure 9.4 is a structure diagram illustrating the processes involved. Using this structure, we can write the following skeleton program:

```
program WordProc (input,output);
procedure InDoc;
  {input document from disk}
    procedure UnFormDoc;
      {input unformatted document from disk}
        procedure GetMargins;
          {input margin positions from keyboard}
        begin {GetMargins}
        end; {GetMargins}
        procedure Format;
        {input, format and display document}
```

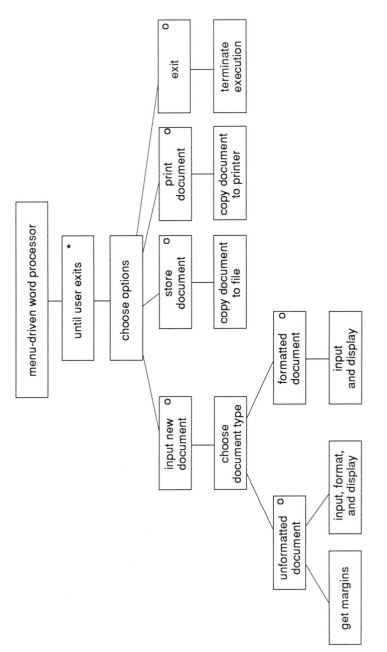

Figure 9.4

```
      begin {Format}
      end; {Format}
   begin {UnFormDoc}
   end; {UnFormDoc}
   procedure FormDoc;
      {input formatted document from disk}
      begin {FormDoc}
      end; {FormDoc}
   begin {InDoc}
   end; {InDoc}
   procedure StoreDoc;
      {store formatted document on disk}
   begin {StoreDoc}
   end; {StoreDoc}
   procedure PrintDoc;
      {print out formatted document}
   begin {PrintDoc}
   end; {PrintDoc}
   begin {main program}
   repeat
      {Allow user to choose options}
   until exit
   end. {main program}
```

CHOOSING DATA STRUCTURES

Assuming that our screen has a width of 80 columns, it would be sensible to store a line of text in a string of length 80 characters. Our document is limited to no more than 100 such lines. We will, therefore, use an array, **DocArray**, of 100 such strings to store the entire document.

We will need to declare two external text files: one from which we can input the unformatted document, and one to which the formatted document can be output. (We may need a third file to represent the printer, this will depend on your computer system.) We will give these two files the identifiers **InFile** and **OutFile**.

INPUTTING AND FORMATTING A DOCUMENT

We will now look in detail at the procedure **Format**. Before we can input a document (either formatted or unformatted) we need to perform some *initialisation* tasks. We need to prepare the input file for reading by resetting it. (Other, implementation-dependent file initialisation may also be necessary.) We will also fill **DocArray** with space characters, so that it will not be necessary to pad out each line with spaces later.

We will declare a procedure, **InitDoc**, to do this. We can then call this procedure before inputting either a formatted or an unformatted document.

We will have to read in the unformatted document character-by-character from the input file. We will, therefore, need a loop which reads in characters up to the end-of-file marker. A **while** loop will enable us to take into account the case where the input file is empty:

```
while not eof (InFile) do
  begin
  {read in characters and put in DocArray}
  end;
```

We will need to go to a new line whenever an end-of-line marker is encountered. So we will need a second, inner, loop which terminates when **eoln (InFile)** becomes **true**:

```
while not eoln (InFile) do
  begin
  {read in characters and put in DocArray}
  end;
```

We will also need to move on to a new line when we have filled the current line up as far as the right margin. In this case, we will also have to check whether or not we have reached the end of a word. If not, we will have to *move* the letters of the incomplete word at the end of the current line on to the next line, and pad out the current line with spaces. Our program will be easier to follow if we use a separate procedure **MoveChars** to perform this operation.

We will declare a char type variable, **ch**, into which we will read each character of the document, before storing it in **DocArray**. This will enable us to 'look beyond' the end of a line of text, and determine whether or not the end of a word has been reached. Whenever we reach the end of a line we will check whether the next character is a space character. If not, then we will call **MoveChars**.

We will need integer variables to store the current line and character positions within **DocArray**. If we use global variables then we can use these to give information about how many lines the document contains in total. We will need to know this whenever we wish to store or print the document. We will give these variables the identifiers **LineIndex** and **CharIndex**.

We will need to take great care to ensure that **LineIndex** and **CharIndex** *always* contain the correct values. **CharIndex** must be incremented every time a character is stored in **DocArray**. **LineIndex** must be incremented whenever a new line is started. In addition, whenever we move on to a new line, **CharIndex** must be set to the value of the left-margin position. We will use **LMargin** and **RMargin** to store the left- and right-margin positions.

We can now fill in the loops:

```
while not eof (InFile) do
  begin
  while not eoln (InFile) do
    begin
    read (InFile,ch);
    if CharIndex < = RMargin {not beyond right
                                       margin}
      then begin
        DocArray [LineIndex,CharIndex] := ch;
        CharIndex := CharIndex+1
                    {increment CharIndex}
      end
    else begin
      CharIndex := LMargin;
              {go back to left margin}
      if ch < > ' '
        then MoveChars;
      if not eoln (InFile)
        then LineIndex := LineIndex+1;
              {move on to next line}
      end;
    end; {while not eoln (InFile)}
  if not eof (InFile) then readln (InFile);
      {prepare to read next line of input}
  LineIndex := LineIndex+1;
      {move on to next line}
```

```
      CharIndex := LMargin;
          {go back to left margin}
end; {while not eof (InFile)}
```

The procedure **MoveChars** needs a little thought. We must work our way *backwards* through the current line of **DocArray** until we find a space character. (We will declare a local variable, i, to hold this index.) We must then *copy* all entries on the current line *beyond* the element containing the space character into elements at the beginning of the next line, starting at the left-margin position. We will declare a second local variable, j, which holds the index to the element which is about to be copied. We will index the element into which a character is to be copied by **CharIndex**. This will ensure that **CharIndex** ends up with the correct value, ready for future use. Finally, we must put the most recently read character (stored in **ch**) into **DocArray**, so as to be ready to read in the next character.

Study **MoveChars** carefully so that you understand exactly what is happening:

```
procedure MoveChars; {moves chars on to next line}
var i, j : integer;
begin {MoveChars}
i := RMargin;
while DocArray [LineIndex, i] < > ' ' do
                {look for beginning of word}
   i := i–1;
for j := i+1 to RMargin do
   begin {copy last word on to next line}
   DocArray [LineIndex+1,CharIndex] :=
      DocArray [LineIndex, j];
   DocArray [LineIndex, j] := ' ';
                {pad current line with spaces}
   CharIndex := CharIndex+1;
   end;
DocArray [LineIndex+1,CharIndex] := ch;
CharIndex := CharIndex+1;
end; {MoveChars}
```

Once the document has been stored in **DocArray**, we can display it on the screen simply by **write**-ing each line to the standard **output** file. We

will do this within another procedure, **DisplayDoc**, which can be called
after inputting either a formatted or unformatted document.

FILLING IN THE BLANKS

You should by now be able to complete most of the procedures in this
program. Try to write code for:

the main body, **GetMargins, FormDoc, StoreDoc, PrintDoc.**

Here is a version of **WordProc** which will work, using Turbo Pascal,
on a PC. Lines of code which are specific to Turbo Pascal are marked
with a comment {Turbo}. If you are using a different version of Pascal
you may have to omit these lines or replace them with alternative code.

To run the program you will need to use your text editor to create an
unformatted file. Remember to use the same name for the file as you use
for the input file in your program!

```
program WordProc (input,output, InFile,OutFile,PrinterFile);
type
  Line = packed array [1..80] of char;
var
  DocArray : array [1..100] of Line;
  exit : boolean;
  InFile,OutFile,PrinterFile : text;
  Choice : char;
  LineIndex, CharIndex : integer;
procedure InDoc;
  procedure InitDoc;
  var i, j : integer;
  begin
  for i := 1 to 100 do
    for j := 1 to 80 do
      DocArray [i, j] := ' ';
  assign (InFile, 'DocFile'); {Turbo}
  reset (InFile);
  LineIndex := 1;
  end; {InitDoc}
  procedure UnFormDoc;
  var
```

```pascal
    LMargin,RMargin : integer;
{input unformatted document from disk}
    procedure GetMargins;
    begin {GetMargins}
    writeln ('please enter position of left margin');
    readln (LMargin);
    while not (LMargin in [1..70]) do
       begin
       writeln ('invalid left margin position.');
       writeln ('Please re-enter.');
       readln (LMargin);
       end;
    writeln ('please enter position of right margin');
    readln (RMargin);
    while not (RMargin in [LMargin + 1..80]) do
       begin
       writeln ('invalid left margin position.');
       writeln ('Please re-enter.');
       readln (RMargin);
       end;
    end; {Get Margins}
    procedure Format;
    var
       ch : char;
    procedure MoveChars; {moves chars on to next line}
    var i, j : integer;
    begin {MoveChars}
    i := RMargin;
    while DocArray [LineIndex,i] < > ' ' do
       i := i–1;
    for j := i+1 to RMargin do
       begin
       DocArray [LineIndex+1,CharIndex] :=
          DocArray [LineIndex, j];
       DocArray [LineIndex, j] := ' ';
       CharIndex := CharIndex+1;
       end;
    DocArray [LineIndex+1,CharIndex] := ch;
    CharIndex := CharIndex+1;
    end; {MoveChars}
```

```
begin {Format}
CharIndex := LMargin;
while not eof (InFile) do
   begin
   while not eoln (InFile) do
      begin
      read (InFile,ch);
      if CharIndex < = RMargin
         then begin
              DocArray [LineIndex,CharIndex] := ch;
              CharIndex := CharIndex+1
              end
         else begin
              CharIndex := LMargin;
              if ch < > ' '
                 then MoveChars;
              if not eoln (InFile)
                 then LineIndex := LineIndex+1;
              end;
      end; {while not eoln (InFile)}
      if not eof (InFile) then readln (InFile);
      LineIndex := LineIndex+1;
      CharIndex := LMargin;
   end; {while not eof (InFile)}
end; {Format}
begin {UnFormDoc}
GetMargins;
InitDoc;
Format;
end;
procedure FormDoc;
var
   i : integer;
begin {FormDoc}
InitDoc;
while not eof (InFile) do
   begin
   for i := 1 to 80 do
      read (InFile,DocArray[LineIndex,i]);
   readln (InFile);
```

```
          LineIndex := LineIndex+1;
          end;
        end; {FormDoc}
        procedure DisplayDoc;
        var i : integer;
        begin
        for i : 1 to LineIndex-1 do
          begin
          writeln (DocArray[i]);
          end;
        end;
      begin {InDoc}
      writeln ('Formatted or unformatted document?');
      writeln ('enter "f"/"u"');
      repeat
        readln (choice)
      until choice in ['f', 'F', 'U', 'u'];
      if choice in ['f', 'F'] then FormDoc
                              else UnFormDoc;
      close (InFile); {Turbo}
      DisplayDoc;
      end; {InDoc}
      procedure StoreDoc;
      var
        i : integer;
      begin {StoreDoc}
      assign (OutFile, 'DocFile'); {Turbo}
      rewrite (OutFile);
      for i := 1 to LineIndex-1 do
        writeln (OutFile,DocArray[i]);
      close (OutFile); {Turbo}
      end; {StoreDoc}
      procedure PrintDoc;
      var i : integer;
        {print out formatted document}
      begin {PrintDoc}
      assign (PrinterFile,'prn'); {Turbo}
      rewrite (PrinterFile);
      for i := 1 to LineIndex-1 do
        writeln (PrinterFile,DocArray[i]);
```

```
close (PrinterFile); {Turbo}
end; {PrintDoc}
begin {main program}
exit := false;
repeat
writeln ('What would you like to do next?');
writeln;
writeln ('1. Input document from disk');
writeln ('2. Store current document');
writeln ('3. Print current document');
writeln ('4. Exit');
writeln;
writeln ('enter number of option you require');
repeat
  readln (choice)
until choice in ['1', '2', '3', '4'];
case choice of
  '1' :   InDoc;
  '2' :   StoreDoc;
  '3' :   PrintDoc;
  '4' :   Exit := true
end; {case}
until exit
end. {main program}
```

MORE ADVANCED TOPICS

Buffer Variables

Each Pascal text file has associated with it a 'buffer variable'. This represents the current character of the file (ie the next available character in the case of a file open for reading). The buffer variable of a file with name **ThisFile** is denoted by **ThisFile^**.

The statement **read (ThisFile,ch)** copies the buffer variable, **ThisFile^**, into **ch** and moves on through the file, so that **ThisFile^** takes the value of the next character in the file. The statement **ch:=ThisFile^** copies **ThisFile^** into **ch**, but *does not* move on to the next character in the file. So, for example, the following program segment will assign *the same* value for each of the variables **ch1**, **ch2**, and **ch3**:

```
ch1 := ThisFile^;
```

```
ch2 := ThisFile^;
ch3 := ThisFile^;
```

It is sometimes useful to examine the contents of the buffer variable of an input file before deciding whether or not to read in the next character. We could, for example, have used the buffer variable in our word processor program when we wished to find out whether or not the next character in the file was a space.

When either of **eof (ThisFile)** or **eoln (ThisFile)** is **true**, the buffer variable, **ThisFile^**, is required by the ISO standard to be the space character. In practice, in some implementations (including Turbo Pascal) this is not the case. When using a version of Pascal which does not adhere to the standard in this respect, it is particularly important to make sure that you never attempt to read beyond the last character on a line of text. If you do then you may inadvertently try to process various characters used to denote the end of a line (carriage-return, linefeed etc) in place of the actual text contained in your file.

When **eof (ThisFile)** is **true** then **eoln (ThisFile)** is always **true** also.

Get and Put

When a text file is open for input, it is possible to move on to the next character in the file *without* reading in the current character. **Get (ThisFile)** has the effect of moving on to the next character and 'throwing away' the current character. Thus

```
ch := ThisFile^;
Get (ThisFile);
```

has exactly the same effect as

```
read (ThisFile);
```

It is sometimes useful to use **get** to skip past unwanted characters in a file.

When a text file is open for output, the buffer variable is undefined until it is assigned a value. We can do this using an assignment statement:

```
ThisFile^ := ch;
```

This copies the value of **ch** into the buffer variable **ThisFile^**. To add this value to the contents of **ThisFile**, we need to use the procedure **put**.

Put (ThisFile) has the effect of adding the value of the buffer variable to the end of **ThisFile**, leaving the buffer variable undefined once more. The combination of statements, **ThisFile^ :=ch, put (ThisFile);**, has exactly the same effect as the single statement, **write (ThisFile,ch);**.

Using our train analogy once more, we can think of the file buffer variable as a siding, large enough to contain one truck (or character). When we write a character to the file, we first shunt it into the siding (ie assign a value to the buffer variable). Then we can couple it to the end of the train (ie use the **put** procedure). Similarly, to **read** a character from a file, we must first uncouple the leading truck and move it into the siding (using **get**). The truck is then ready to be taken away (using an assignment statement).

Note to Turbo Pascal Users

Turbo Pascal does not include the procedures **get** and **put,** or the ability to access the file buffer variable. To add data to a file the **write** procedure must be used. Data can only be read from a file by using the **read** procedure. The only real disadvantage of this limitation is that it is not possible to 'read ahead' from a file without actually inputting the next data item.

Internal and External Files

The files which we have used so far are all *external* files. This means that they exist before (in the case of input) or after (in the case of output) the program is executed. It is possible to declare a file identifier in the variable declaration section of the program *without* listing it in the program header. The resulting file is an *internal* file. An internal file can be used during execution of the program to store data temporarily, but the contents of the file will be lost when the program finishes execution.

One use for an internal file would be to store data until we know whether or not it needs to be stored externally. For example, our word processor program could be modified to cope with larger documents by storing the document in an internal file instead of in an array.

Turbo Pascal does not implement internal files. All file variables (whether or not declared in the program header) will be treated as external.

Reading Numbers from a Text File

It is possible to read in integers or real numbers from a text file. It is important to make sure that a valid sequence of characters corresponding to the type of variable being read is input. Leading spaces are skipped, but trailing spaces are not. Unless you can be absolutely certain that no extra spaces will be included in your file, special care must be taken. Consider the following program segment:

```
reset (InFile);
while not eof (InFile) do
    read (InFile, IntNumber);
```

where **IntNumber** is an integer variable.

If the last number in the file is followed by one or more space characters, then **eof (InFile)** will be false after the last number has been read in. So the loop will be executed again. The remaining spaces will be skipped – up to and *beyond* the end of the file.

There are several possible ways of dealing with this problem, for example:

1) Use a 'rogue value' to terminate the sequence of numbers.
2) Include statements to skip any trailing spaces after each number.

Formatting Output

Integer, real, char and boolean types of data may all be output to a text file. The exact format in which they will be output depends upon your implementation. If the format of output is particularly important (for example, if you are printing a table of values), then the number of character spaces (ie the *width*) taken up by each data item can be specified. This is done by adding the required width after the data item in the **write** or **writeln** statement. For example

write (i:10, ':',Answer[i]:20)

would display the integer variable **i** and the **real** array element **Answer [i]** using widths of 10 and 20 characters respectively.

In the case of real items, a second integer value may be appended. This specifies the number of digits which are to be printed after the decimal point. If this is specified then the item is output in the following way:
<space character> <sign> <integral part> <decimal point> <fractional

part>. If the second value is not given then the item is output with only one decimal place before the decimal point and using the E symbol to give the magnitude. For example, the value 100.23 would be output in the form 1.0023E2.

EXERCISES

1. Look at the following procedure heading:

procedure TestParams (i:integer;b1,b2:boolean;ch:char);

Suppose that the following variable identifiers have been declared:

value, age:integer;
good,stop,goback:boolean;
FirstChar,lastChar:char;

Which of the following procedure calls are correct?

   i)   **TestParams (value,good,stop,'a');**
   ii) **TestParams (1,true,false,age):**
  iii) **TestParams (value+age,not stop,goback,LastChar);**
  iv) **TestParams (age-21,goback,FirstChar);**
   v) **TestParams (10,value=age,age>65,'*');**

2. Write a procedure to display a 10-by-5 rectangle of stars on the screen:

```
* * * * * * * * * *
* * * * * * * * * *
* * * * * * * * * *
* * * * * * * * * *
* * * * * * * * * *
```

Using parameters, modify this procedure so that any size rectangle may be drawn. Write a program, incorporating this procedure, which asks for the dimensions of the rectangle and then displays it on the screen.

3. Write a procedure, **ErrorMessage**, which can be called whenever the user of a program enters inappropriate data. It should display a message on the screen indicating what is wrong. Try to find a way of drawing the user's attention to the problem, by 'beeping' or changing the screen display in a noticeable way. (Use a string parameter to hold the message.)

4. Modify the word-processor program to cope with larger documents by

dealing with a number of 100-line portions. After each portion has been read in and formatted it should be written to a text file (*not* the same file as it was read from!). This second (formatted) text file should then be **reset**, so that its contents may be input line-by-line and sent to the printer if required.

5. Write a program which stores names and addresses in a text file. The user should be given the option of either creating a new file, or adding to a previously created file.

You will need to decide on a way of marking the point at which one entry ends and the next begins – you could, for example, use a special character to denote the end of an entry, or you could specify an exact number of lines for each entry.

To add an entry to a file, you will need to use *two* files. Read in each entry from the input file and copy it into an output file. When you reach the end of the input file, add any entries which the user requires to the output file. You will then need to copy *all* the entries in the output file *back into* the original file.

6. (More difficult.) Suppose that a text file has been created which consists of a number of lines, each of exactly 20 characters. Suppose, further, that the 20-character strings stored in this file are stored in alphabetical order (ie if the first two strings are read into variables **string1** and **string2**, then **string1 < string2** will be true). Write a procedure which will take as a parameter a 20-character string and place it in the file at the appropriate alphabetic place. (Read in each string until you reach one which belongs *after* the parameter string. As in exercise 5, you will need a second, temporary, file.)

Using this procedure, write a program which will allow the user to create and add to a file of 20-character names stored alphabetically.

7. (More difficult.) Write a program to create a text file containing items of the following form:

1st line: **price of house**
2nd line: **vendor's name**
3rd line .. 7th line: **address**

Modify your program, using the technique of exercise 6, to create a file in which the items occur in ascending order of price.

Write a second program which prints out all the houses in a price range specified by the user.

*8. The energy requirements of an individual may be calculated using the following rules:

i) Find basal metabolic rate from tables in Figure 9.5.

i) Add the following percentages according to lifestyle:

mainly sedentary: add 40%
lightly active: add 50%
moderately active: add 60%
regularly active: add 70%
very active: add 80%

(These figures should not be treated as scientifically accurate.)

basal metabolic rate (calories/day) – don't take these seriously, they are purely fictional!

MEN

body weight (kg)	age groups				
	20-29	30-39	40-49	50-59	60+
60-69	1700	1600	1520	1450	1370
70-79	1800	1700	1600	1500	1450
80-89	1900	1800	1720	1650	1500
90+	2100	2000	1940	1890	1800

WOMEN

body weight (kg)	age groups				
	20-29	30-39	40-49	50-59	60+
50-59	1400	1300	1250	1250	1160
60-65	1500	1430	1370	1280	1220
66-69	1600	1500	1420	1330	1300
70+	1700	1610	1520	1430	1360

Figure 9.5

Write a program which will ask the user for the necessary personal details in order to calculate his/her daily energy requirements for each of the above lifestyles. Display the results in the following form:

name: \<name\>
weight: \<weight\> **kg**   **sex:** \<sex\>   **age:** \<age\>
Lifestyle   **energy requirements (cal)**

10 Names and Numbers

INTRODUCTION

In this chapter we will write a program to store data about the customers on an estate agent's mailing list. This will involve defining a suitable Pascal type to store a number of diverse items in a single variable; and the creation of files in which to store such entities.

NEW PASCAL FEATURES

1) Record type definitions
2) Enumerated type definitions
3) Subrange type definitions
4) Constant definitions
5) Files (other than text files)
6) Variable parameters
7) The **with** statement

WHAT INFORMATION DO WE WANT TO STORE?

Suppose that an estate agent wishes to keep the following information about customers on his mailing list:

1) Name
2) Address
3) Telephone number
4) The price range of properties in which the customer is interested
5) Information about which areas of the town are of interest.

Let us first consider what would be the most satisfactory way of storing each of these items individually:

– The name and address can clearly best be stored in character strings.

– The telephone number could be stored *either* as a character string *or* as an integer. Using an integer variable may cause problems in the case of long telephone numbers, since the maximum integer size may be exceeded. Using a string also has the advantage that it will be easy to include information about such things as which part is the actual number, and which is the dialling code for the local exchange. For example, we might use an underline character to separate the digits: '0512_12345 '.

– The price range can best be stored as two integers, giving the upper and lower limits.

– Information about areas of interest can be stored by defining a list of town areas. We can then record which areas are of interest to a particular customer by using a set variable whose elements are the areas of interest. For example, if we divide the town up into areas labelled A, B, C, D, E, then we could indicate interest in areas A, C, and D using the set {'A', 'C', 'D'}.

RECORDS

Pascal allows us to store diverse variable types, such as those listed above, as a single entity using a record. We can define a suitable record type to store the details for our imaginary estate agent like this:

```
CustomerInfo = record
               name: packed array [1..20] of char;
               address: array [1..6] of packed array [1..40] of char;
               TelNumber: packed array [1..15] of char;
               LowPrice,HighPrice : integer;
               Areas: set of char
               end;
```

We can then declare variables of this new type, like this:

FirstCustomer, CurrentCustomer : CustomerInfo;

The above declarations allocate areas in memory to store two records, each containing: a character string of length 20, an array of 6 x 40-character strings, a 15-character string, two integers, and a set of char.

USING RECORDS

We can refer to the components, or *fields*, of a record by using the record identifier, together with the identifier of the required field. For example,

we could assign the name 'John Smith   ',
to the **name** field of **FirstCustomer** using the following statement:

FirstCustomer . name := 'John Smith   ';

Similarly, we could assign the character, **'a'**, to the 10th place in the 2nd line of the **address** field, using the following:

FirstCustomer . address[2,10] := 'a';

We can also copy the *entire* contents of a record into another record *of the same type,* for example:

FirstCustomer := CurrentCustomer;

DESIGNING OUR PROGRAM

We must now give some attention to what our estate agent will want to be able to do with the information which we will store in records such as those declared above. He will probably wish to be able to perform the following operations:

1) Enter a customer's details from the keyboard.
2) Add these details to a file containing details entered previously.
3) Retrieve information from the file and display it.
4) Retrieve information from the file, amend it, and re-store it.
5) Remove records from the file, when they are no longer required.

Since we have a list of alternative operations which the user will wish to choose between, a menu-driven program seems a sensible choice. Figure 10.1 shows the structure which we will use.

Using this structure, we can write the following skeleton program:

```
program CustomerData (input,output);
type
CustomerInfo = record
                name: packed array [1..20] of char;
                address: array [1..6] of
                        packed array [1..40] of char;
                TelNumber: packed array [1..15] of char;
                LowPrice,HighPrice : integer;
                Areas : set of char
            end;
    var
```

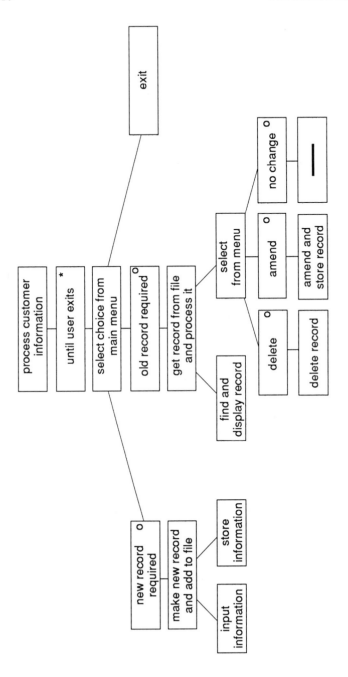

Figure 10.1

```
   exit : boolean;
   CurrentInfo : CustomerInfo;
procedure InputInfo;
begin
   {input customer information from keyboard}
end;
procedure StoreInfo;
begin
   {store record in file}
end;
procedure AddRecord;
begin
   {adds new record to file}
InputInfo;
StoreInfo;
end;
procedure Delete;
begin
   {delete record from file}
end;
procedure Amend;
begin
   {amend record and re-store in file}
end;
procedure DisplayRecord;
begin
   {find and display record from file}
end;
procedure RecordMenu;
begin
   {select operation to be performed on a record}
end;
procedure MainMenu;
begin
   {select operation to be performed on file}
end;
begin  {Main body}
exit := false;
repeat
   MainMenu
```

until exit;
end.

The boolean *flag*, **exit**, will be given the value **true** when the user chooses the exit option from the main menu. This is a means of conveying the information about the user's choice *from* **MainMenu** *to* the main program.

The variable **CurrentInfo** will be used to hold the record which is currently under consideration at any time during execution of the program.

You should, by now, be able to write the procedures **MainMenu** and **RecordMenu**. Remember to include an option in the main menu which sets **exit** to true. Test that your menu procedures do select the correct options by inserting **write** statements into the procedures which they call. For example, if the procedure **AddRecord** is amended like this:

```
procedure AddRecord;
begin
   {adds new record to file}
writeln ('AddRecord');
InputInfo;
StoreInfo;
end;
```

then a message will appear on the screen whenever this procedure is executed.

MORE ABOUT RECORD TYPE DEFINITIONS

We will now leave our programming problem for a while to look more generally at ways of defining record types in Pascal. Here are some more examples of **record** definitions:

```
i)  record
        name : NameType;
        age : integer
    end;
ii) record
        title : String;
        table : array [0..20, 0..10] of integer
    end;
```

iii) **record**
     EmployeeNumber : integer;
     data : record
          name : packed array [1..30] of char;
            age : integer;
            grade : char
          end;
     AttendanceTable : array [1..52, 1..5] of char;
          salary : integer
     end;

As you can see from these examples, it is possible to include type definitions describing the *fields* within a record type definition. The syntax of a record type definition is shown in Figure 10.2.

A type definition such as iii) above, while perfectly acceptable Pascal, is not very easy to understand. There are a number of ways we could improve our presentation:

1) Rather than including additional type definitions *within* a record definition, we could use earlier type definitions to assign a type identifier to any types which we wish to use. For example:

DataType=record
          name : packed array [1..30] of char;
             age : integer;
             grade : char
          end;
AttendTableType= array [1..52, 1..5] of char;

With these definitions, we can then define our employee record type thus:

record
   EmployeeNumber : integer;
   data: DataType;
   AttendanceTable:AttendTableType;
   salary : integer
end;

2) Constant identifiers could be used instead of literal integers when defining the subrange which indexes an array type. This would not only make the program more readable, but also facilitate changes in the size of the array, should they become necessary. Constant declarations are

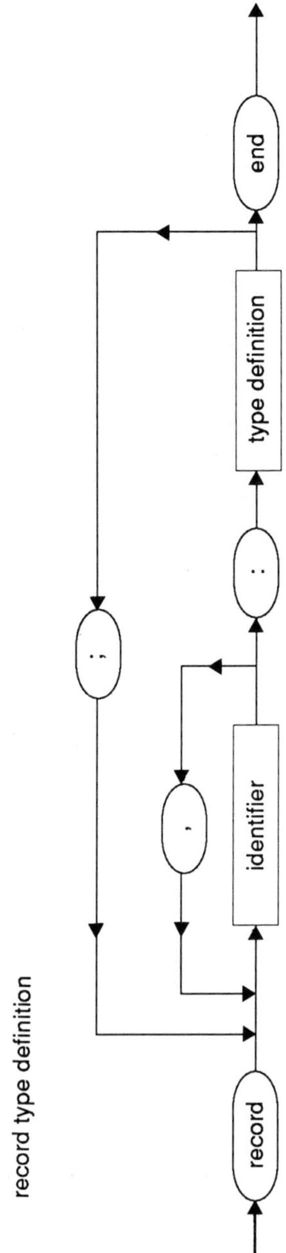

record type definition

Figure 10.2

discussed in the 'more advanced' section of Chapter 8. If you have not already read this section, you should do so now.

Suitable constant declarations would be:

const
  NameLength=30;
  WeeksPerYear=52;

We can then make the following type definitions:

DataType=record
                name : packed array [1..NameLength] of char;
                age : integcr;
                grade : char
              end;
AttendTableType= array [1..WeeksInYear, 1..5] of char;

3) The array type **AttendTableType**, above, is an array indexed by the week of the year and the day of the week. It would be easier to understand which day is being referred to when this array is accessed if the *name* of the day of the week were used, rather than the corresponding number. For example, **AttendTable[23,4]** refers to Thursday of the 23rd week of the year. This would be more immediately apparent if this element of the array could be referred to as **AttendTable[23,Thursday]**.

We could do this by making 5 constant declarations:

const
  Monday=1;
  Tuesday=2;
  Wednesday=3;
  Thursday=4;
  Friday=5;

There is a shorter way of doing this in Pascal: we can define an *enumerated type*. Here is an example:

type
  WeekDay = (Monday,Tuesday,Wednesday,Thursday,Friday);

We can then use this enumerated type to index our array *provided that we define the array to be indexed by this new type.* We can do this like this:

AttendTableType= array [1..WeeksInYear,Monday..Friday] of char;

or, since the subrange which indexes the array is *identical* to the whole enumerated type, like this:

AttendTableType= array [1..WeeksInYear,Weekdays] of char;

Notice that the array **AttendTable** is now indexed by two different types. Our definition specified that the first index must be an integer in the range **1..WeeksInYear**, while the second must be of the enumerated type **WeekDay**.

Enumerated types are *ordinal* (ie there is a definite *order* in which they can be arranged). This means that they can be used as the indices of arrays, and variables of these types can be used to control **for** loops. The order of the members of an enumerated type is the same as the order in which they are listed in the type definition. This means that, with the definition of **WeekDays** given above, the following inequalities are true:

Monday < Tuesday < Wednesday < Thursday < Friday.

The operators **succ** and **pred** (see Chapter 6) may be used on enumerated types. In the above example, **succ(Monday)** = **Tuesday**, **succ(Tuesday)** = **Wednesday, etc.**

IMPROVING THE TYPE DEFINITIONS IN OUR PROGRAM

Let us consider how we can improve the readability of the record type definition in our estate agent program. At present we have the following definition:

```
CustomerInfo = record
                  name: packed array [1..20] of char;
                  address: array [1..6] of
                      packed array [1..40] of char;
                  TelNumber : packed array [1..15] of char;
                  LowPrice,HighPrice : integer;
                  Areas : set of char
               end;
```

We could make this clearer by having separate type definitions for each of the string types, and by using constant definitions to specify the length of each string type. For example:

```
const
  NameLength = 20;
```

```
    LineLength = 40;
    AddrLength = 6;
    TelLength = 15;
type
    NameType = packed array [1..NameLength] of char;
    AddrLine = packed array [1..LineLength] of char;
    AddressType = array [1..AddrLength] of AddrLine;
    TelType = packed array [1..TelLength] of char;
```

It is a little extravagant to use the type **set of char** for our field, **Areas**, when we only in fact have five areas to choose from. We could usefully change to using a *subrange* of the **char** type, such as:

Areas : set of 'A'..'E'

Alternatively, we could choose to use an *enumerated* type, listing *by name* the areas which we wish to include. For example:

type
AreaType=(Appleton,Walton,Grappenhall, Latchford, StocktonHeath);

With this definition, we can declare **Areas** to be of type **set of AreaType**.

We will adopt this second strategy. Our record definition now looks like this:

```
CustomerInfo = record
                name: NameType;
                address: AddressType;
                TelNumber: TelType;
                LowPrice,HighPrice : integer;
                Areas: set of AreaType
            end;
```

INPUTTING THE INFORMATION

We will now look in detail at the procedure **InputInfo**. This procedure must give instructions to the user so that he can enter each item of information as it is required. It must also read in each item of information and store it in the current customer information record. To make our program *user-friendly* we should include some provision for him to correct any mistakes which he may make.

Our record contains three fundamentally different types of data: strings, integers and sets of an enumerated type. We will look at ways of inputting each of these types separately.

Inputting Strings

We have already written procedures to read in strings from the keyboard. The procedure **EnterName** from the program **letter** (listed at the beginning of Chapter 9) can easily be modified to store a name in the **name** field of the current record:

```
procedure EnterName;
var
  i : integer;
begin
  writeln ('Enter name of customer');
  CurrentInfo.Name := '                              ';
  i := 1;
  repeat
    read (CurrentInfo.Name[i]);
    i : =i+1;
  until eoln or (i > Namelength);
  readln;
end;
```

The address can be read in in an exactly similar way, but an additional loop must be included to allow up to six lines to be entered. We must also choose a way for the user to indicate that the last line of the address has been entered, and our program should tell the user what to do. Here is one way of doing this:

```
procedure EnterAddr;
var
  i,LineNo : integer;
begin
  for LineNo := 1 to AddrLength do
    CurrentInfo.Address[LineNo] :=
      '                              ';
  writeln ('Enter address of customer');
  writeln ('Press ENTER twice to end');
  LineNo := 1;
  repeat
```

```
  i := 1;
  repeat
    read (CurrentInfo.Address [LineNo,i]);
    i := i+1;
  until eoln or (i >=LineLength);
  readln;
  LineNo := LineNo+1;
until eoln or (LineNo >=AddrLength);
readln;
end;
```

Validating Data

Inputting the telephone number can be done in the same way. However, in this case we have a very definite idea of what constitutes a 'correct' character. Any character other than one of the digits, '0' .. '9', must be an error. It is, therefore, possible for us to include code which will check each character against a list of valid ones and take appropriate action if an invalid character is typed in. Assuming that the user knows what a telephone number looks like, it is unlikely that he will need to be informed of any mistake that he makes. So we will simply ignore invalid characters and wait for a digit to be entered. Here is a suitable procedure:

```
procedure EnterTel;
var
  i : integer;
  ch : char;
begin
  writeln ('Enter telephone number of customer');
  CurrentInfo.TelNumber := '                    ';
  i := 1;
  repeat
    read (ch);
    if ch in ['0'..'9'] then
      begin
      CurrentInfo.TelNumber[i] :=ch;
      i := i+1;
      end;
  until eoln or (i >TelLength);
  readln;
  end;
```

Inputting Integers

We know how to read in an integer using a **read** statement. However, when we are inputting data which is being typed in by a user, it is not satisfactory to use this facility. This is because a run-time error will occur, and the program will be abandoned, if the user enters a combination of characters which does not constitute a valid integer.

For this reason, we will read in the values of **LowPrice** and **HighPrice** as strings of characters, and then *convert* these strings into the corresponding integer. This will allow us to *ignore* any non-digit characters which may be entered accidentally. We can use a modified version of the procedure for reading in the telephone number to do this.

Since **maxint** (the largest integer allowed on a particular Pascal implementation) is typically 32767, we will use a five character string to store the characters making up our number. So as to ensure that we will only be dealing with integers within the available range, we will ask for prices to be given in terms of multiples of £1000.

Converting from Characters to Integers

The **char** type consists of characters which can be listed in some particular order. The numerical value of the position of a character in this list (ie its *ordinal number*) can be obtained by using the operator **ord**. So, if **ch** is a variable of type **char** and **i** is an **integer** variable, then the statement **i := ord(ch)** assigns the ordinal value of **ch** to **i**.

Since every *ordinal* type can be defined as a list of values occurring in a specified order, this concept of an *ordinal number* is valid for any *ordinal* type. The operator **ord** may, therefore, be used on *any* ordinal type. For example, **ord (false)** = 0, and **ord (true)** = 1.

In the case of the **char** type, there is a corresponding operator, **Chr**, which converts from an integer to the corresponding character value. For example, under implementations which use the ASCII character set, **chr (32)** gives the space character. There is no such 'reverse' conversion operator for any other ordinal type.

The digits '0'..'9' always occupy adjacent positions in the list of characters. In other words, **ord ('1') = ord ('0')+1, ord ('2') = ord ('1')+1**, etc.

So, we can calculate the integer which corresponds to any character in the range '0'..'9' like this:

DigValue := Ord(ch)–Ord('0');

To calculate the *total* value of a string of up to five digits we must take into account the *position* of each digit within the string as well as its value. For example, the integer 12345 is equivalent to 1*10000+ 2*1000+3*100+4*10+5*1. The rightmost digit corresponds to its ordinal value, but the other digits each correspond to their ordinal value *multiplied by* a power of 10. The following procedure performs the conversion process on a string parameter, **NumString**, putting the result in a global variable.

```
Total:
procedure Convert (NumString:NumStringType);
var
   i,TotalSoFar : integer;
begin
i := 1;
TotalSoFar := 0;
while (NumString[i] < > ' ') and (i <=NumLength) do
   begin
   TotalSoFar := TotalSoFar*10 + ord (NumString[i])
                                          – ord ('0');
   i := i+1;
   end;
Total := TotalSoFar;
end;
```

Dry-run this procedure to convince yourself that it does indeed produce the correct result.

We can now write procedures to input each of **LowPrice** and **HighPrice**. For example:

```
procedure EnterLow;
var
   LowString : NumStringType;
   i : integer;
   ch : char;
begin
writeln ('Enter lowest price.');
writeln ('How many thousands of pounds?');
```

```pascal
while not eoln do
  begin
  for i := 1 to NumLength do LowString [i] := ' ';
  i := 1;
  repeat
    read (ch);
    if ch in ['0'..'9'] then
      begin
      LowString [i] := ch;
      i := i+1;
      end;
  until eoln or (i > NumLength);
  if not eoln then
    begin
    writeln ('Too long. Please enter 5-digit integer.');
    readln;
    end;
  end; {while not eoln}
readln;
Convert (LowString);
CurrentInfo.LowPrice := Total;
end;
```

Variable Parameters

The corresponding procedure for inputting **HighPrice** will obviously be identical to that above *except* for the user instructions and the reference to **CurrentInfo.LowPrice**. So it would save a good deal of code if we could use a single procedure to input an integer, and *tell* the procedure where to store the result.

In Chapter 9 we used *value* parameters to pass information *to* a procedure. We will now see how, by using a new kind of parameter (called a *variable parameter*), we can pass information *from* a procedure to the calling program. (Another way of doing this would be to use a *function*. Functions will be discussed in Chapter 11.)

A variable parameter is declared in a procedure heading by including the reserved word, **var**, before the parameter's identifier in the procedure heading. For example, we could use the following procedure heading:

procedure EnterInt (var Total : integer);

This declares a *variable parameter* of type **integer**, for the procedure **EnterInt**.

We could then *call* this procedure, specifying an integer variable, **i**, as the parameter:
EnterInt (i);

When this procedure call is executed, every reference to **Total** within **EnterInt** will be interpreted as a reference to **i**. So, if a value is assigned to **Total** within **EnterInt** then the variable **i** will have that value when execution of **EnterInt** is completed.

When the procedure **EnterInt** is called, a *variable* of integer type must be given to correspond to the *variable* parameter **Total**. This may be simply a variable identifier, or it may be a more complicated variable reference, such as an array element or a record field. (In the case of a *value* parameter only the initial *value* of the parameter is required, so *any* expression of the correct type may be used, *not* necessarily a variable reference.)

The *address* of this variable is then 'handed to' the procedure. Within **EnterInt**, whenever the variable parameter **Total** is referred to, the variable occupying the memory location specified by the given *address* is used. Thus, if a value is assigned to **Total**, within **EnterInt**, then this same value will be assigned to whatever variable was given when the procedure was called.

The following example may help to illustrate the difference between variable and value parameters:

```
program Paramtest (input,output);
var    i : integer;
procedure ValProc (param : integer);
begin
param := param +1;
writeln ('In ValProc para = ',param);
end;
procedure VarProc (var param : integer);
begin
param := param +1;
writeln ('In VarProc param = ',param);
end;
begin {main body}
i := 1;
```

```
writeln ('At start of body i = ', i);
ValProc (i);
writeln ('After ValProc i = ', i);
VarProc (i);
writeln ('After VarProc i = ', i);
end. {main body}
```

The procedure call, **ValProc (i)**, causes **ValProc** to be executed with the current *value* of **i** being given as the starting value for the value parameter **param**. The value of **i** is left *unchanged* after execution of **ValProc**.

The procedure call, **VarProc (i)**, causes **VarProc** to be called with the *address* of **i** being given as the storage location where the variable parameter **param** is to be found. The value of **i** after execution of **VarProc** is *precisely* the final value assigned to **param** within **VarProc**.

Dry-run this program and make a note of what values you would expect to be displayed. Then run it and check your results.

We will now amend the procedures **EnterLow** and **Convert** to create general procedures to handle the input of digits and their conversion:

```
procedure Convert (NumString:NumStringType; var Total :
  integer);
var
  i, TotalSoFar : integer;
begin
i := 1;
TotalSoFar := 0;
while (NumString [i] < > ' ') and (i <=NumLength) do
  begin
  TotalSoFar := TotalSoFar*10 + ord (NumString[i]) –ord ('0');
  i := i+1;
  end;
Total := TotalSoFar;
end;
procedure EnterInt (Message1,Message2:MessageString; var
  Result : integer);
end;
var
  NumString : NumStringType;
  i : integer;
```

```pascal
    ch : char;
begin
writeln (Message1);
writeln (Message2);
while not eoln do
    begin
    for i := 1 to NumLength do NumString [i] := ' ';
    i := 1;
    repeat
      read (ch);
      if ch in ['0'..'9'] then
        begin
        NumString [i] :=ch;
        i : =i+1;
        end;
    until eoln or (i >NumLength);
    if not eoln then
      begin
      writeln ('Too long. Please enter 5-digit integer.');
      readln;
      end;
    end; {while not eoln}
readln;
Convert (NumString,Result);
end;
```

MessageString is a type identifier which must be defined at a level
which includes *both* the procedure **EnterInt** *and* any procedure which
calls **EnterInt**. It must be a packed array of sufficient length to hold
whatever messages may be required to inform the user what he must
enter next. We will use the following type definition:

```pascal
type
    MessageString=packed array [1..40] of char;
```

We can now write a procedure to input the price limits:

```pascal
procedure EnterPrices;
begin
EnterInt ('Please enter lowest price    ',
    'How many thousands of pounds? ', CurrentInfo.LowPrice);
EnterInt ('Please enter highest price ',
```

'How many thousands of pounds? ', CurrentInfo.HighPrice);
end;

INPUT AND OUTPUT OF VARIABLES OF ENUMERATED TYPES

It is *not* possible to input or output the *names* corresponding to the values of an enumerated type. For example, if we have the following type and variable declarations:

```
type
   AreaType=(Appleton,Walton,Grappenhall,Latchford,
      StocktonHeath);
var
   place : AreaType;
```

then the statement **write (place)** would result in a compiler error.

We can get round this problem by declaring an array of strings, in which we will store the names which define our enumerated type. We will use the enumerated type itself to index the array:

```
var
   AreaNames : array [AreaType] of NameType;
procedure InitAreas;
begin
AreaNames [Appleton]       := 'Appleton           ';
AreaNames [Walton]         := 'Walton             ';
AreaNames [Grappenhall]    := 'Grappenhall        ';
AreaNames [Latchford]      := 'Latchford          ';
AreaNames [StocktonHeath]  := 'StocktonHeath      ';
end;
```

We can now easily write a procedure to allow the user to enter areas of interest:

```
procedure InAreas;
var
   Reply : char;
   Area : AreaType;
begin
writeln ('Which areas are of interest?');
writeln ('Enter Y or N for each, as it is displayed.');
CurrentInfo.Areas := [];
```

```
for area := Appleton to StocktonHeath do
  begin
  write (Areanames [area], '? ');
  repeat
    readln (reply);
  until reply in ['y', 'Y', 'N', 'n'];
  writeln;
  if reply in ['y', 'Y'] then
    CurrentInfo.Areas := CurrentInfo.Areas + [area];
  end;
```

The set of areas of interest is created by first assigning to
CurrentInfo.Areas the value of the *empty set* (ie a set containing no
elements), and then adding each element which receives a positive
response. Set operations are discussed in some more detail in the 'more
advanced' section of this chapter.

It would be useful for the user if, once he has entered the details for a
record, the whole record is displayed for him to check. He might then
wish to alter some of the fields, if he has made any errors. We will write
two procedures: one to display the fields of the current record, and one
to allow the user to make alterations to them.

Using With to Access the Fields of a Record

The following procedure displays the fields of the current record:

```
procedure ShowCurrentRecord;
var
  i : integer;
  area : AreaType;
begin {ShowCurrentRecord}
writeln;writeln;writeln ('details of current customer');
with CurrentInfo do
  begin {with}
  writeln;writeln ('NAME          'name);
  writeln ('ADDRESS       ');
  for i := 1 to AddrLength do
  writeln ('              ', address[i]);
  writeln ('TELEPHONE     ',TelNumber);
  writeln ('PRICE RANGE   ',LowPrice,' to ', HighPrice,
                             ' thousand pounds');
```

```
writeln ('Areas of interest:');
for area := Appleton to StocktonHeath do
  if area in Areas
  then writeln (' ',AreaName[area]);
  end {with};
end; {ShowCurrentRecord}
```

Notice the statement **with CurrentInfo do**. This tells the compiler that we wish to refer to fields of the record **CurrentInfo**. Any identifiers which occur in the following statement (in this case the compound statement delimited by **begin {with}** and **end {with}**) will first be compared with the field identifiers of the record given in the **with** statement. If an identifier *is* the same as one of the fields of the record then the compiler will assume that it is this field which is being referred to.

Using a **with** statement shortens the source code whenever we wish to refer to a number of fields of a record within a short space of time. It may also speed up execution, since the address of the record may not now have to be loaded each time a field is accessed.

If we are dealing with a number of different record types we may sometimes wish to refer to the fields of two or three different records in a short segment of code. It is possible to list more than one record in a **with** statement. The following short program illustrates this:

```
program RecordDemo (input,output);
type
  FirstRec = record
               number : integer;
               letter : char
             end;
  SecondRec = record
                name : packed array [1..20] of char;
                int : integer
              end;
var
  f : FirstRec;
  s : SecondRec;
  i : integer;
begin
with f, s do
```

```
    begin
    writeln ('enter number');
    read (number);
    int := number;
    writeln ('enter name');
    i := 1;
    repeat
      read (name[i]);
      i := i+1;
    until eoln or (i >20);
    letter := name[1];
    end;
  end.
```

The statement **with f, s do** is exactly equivalent to the statements:

with f do
  with s do

Care must be taken when using **with** that none of the variable identifiers which we may wish to use are identical with any of the record field identifiers. For example, we could legally declare a local variable, **name**, within **ShowCurrentRecord**. But we can only use this variable *outside* the **with** statement, since within the **with** statement the identifier name is associated with the field **name** of the record **CurrentInfo**.

Allowing Fields to be Altered

We will use a menu to allow the user to alter fields of the current record:

```
procedure AmendMenu;
var
  ch : char;
  Stop : boolean;
begin {AmendMenu}
Stop := false;
repeat
  writeln;writeln ('Which field do you wish to amend?');
  writeln ('Enter number to select option.');
  writeln;writeln ('1. NAME');
  writeln ('2. ADDRESS');
  writeln ('3. TELEPHONE');
  writeln ('4. PRICE RANGE');
```

```
writeln ('5. AREAS OF INTEREST');
writeln ('6. no further amendments');
repeat
  readln (ch);
until ch in ['1'..'6'];
case ch of
  '1' : EnterName;
  '2' : EnterAddr;
  '3' : EnterTel;
  '4' : EnterPrices;
  '5' : EnterAreas;
  '6' : Stop := true
end {case};
until Stop;
end {Amendmenu};
procedure AmendCurrentRecord;
var
  ch : char;
begin {AmendCurrentRecord}
writeln;writeln;
writeln ('Do you wish to amend this information?');
writeln ('Enter Y or N');
repeat
  readln (ch);
until ch in ['Y', 'y', 'N', 'n'];
if ch in ['Y', 'y'] then
  AmendMenu;
end; {AmendCurrentRecord};
procedure StoreInfo;
begin
ShowCurrentRecord;
AmendCurrentRecord;
AddRec;
end;
```

FILES OF RECORDS

We have now completed most of the parts of our program which involve manipulating the data contained in a record. All that remains is to write code to store and retrieve this information using a file. We can declare a suitable file like this:

var
   CustomerFile : file of CustomerInfo;

This declares an identifier **CustomerFile**, which describes a file containing records of the type **CustomerInfo**. Whereas a text file consists of a list of characters (the *elements* of the file), **CustomerFile** contains a list of records of the type specified by **CustomerInfo**.

We can **read** and **write** elements of a file of records, just as we did with the characters of a text file. However, **readln** and **writeln** cannot be used, since the concept of a *line* of elements in a file of records is meaningless. For the same reason, **eoln** cannot be used on a file other than a text file. **Eof**, however may be used on files of any kind. **Eof** (**CustomerFile**) will become true when the last record in the file is read in.

Get and **Put** may also be performed on files of records, and the file buffer variable may be used. The buffer variable, **CustomerFile^**, refers to an *entire record* of the type **CustomerInfo**.

ADDING RECORDS TO AN EXISTING FILE

It is not possible in Pascal to append records to an existing file directly. In order to do this, it is necessary to *read in the entire file* and store the contents in a temporary file. The new elements can then be written to the temporary file. The contents of the temporary file can then be copied *element by element* back into the original file.

Here is a procedure which appends the current record to an existing file of customer records:

```
procedure AddRec;
var
  TempRec : CustomerInfo;
begin
reset (CustomerFile) {prepare for input};
rewrite (TempFile) {prepare for output};
while not eof (CustomerFile) do
  begin
  read (CustomerFile,TempRec);
  write (TempFile,TempRec);
  end;
write (TempFile,CurrentInfo) {add current info};
```

```
reset (TempFile) {prepare for input};
rewrite (CustomerFile) {prepare for output};
while not eof (TempFile) do
   begin
   read (TempFile,TempRec);
   write (CustomerFile,TempRec);
   end;
end;
```

FINDING A PARTICULAR RECORD IN A FILE

In order to find a specific record in a file, we must read in records from the file until we come to the required one. We will need a way of recognising when we have found the right record. Usually this will involve looking at one particular field of each record and comparing it with a given value. We might, for example, wish to find all the customers who are interested in houses in a particular area or within a particular price range.

In our current example, we wish to identify the record of a single customer. So searching by name will be the most satisfactory method. Here is a procedure which searches for the records of a customer whose name is given in a parameter, **CustName**. After each record is read in, it is stored in a temporary file. This will allow us to amend the information in the customer's record and re-store it if required. If the required record is found, it is copied into **CurrentInfo** ready for processing as the current record.

```
procedure FindInfo (CustName:NameType);
var
   TempRec : CustomerInfo;
   Found : boolean;
begin
reset (CustomerFile);
rewrite (TempFile);
found := false;
while not (eof (CustomerFile) or found) do
   begin
   read (CustomerFile,TempRec);
   if TempRec.name = CustName
      then found := true
```

```
      else write (TempFile,TempRec);
    end {while};
  if found
    then CurrentInfo := TempRec
    else writeln ('Customer not found');
  end;
```

DELETING A RECORD FROM A FILE

Once a record has been found in a file using the method above, it may be deleted simply by *not* writing it to the temporary file.

COMPLETING OUR PROGRAM

We have now written most of the components of our program. With a few additions, we can 'glue them together' to give a completed version. The listing below will run using Turbo Pascal. Two lines (marked {Turbo}) have been added to enable Turbo Pascal to assign external names to the files used. You may need to make similar slight amendments to suit your own implementation.

```
program CustomerData (input,output,CustomerFile,TempFile);
const
  NameLength = 20;
  LineLength = 40;
  AddrLength = 6;
  TelLength = 15;
  NumLength = 5;
type
  NameType = packed array [1..NameLength] of char;
  AddrLine = packed array [1..LineLength] of char;
  AddressType = array [1..AddrLength] of AddrLine;
  TelType = packed array [1..TelLength] of char;
  NumStringType = packed array [1..5] of char;
  MessageString = packed array [1..40] of char;
  AreaType =
  (Appleton,Walton,Grappenhall,Latchford,StocktonHeath);
  CustomerInfo = record
                   Name : NameType;
                   address : AddressType;
                   TelNumber : TelType;
```

```
                    LowPrice,HighPrice : integer;
                    Areas : set of AreaType
                 end;
var
  CustomerFile,TempFile : file of CustomerInfo;
  exit : boolean;
  CurrentInfo : CustomerInfo;
  AreaNames : array [AreaType] of NameType;
procedure InitAreas;
begin
AreaNames [Appleton]          := 'Appleton              ';
AreaNames [Walton]            := 'Walton                ';
AreaNames [Grappenhall]       := 'Grappenhall           ';
AreaNames [Latchford]         := 'Latchford             ';
AreaNames [StocktonHeath]     := 'StocktonHeath         ';
end;
procedure EnterName (var name : NameType);
var
  i : integer;
begin
  writeln ('Enter name of customer');
Name := '                        ';
i := 1;
repeat
  read (Name[i]);
  i := i+1;
until eoln or (i >=NameLength);
readln;
end;
procedure EnterAddr;
var
  i, LineNo : integer;
begin
for LineNo := 1 to AddrLength do
  CurrentInfo.Address[LineNo] :=
             '                                    ';
writeln ('Enter address of customer');
writeln ('Press ENTER twice to end');
LineNo := 1;
repeat
```

```
    i := 1;
    repeat
      read (CurrentInfo.Address[LineNo,i]);
      i := i+1;
    until eoln or (i >=LineLength);
    readln;
    LineNo := LineNo+1;
  until eoln or (LineNo >= AddrLength);
  readln;
  end;
  procedure EnterTel;
  var
    i : integer;
    ch : char;
  begin
  writeln ('Enter telephone number of customer');
  CurrentInfo.TelNumber := '                  ';
  i := 1;
  repeat
    read (ch);
    if ch in ['0'..'9'] then
      begin
      CurrentInfo.TelNumber [i] := ch;
      i := i+1;
      end;
  until eoln or (i >=TelLength);
  readln;
  end;
  procedure Convert (NumString:NumStringType; var Total :
    integer);
  var
    i, TotalSoFar : integer;
  begin
  i := 1;
  TotalSoFar := 0;
  while (NumString [i] < > ' ') and (i <=NumLength) do
    begin
    TotalSoFar := TotalSoFar*10 + ord (NumString[i] – ord ('0');
    i := i+1;
    end;
```

```pascal
  Total := TotalSoFar;
end;
procedure EnterInt (Message1,Message2:MessageString; var
  Result : integer);
var
  NumString : NumStringType;
  i : integer;
  ch : char;
begin
writeln (Message1);
writeln (Message2);
while not eoln do
  begin
  for i := 1 to NumLength do NumString[i] := ' ';
  i := 1;
  repeat
    read (ch);
    if ch in ['0'..'9'] then
      begin
      NumString[i] := ch;
      i := i+1;
      end;
  until eoln or (i >NumLength);
  if not eoln then
    begin
    writeln ('Too long. Please enter 5-digit integer.');
    readln;
    end;
  end; {while not eoln}
  readln;
Convert (NumString,Result);
end;
procedure EnterPrices;
begin
EnterInt ('Please enter lowest price   ',
  'How many thousands of pounds?  ',CurrentInfo.LowPrice);
EnterInt ('Please enter highest price  ',
  'How many thousands of pounds?   ', CurrentInfo.HighPrice);
end;
procedure EnterAreas;
```

```
var
  Reply : char;
  Area : AreaType;
begin
writeln ('Which areas are of interest?');
writeln ('Enter Y or N for each, as it is displayed.');
CurrentInfo.Areas := [];
for area := Appleton to StocktonHeath do
  begin
  write (Areanames[area]. '? ');
  repeat
    readln (reply);
  until reply in ['y', 'Y', 'N', 'n'];
  writeln;
  if reply in ['y', 'Y'] then
    CurrentInfo.Areas := CurrentInfo.Areas + [area];
  end;
end;
procedure InputInfo;
  begin
  Entername (CurrentInfo.name);
  EnterAddr;
  EnterTel;
  EnterPrices;
  EnterAreas;
  end;
procedure ShowCurrentRecords;
var
  i : integer;
  area : AreaType;
begin {ShowCurrentRecord}
writeln;writeln;writeln ('details of current customer');
with CurrentInfo do
  begin {with}
  writeln;writeln ('NAME            ',name);
  writeln ('ADDRESS ');
  for i := 1 to AddrLength do
    writeln ('                       ', address[i]);
  writeln ('TELEPHONE     ',TelNumber);
  writeln ('PRICE RANGE ', LowPrice,' to ', HighPrice,
```

```
                                          ' thousand pounds');
      writeln ('Areas of interest : ');
      for area := Appleton to StocktonHeath do
        if area in Areas
          then writeln (' ', AreaNames[area]);
      end {with};
    end; {ShowCurrentRecord}
    procedure CopyToTemp;
    var TempRec : CustomerInfo;
    begin
    while not eof (CustomerFile) do
      begin
      read (CustomerFile,TempRec);
      write (TempFile,TempRec);
      end;
    end;
    procedure CopyFromTemp;
    var TempRec : CustomerInfo;
    begin
    reset (TempFile) {prepare for input};
    rewrite (CustomerFile) {prepare for output};
    while not eof (TempFile) do
      begin
      read (TempFile,TempRec);
      write (CustomerFile,TempRec);
      end;
    end;
    procedure AddRec;
    var ch : char;
    begin
    writeln ('Create new file or add to old one?');
    writeln ('enter n for new o for old');
    repeat
      readln (ch)
    until ch in ['N', 'n', 'O', 'o'];
    if ch in ['O', 'o']
      then begin
            reset (CustomerFile) {prepare for input};
            rewrite (TempFile) {prepare for output};
            CopyToTemp;
```

```pascal
            write (TempFile,CurrentInfo) {add current info};
            CopyFromTemp;
            end
      else begin
            rewrite (CustomerFile);
            write (CustomerFile,CurrentInfo)
            end;
   end;
   procedure AmendMenu;
   var
      ch : char;
      Stop : boolean;
   begin {AmendMenu}
   Stop := false;
   repeat
      writeln;writeln; ('Which field do you wish to amend?');
      writeln ('Enter number to select option.');
      writeln;writeln; ('1. NAME');
      writeln ('2. ADDRESS');
      writeln ('3. TELEPHONE');
      writeln ('4. PRICE RANGE');
      writeln ('5. AREAS OF INTEREST');
      writeln ('6. no further amendments');
      repeat
        readln (ch);
      until ch in ['1'..'6'];
      case ch of
         '1' : EnterName (CurrentInfo.name);
         '2' : EnterAddr;
         '3' : EnterTel;
         '4' : Enterprices;
         '5' : EnterAreas;
         '6' : Stop := true
      end {case};
      if not stop then ShowCurrentRecord;
      until Stop;
   end {Amendmenu};
   procedure AmendCurrentRecords;
   var
      ch : char;
```

```pascal
begin {AmendCurrentRecord}
writeln;writeln;
writeln ('Do you wish to amend this information?');
writeln ('Enter Y or N');
repeat
  readln (ch);
until ch in ['Y', 'y', 'N', 'n'];
if ch in ['Y','y'] then
  AmendMenu;
end {AmendCurrentRecord};
procedure StoreInfo;
begin
ShowCurrentRecord;
AmendCurrentRecord;
AddRec;
end;
procedure AddRecord;
begin
InputInfo;
StoreInfo;
end;
procedure FindInfo (CustName:NameType);
var
  TempRec : CustomerInfo;
  Found : boolean;
begin
reset (CustomerFile);
rewrite (TempFile);
found := false;
while not (eof (CustomerFile) or found) do
  begin
  read (CustomerFile,TempRec);
  if TempRec.name = CustName
    then found := true
    else write (TempFile,TempRec);
end {while};
if found
then CurrentInfo := TempRec
else writeln ('Customer not found');
end;
```

```
procedure Delete;
begin
CopyToTemp;
CopyFromTemp;
end;
procedure Amend;
begin
AmendMenu;
write (TempFile,CurrentInfo);
CopyToTemp;
CopyFromTemp;
end;
procedure DisplayRecord;
var
  RequiredName:NameType;
begin
EnterName (RequiredName);
FindInfo (RequiredName);
ShowCurrentRecord;
end;
procedure RecordMenu;
var
  ch : char;
begin
writeln ('enter number to select option: ');
writeln ('1. delete record ');
writeln ('2. amend record');
writeln ('3. leave record unchanged');
repeat
  readln (ch);
until ch in ['1'..'3'];
case ch of
  '1' : delete;
  '2' : amend;
  '3' :
end;
end;
procedure MainMenu;
var
  ch : char;
```

```
begin
writeln ('CUSTOMER INFORMATION');
writeln;writeln ('Do you wish to :');
writeln;writeln ('1. add a new customer');
writeln ('2. display existing customer');
writeln ('3. exit from this program');
writeln;writeln ('enter number to select option');
repeat
   readln (ch);
until ch in ['1', '2', '3'];
case ch of
   '1' :  AddRecord;
   '2' :  begin
            DisplayRecord;
            Recordmenu
          end;
   '3' :  exit := true
end;
end;
begin {Main body}
exit := false;
InitAreas;
assign (CustomerFile, 'a:Cust'); {Turbo}
assign (TempFile, 'a:temp'); {Turbo}
repeat
   MainMenu
until exit;
end.
```

MORE ADVANCED TOPICS

Record with Variants

Occasionally the nature of the information which is to be stored in a
record will vary. For example, a record containing information about
members of a group of people might include a field giving their marital
status. Dependent upon this, additional fields could give the following
information:

   1) In the case of a married person, the spouse's name.
   2) In the case of a divorced person, the date of the divorce.

We could store this information using the following type definitions:

```
MaritalStatus = (Single,Married,Divorced);
NameType = packed array [1..30] of char;
DateType = array [1..3] of integer;
PersonalRecord = record
                    Status : MaritalStatus;
                    SpouseName : NameType;
                    DivorceDate : DateType
                 end;
```

Now that memory space is comparatively cheap and plentiful, this would usually be a perfectly satisfactory way of storing the information. However, if memory space is limited then it is wasteful to take up space for two fields, **SpouseName** and **DivorceDate**, *both* of which will never be required. Pascal allows us to use *the same memory space* for both fields by declaring them as *variants*. Here is a type definition which stores the same information, but instructs the compiler to reserve only as much space as is required for the *larger* of the two variants, rather than a separate space for each:

```
PersonalRecord = record
                    case  Status : MaritalStatus of
                    Single : ( );
                    Married : (SpouseName:NameType);
                    Divorced : (DivorceDate:DateType)
                 end;
```

The field, **Status**, which determines which of the variant fields is currently in use, is called the *tag* field.

Inexperienced programmers are well advised to avoid the use of variant record fields. For this reason, they are described only briefly here. Students who require a full discussion of variant fields and their uses should consult a more advanced text book. Several suitable books are listed in the bibliography. For completeness, the syntax of a field list including variants is given in Figure 10.3.

Set Operators

In our example program for this chapter, we used the operator, +, to add an element to a set. This is just one of the operators which can be used on variables of set types. The full list of set operators is:

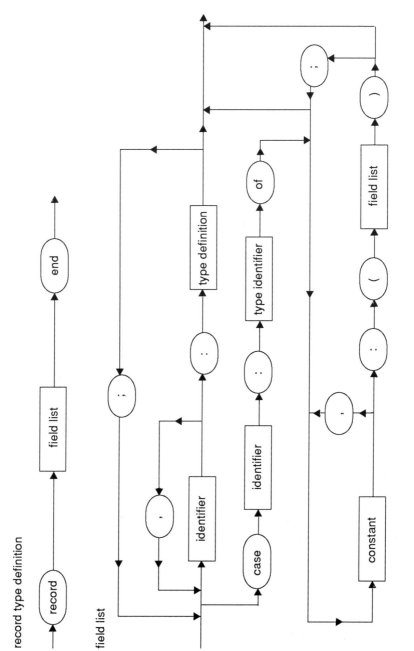

Figure 10.3

relational operators:

= < >	equality/non-equality
<= >=	inclusion

set manipulation operators:

+	union
*	intersection
−	difference

If **A** and **B** are items of some set type, then:

i)   A=B is **true** if, and only if, the elements of **A** are *identical* with the elements of **B**.

ii) A< >B is **true** if any element of A is *not* an element of B *or* if any element of **B** is *not* an element of **A**.

iii) A<=B is **true** if **all** the elements of A are also elements of **B**.

iv) A>=B is **true** if **all** the elements of B are also elements of **A**.

v)   **A+B** is the set containing *every* element belonging to *either* **A** *or* **B** (or both).

vi) **A*B** is the set containing every element belonging to *both* **A** *and* **B**.

vii) **A–B** is the set containing every element of **A** which is *not* an element of **B**.

Suppose that the following type definitions and variable declarations have been made:

type
    Days = (**Sunday,Monday,Tuesday,Wednesday,Thursday,**
                Friday,Saturday);
var
    Today,AnotherDay:days;
    Weekdays,WeekEnd : set of days;

If we assign values to **Weekdays** and **WeekEnd**, like this:

Weekdays := [Monday..Friday];
Weekend := [Sunday,Saturday];

then the following boolean expressions are true:

WeekDays < > Weekend
Weekend = [Saturday,Sunday]
Weekdays <= [Sunday..Saturday]
[Friday,Saturday,Sunday] >= Weekend

(WeekEnd + [Thursday,Friday,Saturday]) =
[Sunday,Thursday,Friday,Saturday]

(Of course, since the *order* in which the elements of a set are listed is immaterial, it does not matter that the elements **Thursday** and **Friday**, which occur earlier in the ordinal list than **Sunday**, have been added later.)

(Weekend * [Tuesday,Saturday]) = [Saturday]
(WeekDays – [Friday,Saturday]) = [Monday..Thursday]

EXERCISES

1. Amend the estate agent's program to include the following improvements:
   i)   Give a warning message, and allow the user to re-enter an address which is longer than six lines.
   ii) Give a warning, and allow the user to re-enter the values, if the lower price bound is higher than the upper bound.
   iii) Give a warning, and allow the user to re-enter the telephone number if it exceeds the allowed length.

2. Write a procedure which will search for all the customers who are interested in houses in a particular area and display them on the screen.

3. Write a procedure which will list all the customers who would be interested in houses at a particular price.

*4. Amend the program so that the customer records are stored in alphabetical order of name.

5. Define suitable record types to store the following information:
   i)   The name, sex, course name, year of study, and name of personal tutor, for a group of students.
   ii) The age, sex, height and weight of a group of people, together with a code giving their physical fitness on a scale of 1 to 5.
   iii) The author, title and ISBN of the books in a library.

6. A bird watcher wishes to store information about the nesting sites of a number of species of birds. He wishes to be able to enter the following information for each nesting site which he discovers:
   i)   The species of bird.
   ii) The map grid reference.
   iii) The date when the site was discovered.

iv) The number of pairs using the site.

v) Whether or not the birds used the site in the previous breeding season.

Write a program which will enable him to create a file which will store this information. He should also be able to update the file by:

i)   Adding new records.

ii) Amending existing records.

iii) Deleting records.

Write a further program which will allow the bird watcher to enter the name of a bird species and get a printout of all the records concerned with this species.

*7. The students union at a college wishes to store information about the leisure interests of its members. Each student is asked to indicate whether or not they are interested in each of the following: football, hockey, netball, basketball, cricket, tennis, athletics, swimming, dancing, listening to music, singing, playing musical instruments, debating, drama, rock climbing, hang gliding, reading, gymnastics, rowing, sailing, watching television, community service, religious activities, politics.

Define a suitable record type to store the following information about each student: name, age, year of Course, leisure interests.

Write a program to create a file of such records, and to allow the file to be amended.

Write a procedure which will list all the students who are interested in a particular activity or group of activities. For example, the user should be able to obtain a list of all those interested in drama *and* rock climbing.

*8. Using the program from *7 to help you, write a computer-dating program. You should create two files : one of men and one of women. The user should then be able to select a record from one of the files, and be given a list of people from the other file who have similar interests.

You may like to make this more sophisticated by including additional information or by making additional rules of 'compatibility' – a shared interest in politics, for example, may or may not indicate a meeting of minds!

9. Write a program which will allow our estate agent to store brief details about the houses which he is selling. Use a file, **PropertyFile**, of records

of the following type:

```
PropertyInfo = record
                 Identity : AddrLine;
                 Price,Beds,Receps : integer;
                 Area : AreaType
              end;
```

to store the first line of address, the price, the numbers of bedrooms and reception rooms, and the area where the house is situated.

11 Let's Get Moving

INTRODUCTION

In this chapter we will write a program which can be used, in conjunction with the estate agent's customer information program from Chapter 10, to match up customers with suitable properties.

The program will read the details of a customer from a file, and will then display a list of suitable houses. We will discuss ways of improving and extending this program to allow more factors to be taken into account. We will also look at additional programs which could be incorporated into a software package for an estate agent.

The reader is encouraged to use the suggestions outlined in this chapter, together with his own ideas, to write such a package for himself.

We will then look at the use of *functions* in performing calculations, and at some of the standard functions provided in Pascal.

NEW PASCAL FEATURES

1) Functions
2) The **real** type
3) Standard functions

DEFINING THE PROBLEM

In Chapter 10 we wrote a program which can be used to produce a file, **CustomerFile**, of records containing information about each of the customers on an estate agent's mailing list. If you have done exercise 9 in that chapter you will also have a program which produces a file of information about the houses on the estate agent's books. If not, you will find a suitable one listed in the solutions section.

We will now write a program which will allow the user to select a customer from the file of customer records, and will then examine the property records file to find houses which suit the needs of that customer. Finally, a list of suitable houses will be displayed.

Figure 11.1 shows the structure which we will use in designing this program. Using this structure, we can write the following skeleton program:

```pascal
program PropertyList (input,output, CustomerFile,PropertyFile);
const
   NameLength = 20;
   LineLength = 40;
   AddrLength = 6;
   TelLength = 15;
   NumLength = 5;
type
   NameType = packed array [1..NameLength] of char;
   AddrLine = packed array [1..LineLength] of char;
   AddressType = array [1..AddrLength] of AddrLine;
   TelType = packed array [1..TelLength] of char;
   NumStringType = packed array [1..5] of char;
   MessageString = packed array [1..40] of char;
   AreaType = (Appleton,Walton,Grappenhall,Latchford,
      StocktonHeath);
   CustomerInfo = record
                    name : NameType;
                    address : AddressType;
                    TelNumber : TelType;
                    LowPrice,HighPrice : integer;
                    Areas : set of AreaType
                  end;
   PropertyInfo = record
                    Price,Beds,Receps : integer;
                    Area : AreaType
                  end;
var
   CustomerFile : file of CustomerInfo;
```

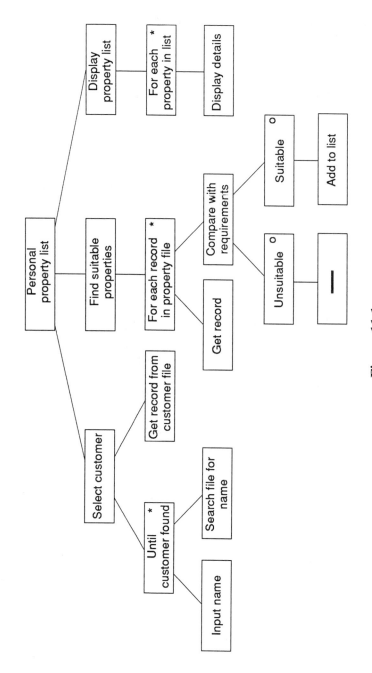

Figure 11.1

```pascal
PropertyFile : file of PropertyInfo;
Customer : CustomerInfo;
CustomerName : NameType;
procedure InName (var name : NameType);
  {Inputs the name of the required customer}
begin
end;
procedure GetCustomer (name : NameType; var customer :
  CustomerInfo; var found : boolean);
  {gets customer with required name from file}
  {sets found to false if name not found}
begin
end;
procedure AddProp (property : PropertyInfo);
  {adds property to list of suitable houses}
begin
end
procedure Suitable (Customer : CustomerInfo; property :
  PropertyInfo);
  {determines whether or not property is suitable for customer}
begin
end
procedure FindProps (Customer : CustomerInfo);
  {finds all the properties suitable for customer}
var
  ThisProp : PropertyInfo;
begin
reset (PropertyFile);
  while not eof (PropertyFile) do
    begin
    read (PropertyFile,ThisProp);
    suitable (Customer,ThisProp);
    if {property is suitable}
      then AddProp (ThisProp);
    end;
end;
procedure DisplayProp (property : PropertyInfo);
  {displays details of property}
begin
end;
```

```
procedure DisplayList;
begin
{while not at the end of the list}
  DisplayProp ({next property in the list});
end;
begin {main body}
repeat
  InName;
  GetCustomer;
until {name in customer file or user wishes to give up}
FindProps;
DisplayList;
end.
```

You should be able to fill out the procedures, **InName**, **GetCustomer**, and **DisplayProp**.

Let us give some attention to the main body of the program first. We will declare a global boolean variable **CustomerFound** to store information about whether or not we have been able to find the customer record which was wanted. If the name given does not correspond to a name in the customer file, we will give the user the opportunity *either* to enter a different name *or* to exit from the program. We will declare a **char** variable, **ch** to store his reply, and a **boolean** variable, **GiveUp** to register whether or not to continue. The main body can then be completed like this:

```
begin
GiveUp := false; {initialise GiveUp}
repeat
  InName (CustomerName);
  GetCustomer (CustomerName,Customer,CustomerFound);
  if not CustomerFound {name is not in customer file}
    then begin
      writeln ('No customer of this name. Try again?');
      repeat
        readln (ch)
      until ch in ['Y', 'y', 'N', 'n'];
      if ch in ['N', 'n'] then GiveUp := true;
    end;
until CustomerFound or GiveUp;
            {name in file or user wishes to give up}
```

```
if not GiveUp then
  begin
  FindProps (Customer);
  DisplayList;
  end;
end.
```

FINDING A SUITABLE HOUSE

Before we can complete the remainder of the program, we need to consider what criteria should be satisfied in order for a house to be deemed 'suitable' for a particular customer.

At present the only pieces of information which we have concerning the requirements of a customer are: the price range and the areas of town in which he is interested. So we will define a suitable house as being any house which is *both* within the specified price range and in one of the chosen areas.

The procedure **Suitable** must, therefore, make the following comparisons:

(Property.Price>=Customer.LowPrice) and (Property.Price<= Customer. HighPrice)

and

Property. area in Customer.Areas

If both of these expressions are true then the house is suitable. Otherwise it is not. The procedure, **Suitable**, needs therefore to pass back a boolean value to indicate this.

We could use a variable parameter to pass back this information, but, in a case like this, where only one result is to be passed back, it is often simpler to use a *function* rather than a procedure.

FUNCTIONS

We have already met some functions. The Pascal language includes a number of *pre-defined* functions, among them **eoln, eof, ord, chr**. Each of these operates on a parameter, and returns a result. In the case of **eoln** and **eof** the result is of **boolean** type, **ord** gives an **integer** result, and **chr** a **char** result.

A *function* can be thought of as a special sort of procedure. It is defined in a very similar way to that of a procedure. The difference between functions and procedures is that, when it is executed, a function returns a value, called the *result* of the function. The *type* of the result must be given in the function heading. For example, we could define the *function* **Suitable** like this:

```
function Suitable (Customer:CustomerInfo; Property:Property
    Info) : boolean;
begin
with Customer, Property do
    Suitable := (Price>=LowPrice) and (Price<=HighPrice)
                                and (area in areas);
    end;
```

The *identifier* **Suitable** may be used within the *function* **Suitable** exactly as if it were a local variable. The result which will be returned by the function is the final value assigned to **Suitable** before execution of the function is completed. If the value of a function is left undefined when execution is completed then a run time error *should* occur. However, many implementations will simply allow execution to continue – with totally unpredictable results! In either case, it is important to make sure that a value will be assigned to the result variable *regardless of which route is followed* within a function.

A function may be of any *ordinal* type, or of the type **real**. (The **real** type is discussed briefly in the 'more advanced' section of Chapter 4, and more fully later in this chapter.) A function *cannot* be of *structured* type (ie a type which can be broken down into components of a simpler type). Arrays, records and sets are all examples of structured types.

The syntax of a function header is given in Figure 11.2.

Function header

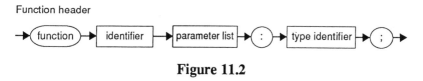

Figure 11.2

STORING THE LIST OF SUITABLE HOUSES

We will now consider how we are going to store the list of houses which are found to be suitable for our customer. We need to declare a data structure which will allow us to store the details of each house, and to output the information about each house in turn.

We do not know how long the list is going to be. It *could* be as long as the entire file of property records (if we have a peculiarly accommodating customer!), or it could be empty. The most straightforward way of storing the list would be to declare an array of records. Each element of this array would be of type **PropertyInfo**. But how large should the array be? If we insist on being able to store a record of *every* suitable house, then our array will have to be extremely large.

Alternatively, we could use a temporary file in which to store the list of properties. This avoids having to set a limit on the size of the list. However, in most implementations, including Turbo Pascal, execution time will be slowed considerably because the file will be stored on disk, rather than in the computer memory.

To decide which alternative storage method is appropriate, we need to consider whether or not the ability to store virtually unlimited numbers of records is crucial to the task which our program is designed to perform. In this case the answer is clear: customers will not welcome excessively long lists of houses to look at. Our estate agent will be more likely to sell a house to a customer who is provided with a reasonable number of well-selected houses than to someone who is bombarded with hundreds of property records. So, we can easily set a limit on the number of records which we wish to keep in the list.

We will, therefore, declare an array of records to store the suitable house details:

```
const
  HouseListLength = 40;
var
  HouseList : array [1..HouseListLength] of PropertyInfo;
  ListIndex : integer;
```

By using the constant, **HouseListLength**, we have made it easy to change the length of the list if we wish to.

We can now complete the procedure **AddProp** and **FindProps**:

```
procedure AddProp (property : PropertyInfo);
  {adds property to list of suitable houses}
begin
```

```
ListIndex := ListIndex+1;
if ListIndex <= HouseListLength
  then HouseList [ListIndex] := property;
end
procedure FindProps (Customer : CustomerInfo);
  {finds all the properties suitable for customer}
var
  ThisProp : PropertyInfo;
begin
reset (PropertyFile);
ListIndex := 0;
  while not eof (PropertyFile) do
    begin
    read (PropertyFile,ThisProp);
    if suitable (Customer,ThisProp)
      then AddProp (ThisProp);
    end;
end;
```

At present, if more than **HouseListLength** suitable houses are found then only the first **HouseListLength** such property records are added to the list. We will look later at better ways of selecting which records are to be left off the list.

You should now be able to complete the last remaining procedure, **DisplayList**. Test your program using a variety of different data. A working version of this program is listed below. Lines marked {Turbo} are additional lines needed when using Turbo Pascal.

```
program PropertyList (input,output, CustomerFile,PropertyFile);
const
  NameLength = 20;
  LineLength = 40;
  AddrLength = 6;
  TelLength = 15;
  NumLength = 5;
  HouseListLength = 40;
type
  NameType = packed array [1..NameLength] of char;
  AddrLine = packed array [1..LineLength] of char;
  AddressType = array [1..AddrLength] of AddrLine;
```

```
    TelType = packed array [1..TelLength] of char;
    NumStringType = packed array [1..5] of char;
    MessageString = packed array [1..40] of char;
    AreaType = (Appleton,Walton,Grappenhall,Latchford,
      StocktonHeath);
  CustomerInfo = record
                    name : NameType;
                    address : AddressType;
                    TelNumber : TelType;
                    LowPrice,HighPrice : integer;
                    Areas : set of AreaType
                 end;
  PropertyInfo = record
                    Identity : AddrLine;
                    Price,Beds,Recepts : integer;
                    Area : AreaType
                 end;
var
  CustomerFile : file of CustomerInfo;
  PropertyFile : file of PropertyInfo;
  HouseList : array [1..HouseListLength] of PropertyInfo;
  ListIndex : integer;
  Customer : CustomerInfo;
  CustomerName : NameType;
  CustomerFound, GiveUp : boolean;
  ch : char;
procedure InName (var name : NameType);
  {Inputs the name of the required customer}
var
  i : integer;
begin
  writeln ('Enter name of customer');
  Name := '                       ';
  i := 1;
  repeat
    read (Name[i]);
    i := i+1;
  until eoln or (i >=NameLength);
  readln;
end;
```

```
procedure GetCustomer (name : NameType; var Customer :
   CustomerInfo; var found : boolean);
   {gets customer with required name from file}
begin
assign (CustomerFile, 'b:cust'); {Turbo}
reset (CustomerFile);
found := false;
while not (eof (CustomerFile) or found) do
   begin
   read (CustomerFile,Customer);
   if name = Customer.name then found := true;
   end;
end;
procedure AddProp (property : PropertyInfo);
   {adds property to list of suitable houses}
begin
ListIndex := ListIndex+1;
if ListIndex <=HouseListLength
   then HouseList [ListIndex] := property;
end;
function Suitable (Customer : CustomerInfo; Property :
   PropertyInfo) : boolean;
begin
with Customer, Property do
   Suitable := (Price>=LowPrice) and (Price<=HighPrice)
                   and (area in areas);
end;
procedure FindProps (Customer : CustomerInfo);
   {finds all the properties suitable for customer}
var
   ThisProp : PropertyInfo;
begin
assign (PropertyFile, 'b : prop'); {Turbo}
reset (PropertyFile);
ListIndex := 0;
   while not eof (PropertyFile) do
      begin
      read (PropertyFile,ThisProp);
      if suitable (Customer,ThisProp)
        then AddProp (ThisProp);
```

```
      end;
  end;
  procedure DisplayProp (property : PropertyInfo);
    {displays details of property}
  begin
  with property do
    begin
    writeln;writeln (Identity);
    writeln ('price :                    ',price);
    writeln ('bedrooms :                 ',beds);
    writeln ('reception rooms :          ',receps);
    end;
  end;
  procedure DisplayList;
  var i : integer;
  begin
  for i := 1 to ListIndex do
    DisplayProp (HouseList[i]);
  end;
  begin {main body}
  GiveUp := false;
  repeat
    InName (CustomerName);
    GetCustomer (CustomerName,Customer,CustomerFound);
    if not CustomerFound then
      begin
      writeln ('No customer of this name exists. Try again?');
      repeat
        readln (ch);
      until ch in ['y', 'Y', 'N', 'n'];
      if ch in ['n', 'N'] then GiveUp := true;
      end;
  until CustomerFound or GiveUp;
  if not GiveUp then
    begin
    FindProps (Customer);
    DisplayList;
    end;
  end.
```

IMPROVEMENTS TO OUR ESTATE AGENT PACKAGE

There are many ways in which the programs in our package could be improved and extended. A few of them are listed below. Some involve trivial alterations to the existing program, while others are quite tricky to implement.

1. Creating an Ordered File

If our file of properties becomes large it will take a long time to find all the suitable houses for a customer, since we will have to compare the details of *every* house with his requirements. We could reduce the average execution time by storing the property records *in order of price* within the file. This means that, once all the houses in the required price range have been checked, no further property records need be scrutinised. Since the records are listed in *sequence*, we may refer to this as a *sequential* file.

Figure 11.3 shows a structure diagram for adding a record to a file of property records, which are stored in ascending order of price. Using this as a guide, we can use the following procedures to create such a file:

```
procedure CopyToTemp;
var TempRec : propertyInfo;
begin
if not eof (PropertyFile) then
  repeat
  read (PropertyFile,TempRec);
  if (TempRec.price > CurrentInfo.price) then
    write (TempFile,CurrentInfo);
  write (TempFile,TempRec);
  until eof (PropertyFile) or (TempRec.price>CurrentInfo.price);
while not eof (PropertyFile) do
  begin
  read (PropertyFile,TempRec);
  write (TempFile,TempRec);
  end;
end;
procedure CopyFromTemp;
var TempRec : propertyInfo;
begin
reset (tempFile) {prepare for input};
```

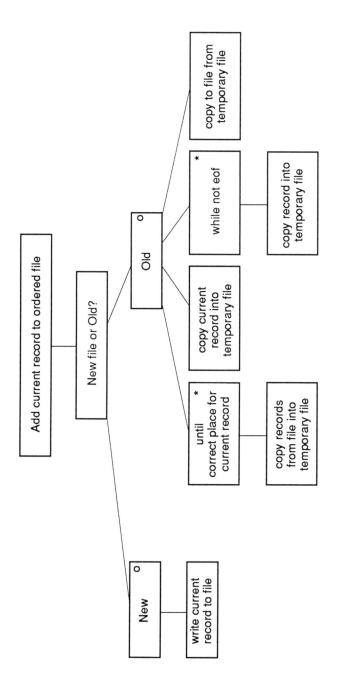

Figure 11.3

```
rewrite (propertyFile) {prepare for output};
while not eof (TempFile) do
  begin
  read (TempFile,TempRec);
  write (propertyFile,TempRec);
  end;
end;
procedure AddRec;
var ch : char;
begin
writeln ('Create new file or add to old one?');
writeln ('enter n for new or o for old');
repeat
  readln (ch)
until ch in ['N', 'n', 'O', 'o'];
if ch in ['O', 'o']
  then begin
    reset (propertyFile) {prepare for input};
    rewrite (TempFile) {prepare for output};
    CopyToTemp;
    CopyFromTemp;
    end
  else begin
    rewrite (propertyFile);
    write (propertyFile,CurrentInfo)
    end;
end;
```

2. Allowing Input from the Keyboard

Sometimes the user may wish to obtain a list of suitable houses for a customer whose details are not in the customer records file. You should be able to modify the program, **PropertyList**, to give the user the choice of either giving the name of a customer whose details are stored in the customer file, or entering the customer's details from the keyboard.

3. Allowing the User to View the Records in a File

Sometimes the user may not be able to remember the exact name of a customer or identification of a property. It would be useful if he could select the record he wants from a list of the records in the file. For example, the name of each customer could be displayed, and the user asked to indicate whether this was the required customer record.

You should be able to introduce this option by writing a procedure which reads in records from a file and displays one or more fields of the current record as it does so. The procedure should stop reading when *either* the end of file is reached *or* the user indicates that the current record is the one which he requires.

4. Including Additional Information

The customer would find the package more useful if more information about his requirements were taken into account in selecting suitable properties. He could, for example, be asked to give a minimum (and, perhaps, a maximum) number of bedrooms; a preference for a house, bungalow or flat; special requirements (such as a double garage or central heating).

To implement this, you will need to change the definitions of both the customer and property records, so as to store the necessary additional information.

5. Dealing With Too Many Suitable Houses

When the number of suitable properties turns out to be greater than the maximum list size, some action should be taken to determine which properties are included. At present our program simply stops looking for suitable properties once the list is full.

One option would be to print out the full list, and then go on looking for further properties, printing out the details in batches. (This is what we did with the standard letters in our program, **Letter**, in Chapter 9.)

Alternatively, some criteria could be used to determine which houses are left out of the list. If we were writing this package for an actual estate agent, we would need to consult him as to which criteria should be taken into account. He might consider that it is best to give the customer details of only the most expensive properties, in the hope that he will choose one of these – or he might wish to include a field within each property record indicating how urgent it is to sell this particular house, and then choose to list the most urgent ones. His customers, on the other hand, might prefer to be given the cheapest houses, or those with the largest number of rooms.

Whatever criteria are chosen, once the list of suitable properties is full, each new suitable property must be compared with those already in the list. If the new property proves to be more desirable than any already in the list then ideally it should be inserted into the list to replace the *least* desirable property. However, it may not always be easy to work out which *is* the least desirable element of the list. A reasonable compromise would be to compare the new property with each element in the list until an element is found which is less desirable than the new property. Then replace this element with the new record.

6. Dealing With an Empty List

Sometimes it may be that there are no properties which fully satisfy a customer's requirements. It may then be desirable to provide a list of 'near misses'. You could, for example, include houses which fall slightly outside his price range, or which are slightly smaller than he would prefer.

You could create this list by writing a procedure which slightly modifies the customer's requirements (but does *not* put the new requirements in the customer record file). After this procedure has been executed, the new list can be created by executing the normal property selection procedures.

You will have to decide on suitable modifications to the customer's requirements – or should the user be permitted to make his own suggestions? Remember that it is better to provide a short list of reasonably suitable houses than a long list which almost ignores his preferences!

THE FINAL PACKAGE

You should be able to adapt the programs in our estate agent's package to include improvements 1, 2, 3 and 4. Improvements 5 and 6 are more difficult. You will need to spend some time thinking out exactly what you want to achieve before attempting to write code to implement these.

You will, no doubt, be able to think of many more improvements. Use your imagination to design new features which will benefit the estate agent and his clients. When your package is complete, ask a friend to try using it. It should be easy to use, and hard to crash!

STANDARD PROCEDURES AND FUNCTIONS

Pascal has a number of pre-defined procedures and functions. We have already met a number of them, including **write, writeln, read, readln, succ, pred, ord, chr.**

The identifiers which name these differ from *reserved words* in that they may be *re-defined* within a program. For example, in a program where the pre-defined procedure, **writeln**, was *never* required, we could define a variable whose identifier was **writeln**. This is unlikely to be useful, and, in general it is best to avoid using identifiers which have pre-defined meanings as names in your program. However, it is as well to be aware that such re-definition is allowed, since you may sometimes *accidentally* use pre-defined names. In this case, no error will be reported, but you will experience problems if you subsequently wish to use their *pre-defined* meaning in the same program.

Lists of all the pre-defined identifiers, and their meanings, may be found in Appendix C.

PERFORMING CALCULATIONS IN PASCAL

Suppose that we have been asked to write a program which will allow the user to enter the results of an opinion poll, and will calculate the percentage of votes for each party. We will assume that we have already written an input section of the program, which will store the results in an array, **Votes**, of integers, indexed by the enumerated type,

PartyType=(DontKnow, BlackParty, OrangeParty, PinkParty, WhiteParty, YellowParty)

To calculate the percentage of votes for each party we must:

i)   Calculate the total number of votes cast.
ii)   Divide the number of votes for each party by the total.
iii) Multiply the result from ii) by 100.

So far, all our calculations have involved only *integers*. We can divide two integers to produce an integer result using the **div** operator. For example, if we declare an array, **Percent : array [PartyType] of integer**, then we might attempt to calculate the required percentages like this:

Percent [i] := (Votes [i] div TotalVotes) * 100

If you think that this is right then try running the following:

```
program PercentVote (input,output);
type
  PartyType=(DontKnow, BlackParty, OrangeParty, PinkParty,
WhiteParty, YellowParty);
  NameType = packed array [1..12] of char;
var
  Votes, Percent : array [PartyType] of integer;
  PartyNames : array [PartyType] of NameType;
procedure InitPartynames;
begin
PartyNames [DontKnow] := 'Don' 't know ';
PartyNames [BlackParty] := 'Black Party ';
PartyNames [OrangeParty] := 'Orange Party';
PartyNames [PinkParty] := 'Pink Party ';
PartyNames [WhiteParty] := 'White Party ';
PartyNames [YellowParty] := 'Yellow Party';
end;
procedure InVotes;
var party : PartyType;
begin
for party := DontKnow to YellowParty do
  begin
  writeln ('Enter number of votes for ', PartyNames[party]);
  readln (Votes[party]);
  end;
end;
procedure CalcPercent;
var
  party : PartyType;
  Total : integer;
begin
Total := 0;
for party := DontKnow to YellowParty do
  Total := Total + Votes [party];
for party := DontKnow to YellowParty do
  Percent [party] := (Votes [party] div TotalVotes) * 100;
end;
procedure DisplayPercent;
```

```
var party : PartyType;
begin
for party := DontKnow to YellowParty do
    writeln ('Percentage votes for ', PartyNames [party], ' ', Percent
        [party]);
end;
begin {main body}
InitPartynames;
InVotes;
CalcPercent;
DisplayPercent;
end.
```

Did you get the results you were expecting? What has gone wrong?

The problem is caused by our use of the **div** operator. The operation, integer1 div integer2 gives the number of times which integer1 may be divided *exactly* by integer2, ignoring any remainder. For example, 3 div 2=1, 4 div 2=2, 1 div 4=0.

Since **TotalVotes** is always *at least* as large as **Votes [i]**, the result, **Votes [i] div TotalVotes**, will always be zero (unless **Votes [i]** is *equal* to **TotalVotes**, in which case the result will be 1).

We can get round this problem by performing the *multiplication* first:

Percent [party] := (Votes [party] * 100) div TotalVotes;

Alter the program listed above in this way, and try running it using the following sets of data:

i)	Don't Know	: 2 votes
	Black	: 1 vote
	Orange	: 1 vote
	Pink	: 5 votes
	White	: 0 votes
	Yellow	: 1 vote
ii)	Don't Know	: 1760 votes
	Black	: 5001 votes
	Orange	: 2543 votes
	Pink	: 531 votes
	White	: 1021 votes
	Yellow	: 19 votes

Has something gone wrong again? The problem this time is that some of the numbers which we are attempting to calculate are too big. Whenever we use integer variables we must be sure that they will never need to take values greater than **maxint** (the pre-defined identifier denoting the largest available integer), or less than **−maxint**.

We need a way of storing numbers outside the range of valid integers. We can do this in Pascal using the standard type **real**.

THE REAL TYPE

We can declare a variable of type **real** like this:

var
  x : real;

Examples of **real** constants are:

  1.0
  −2.34
  4.78E9
  764.0003
  −11.6E4
  4.2E−10

The letter E is used for convenience when writing very large or very small numbers. The integer following the letter E gives the number of decimal places to the right (or, if negative, to the left) which the decimal point should be moved. For example:

1.2E10 is equivalent to 12000000000
4.9E−7 is equivalent to 0.00000049

The general form of a **real** constant is given in Figure 11.4.

The values of **real** variables are stored only approximately. The degree of accuracy will depend on your implementation. This means that you should never attempt to compare two **real** expressions for equality, since expressions which are mathematically equal may not appear equal when calculated by your computer.

The operators +, − and * can all be used in expressions of **real** type. However, the operator **div** only applies to **integer** expressions. To perform real division a slash, /, is used. For example: **x := x/2.16.**

The types **integer** and **real** are not strictly compatible. It is, for

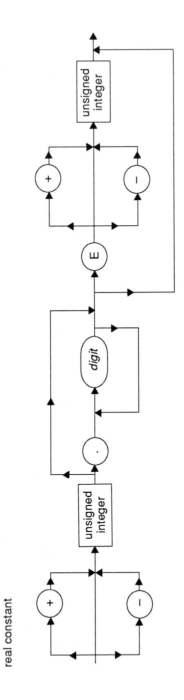

Figure 11.4

example, an error to attempt to assign a **real** value to an **integer** variable. However, **integer** constants, variables and subexpressions may be used within **real** expressions. The **integer** values will be automatically converted to their corresponding **real** values.

CONVERTING FROM REAL TO INTEGER TYPE

So we can calculate the percentage of votes scored by a particular party using the **real** expression: **(Votes[party] * 100) /Total,** but we *cannot* store this value in our array **Percent,** since it is **real** and therefore of the wrong type.

There are two standard functions which may be used to convert **real** values to **integer** type:

1) **trunc (x)** yields the integer part of **x**, throwing away the fractional part. For example:

trunc (1.8) = 1
trunc (–6.2) = –6

2) **round (x)** yields the nearest integer value to **x**. For example:

round (4.6) = 5

In the case where **x** is *exactly* 0.5 greater than some integer, then the result is rounded *up* in the case of positive numbers, and *down* in the negative case. For example:

round (4.5) = 5
round (–4.5) = –5

We can now complete our percentage program by substituting the following statement in procedure **CalcPercent:**

Percent [party] := round ((Votes [party] * 100) /Total);

Try running the amended version using the figures which caused us trouble above. If you are lucky the calculations will now be performed correctly. However, many compilers (including Turbo Pascal) will persist in using integer arithmetic until forced to convert to real by the / operator. This means that, despite the fact that it is calculating part of a real expression, the value of **Votes [party] * 100** may be calculated as an integer. Since this value is sometimes greater than **maxint,** an error will result. If you encounter this problem, you can force the compiler to use real arithmetic by altering the order of the operators:

Percent [party] := round ((Votes [party] /Total) * 100);

MORE ADVANCED TOPICS

Procedure and Function Parameters

There is another type of parameter which we have not yet mentioned. It is possible for procedures or functions to have parameters which are themselves procedures or functions. We can declare such parameters like this:

```
procedure Example1 (procedure x);
procedure Example2 (function y : integer);
procedure Example3 (function a, b : char; procedure q);
function Example4 (procedure proc1, proc2, proc3);
```

The complete syntax of a parameter list is given in Figure 11.5.

Notice that only a name and, in the case of a function parameter, a type identifier is given for each parameter. The number and types of any parameters which may be required when the procedure or function is called are not specified in the parameter list. The programmer is responsible for ensuring that the correct parameters are used when the procedure or function is called.

An example may make use of such parameters easier to understand. The procedure below will display a (sideways) graph of the function sin (x), by writing a star on each line of output:

```
procedure GraphSin (XScale : real);
const
  PageWidth = 75;
  LinesOnPage = 20;
var
  scale,RealX,min,max : real;
  x,y,i : integer;
begin
min := -1;
max := 1;
scale := PageWidth/ (max-min);
for x := 1 to LinesOnPage do
  begin
```

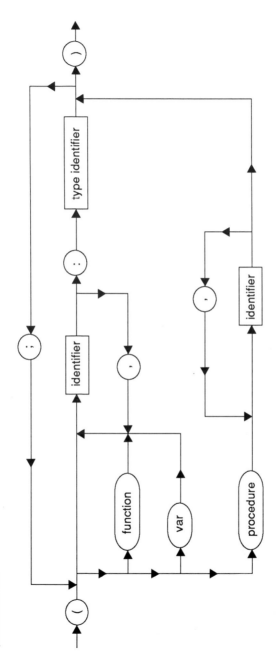

Figure 11.5

```
    RealX := x*XScale;
    y := round ((sin(RealX)-min)*scale);
    for i := 1 to y do
      write (' ');
    writeln ('*');
    end;
  end;
```

We can modify this procedure so that it can be used to draw a graph of any function we may choose, by using a function parameter. We will also need to pass as parameters the minimum and maximum values taken by the chosen function; and it may also be convenient to pass the information regarding the page size as parameters so as to make the graph-drawing procedure as versatile as possible.

We can, for example, draw a graph of $x^3 - 4x$ using the following program:

```
program Graphtest (input,output);
const
  PWidth = 75;
  LsOnPage = 20;
var
  ScaleFactor,fmin,fmax : real;
procedure Graph (function func : real; XScale,min,max : real;
                              PageWidth,LinesOnPage : integer);
var
  scale,RealX : real;
  x,y,i : integer;
begin {graph}
scale := PageWidth / (max-min);
for x := 1 to LinesOnPage do
  begin
  RealX := x*XScale;
  y := round ((f(RealX)-min)*scale);
  for i := 1 to y do
    write (' ');
  writeln ('*');
  end;
end; {graph}
function Cubic (x:real) :real;
```

```
begin
cubic := x*x*x-4*x;
end;
begin {main body}
ScaleFactor := 0.15;
fmin := Cubic (sqrt (4/3));
fmax := Cubic (LsOnPage*ScaleFactor);
Graph (Cubic,ScaleFactor,fmin,fmax,PWidth,LsOnPage);
end.
```

Many Pascal implementations do not include the ability to pass procedures and functions as parameters. Turbo Pascal versions 3.0 and 4.0 do *not* include this facility. Version 5 *does* allow procedures and functions to be passed as parameters, but in a non-standard way. If you wish to use them you should consult the manual. The following program is a version of the above which works under Turbo Pascal version 5:

```
{$F+} program Graphtest (input,output);
const
  PWidth = 75;
  LsOnPage = 20;
type
  func = function (x:real):real; {Turbo requires a function type to
  be declared for passing function parameters}
var
  ScaleFactor,fmin,fmax : real;
procedure Graph (f : func;XScale,min,max : real;
                              PageWidth,LinesOnPage : integer);
    {Notice the non-standard parameter declaration}
var
  scale,RealX : real;
  x,y,i : integer;
begin {graph}
scale := PageWidth/ (max-min);
for x := 1 to LinesOnPage do
  begin
  RealX := x*XScale;
  y := round ((f (RealX) -min) *scale);
  for i := 1 to y do
    write (' ');
  writeln ('*');
```

```
   end;
end; {graph}
function Cubic (x:real) :real;
begin
cubic := x*x*x–4*x;
end;
begin {main body}
ScaleFactor := 0.15;
fmin := Cubic (sqrt (4/3));
fmax := Cubic (LsOnPage*ScaleFactor);
Graph (Cubic,ScaleFactor,fmin,fmax,PWidth,LsOnPage);
readln; {This is necessary in order to prevent Turbo 5 from
clearing the screen as soon as execution is complete}
end.
```

Recursion

Since the scope (see Chapter 6) of a procedure includes its own body, it is possible for a procedure, or function, to be called from within itself. This is called *recursion*. It is used when part of the process carried out by the procedure is to perform an amended version of itself (usually using different values in its parameters).

We can solve a problem recursively if the solution of the problem may be described in terms of simpler versions of the same problem.

For example, suppose we wish to find the sum of the first n integers (where n is a positive integer). We could define a function **sum(n)** which returns, as its result, the sum $1+2+3+4+...+n$. This could also be expressed like this: $(1+2+3+4+...+(n-1))+n$. In other words, $sum(n)=sum(n-1)+n$.

We can see immediately that sum (1)=1. So we can now find sum (n) for *any* value of n by calling sum (n) *recursively* until we reach the stage where we call sum (1):

```
program FindSum (input,output);
var
  Number, SumToN:integer;
function sum (n:integer) : integer;
begin
if n=1 then Sum:=1
```

```
    else Sum := Sum(n–1) + n;
    end;
    begin {main body}
    writeln ('Please enter number');
    readln (Number);
    if Number <=0 then writeln ('Don't be silly! Enter a positive
    integer.');
    else writeln ('The sum of the first ',Number, ' integers is ',
    Sum(Number));
    end.
```

Beginners should approach the use of recursion with caution. In particular you must be careful to ensure that the recursion *will* terminate. Notice the **if** statement in the program above, which ensures that the function **sum** will *never* be called with a negative parameter, since, if it were, the recursion would continue interminably. It is all too easy to write a procedure which continues to call itself for ever! The use of variable parameters in procedures which are to be called recursively is extremely dangerous, since it is then almost impossible to keep track of what values have been assigned to which variables.

Forward References

A procedure or function must have been declared at a point earlier in the text of the program than any of the calls to that procedure. However, this may be inconvenient if there is some reason for arranging the procedures of a program in a particular order. This might be, for example, so as to group together all the procedures concerned with some particular process so as to make them easier to find.

We can get round this difficulty by using a *forward reference*. A procedure, or function, may be declared as **forward,** by adding the qualifier **forward** after the procedure heading. This tells the compiler that the body of the procedure is to be found later in the text. At the point where the body of the procedure occurs, a second procedure heading is used, but this time neither the result type nor the parameter list is included.

The following skeleton program may help to make this clearer:

```
    program ForwardRef (input,output);
    procedure ListedFirst (i,j : integer; var q : boolean); forward;
```

```
function ForwardFunc (c : char) : boolean; forward;
procedure ListedLast;
  var boolvar : boolean;
  begin

  boolvar := ForwardFunc;

  ListedFirst (1,1,boolvar);

  end;
procedure ListedFirst;
  begin

  end;
procedure ForwardFunc;
  begin

  end;
  begin {main body}

end.
```

Mutual Recursion

Sometimes two (or more) procedures may call each other. They are then said to be *mutually recursive*. In order to use mutual recursion between procedures at the same level in Pascal one of the procedures must be declared using a forward reference (see above).

For example, suppose that we have two functions, f and g, related in the following way:

$$f(n) = f(n-1) + g(n-2)$$
$$g(n) = 2g(n-1) + f(n-1)$$

Suppose further that we are given that $f(1) = 0, g(0) = 2, g(1) = 4$. Then we can find the values of f (n) and g (n) for any n using the following program:

program Mutual (input,output);

```
var number : integer;
function f (n : integer) : integer; forward;
function g (n : integer) : integer;
begin {g}
if n = 0 then g := 2
else if n = 1 then g := 4
    else g := 2*g (n–1) + f (n–1);
end; {g}
function f;
begin {f}
if n = 1 then f := 0
else f := f (n–1) + g (n–2);
end; {f}
begin {main body}
writeln ('please enter a positive integer');
readln (number);
writeln ('f (', number, ') = ',f (number) );
writeln ('g (', number, ') = ',g (number) );
end.
```

Care must be taken not to abuse the use of mutual recursion. You must *always* check that the recursion process will terminate properly. The danger of allowing procedures to call each other over and over again without stopping is even greater than in the case of normal recursion. Remember that calling procedure **a** from *within* procedure **b** does *not* have the same effect as exiting from **b** and *then* entering **a**. At run time, every time a procedure is called, some of the computer's memory is used to store copies of value parameters, local variables and information about what it must do when it exits from the procedure. If you repeatedly enter more and more procedures you will eventually run out of storage space and your program will crash!

In general, if you can think of a way of solving your problem *without* using mutual recursion then that is almost certainly the better choice.

EXERCISES

1. Write functions to return the following results:

   i)   The length of the straight line joining two points whose x and y co-ordinates are given as parameters.

   ii) The value **true** whenever two arrays, a and b, each containing 10 integers, have at least 1 element in common (ie for some value of i, a [i]=b [i]); and the value **false** otherwise.

iii) The lower-case letter corresponding to a capital letter given as a char type parameter.

iv) The index to the largest element in an array of 50 real numbers. (If two elements are exactly equal, choose the lower index.)

v) The value true if the string 'Pascal' occurs anywhere within an array of 100 characters (given as a parameter); and the value **false** otherwise.

2. The following program should calculate the mean value (to the nearest integer) of a number of positive integers entered from the keyboard:

```pascal
program CalcMean (input,output);
var
   ThisInt,Total,HowMany, Mean : integer;
   Stop : boolean;
begin
stop := false;
Total := 0;
HowMany := 0;
repeat
   writeln ('Please enter next integer or -1 to stop');
   readln (ThisInt);
   if ThisInt = -1
     then stop := true
     else begin
         Total := Total+ThisInt;
         HowMany := HowMany+1
         end;
   until stop;
Mean := Total div HowMany;
writeln ('Mean value = ', Mean);
end.
```

It does not work correctly on my computer. Why do you think this is? Amend the program and test it using a variety of different data.

What happens if you enter -1 as the *first* integer? Amend your program to avoid this problem.

*3. Write a program to solve the 'Tower of Hanoi' problem by calling a procedure recursively.

The Tower of Hanoi Problem:

You have a pile of discs (see Figure 11.6), and 3 mats (A,B,C) on which they may be placed. The problem is how to move the whole pile of discs from A to C under the following rules:

  i)   Only 1 disc may be moved at a time.
  ii) A disc may only be placed *either* on an empty mat
                              or on a disc larger than itself.

(Hint: write a procedure Move (Start,Finish,N), which moves a pile of N discs from the mat labelled Start to the mat labelled Finished.)

(Note: If you get very frustrated with this problem, complete solutions appear in many books.)

*4. The following procedure inserts a record into the correct place in an array of records arranged in numerical order of the field **Mark**:

```
type
  MarkRec = record
              Mark : integer;
              name : packed array [1..20] of char;
            end;
  RecList = array [1..1000] of MarkRec;

procedure Insert (var MarkList : RecList; ThisRec : MarkRec;
                  Var RecsInList : integer);
var i, j : integer;
begin
i : = 1;
```

Tower of Hanoi

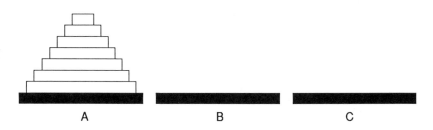

A   B   C

Figure 11.6

```
while (i <= RecsInList) and
                    (MarkRec.Mark) < (MarList [i].Mark) do
   i := i+1;
  for j := RecsInList downto i do
    MarkList [j+1] := MarkList [j];
  MarkList [i] := MarkRec;
  RecsInList := RecsInList+1;
end;
```

Using this to help you, write a program which can sort up to 1000 records in an array by calling recursively a procedure which can sort the first N records and insert the N+1th record into its correct place.

12 Please Form a Queue

INTRODUCTION

In this chapter we will look at the problem of storing information about patients on a hospital waiting list. We will need to include facilities to add and remove patients from the list.

NEW PASCAL FEATURES

1) Pointer variables

DEFINING THE PROBLEM

We wish to store records containing information about the patients on a hospital waiting list. For the present, we will assume that patients are dealt with on a strictly first-come-first-served basis. This means that new patients will be added to the end of the list, and patients will be removed (as hospital beds become available) from the head of the list. (This is clearly an over-simplification of the problem. We will look at ways of making our program more realistic later in the chapter.) This sort of list is known as a queue, because it is like a queue in a shop, where each person moves forward as customers ahead of them are served.

The user of the program will want to be able to choose the following options:

1) Add a patient to the list.
2) Remove a patient from the list.
3) Display information about a particular patient.
4) Read the list from a file.
5) Write the list to a file.

The obvious way to implement this choice is by using a menu-driven program. Figure 12.1 gives a structure diagram showing the main processes which will be required.

CHOOSING SUITABLE DATA STRUCTURES

Clearly the administrators of our fictional hospital will want to be able to store this information *permanently*. It would be of little use to them if the records were lost every time the computer was switched off. So we will have to store the records in a file.

However, a file is not a very convenient data structure. Accessing a record in a file is slow, particularly if the file is large. Adding or removing records from a file involves copying the *entire file contents*. So, it would be better if we could store the contents of all, or part, of our file in the computer memory temporarily, while it is in use. We could then copy the information to the disk file at a convenient time.

Having decided to do this, we then need to consider how we can allocate this temporary storage space. We could use an array, but we then have to decide *how big* it is to be. Our waiting list could vary in size enormously from time to time.

Another problem with using an array is: how do we remove patients from the list? If we want to keep the first patient in the list stored in the first element of the array, then every time a patient leaves the list we will have to copy *every* patient record into the position above them in the list. If the list is long this will be hideously time-consuming.

What we really need to be able to do is to allocate storage space for each record *at run time*, so that we use only the amount of memory that we really need. And we need to be able to link these areas of memory together *in order* so that we know which patient is due to leave the list next. We can do both these things using *pointers*.

THE POINTER TYPE

Suppose that we have defined a type, **PatientRec**, to hold information about a patient. Then we can define a type **PatientPointer** like this:

PatientPointer = ^PatientRec;

We can then declare a variable, **TopOfList**, which is a pointer to a variable of type **PatientRec**, like this:

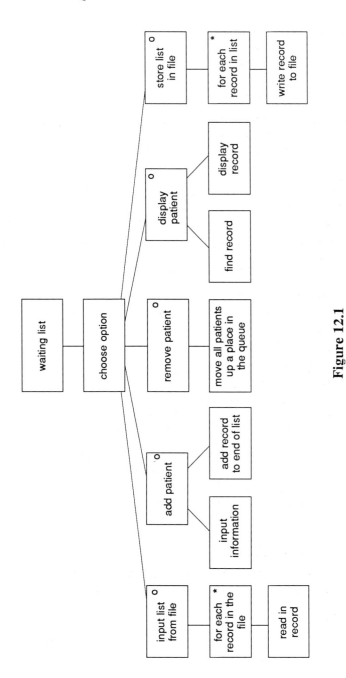

Figure 12.1

var
  TopOfList : PatientPointer;

This means that we are asking the compiler to allocate a storage space large enough to store *the address* of another storage space; and we are informing it that the item stored at that *address* will be of type **PatientRec**.

At execution time, the value of **TopOfList** will initially be undefined (as with variables of all types). In order to use this pointer variable we must allocate a suitable storage space to store a variable of type **PatientRec**, and copy the address of this storage space into **TopOfList**. These two operations are done by calling the standard procedure **New**.

The statement, **New (TopOfList)**, allocates a storage location to store a record of type **PatientRec**, and puts the address of that location in the pointer variable, **TopOfList**. We can then access this new storage location by using the construction **TopOfList^**.

DYNAMIC AND STATIC VARIABLES

All the variables which we have come across up to now have been *static*. This means that the memory which is required to store them is allocated at compile-time.

At run-time, static variables come into existence when the procedure or function within which they were declared is entered. When execution of a procedure or function is completed the variables local to it cease to exist.

The storage space is allocated in an orderly fashion, with local variables being added when a procedure is entered, and then removed on exiting from the procedure. We can think of them as being added to a *stack* of variables, one on top of another. The variables which are declared in the outer levels of the program are 'stacked' beneath those declared at inner levels. Thus, on exiting from a procedure, the program simply 'unstacks' the local variables from the 'top' of the stack. Figure 12.2 illustrates this.

Variables created by the procedure **New** are known as *dynamic* variables. The space in which these are stored is allocated at *run-time*. The area of memory where space is allocated for dynamic variables is called the *heap*. This is in contrast to the *stack* where static variables are

Diagram illustrating the use of the stack during execution of a Pascal program

The variables shown are those which are on the stack when each of the numbered statements in the program on the left has been executed. The arrow represents the 'stack pointer' – a variable which records the current position of the 'top' of the stack throughout execution of the program.

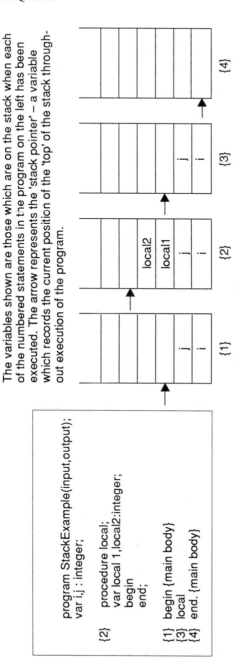

Figure 12.2

stored. The storage space on the heap is allocated, in a rather haphazard way, whenever the procedure **new** is called. It is as though we were 'heaping together' a pile of variables, adding an extra one whenever we need it.

LINKING TOGETHER DYNAMIC VARIABLES

We would like to be able to create a number of patient records at run time, and make them into a list in the order in which they were created. We can do this by 'linking' each record to the next one in the list using a pointer. Suppose that our patient record type is defined like this:

```
PatientRec = record
                Name, Doctor : NameType;
                Age : integer;
                Treatment : TreatmentCode
             end;
```

We could link the records together in a list if we could add a new field, **Next**, of type ^**PatientRec** (pronounced 'pointer-to-PatientRec') like this:

```
PatientRec = record
                Name, Doctor : NameType;
                Age : integer;
                Treatment : TreatmentCode;
                Next : ^PatientRec
             end;
```

But, there is a problem here, because normally an identifier cannot be used in a type definition unless it has previously been declared. So, we need to declare the type **PatientRec** *before* declaring **Next : ^PatientRec,** but **next** is *actually part of the definition* of **PatientRec**.

To get round this apparent impasse, Pascal allows *one* exception to the rule that identifiers must be declared before they are used: pointer types may be declared as pointing to a type which has not yet been defined. So, we can make the following type definitions:

```
type
PatientPointer = ^PatientRec;
PatientRec = record
```

```
          Name,Doctor : NameType;
          Age : integer;
          Treatment : TreatmentCode;
          Next : ^PatientRec
       end;
```

We can now make a *linked list* of patient records by creating a record, on the heap, for each patient. **TopOfList** will be set to point to the first patient record in the list, and the field **next** of each record will be set to point to the *next* record in the list. Figure 12.3 may help you to see what is involved.

The following procedure reads in records from a file of patients' records and stores them in a linked list of dynamic variables:

```
procedure InputList;
var
   CurrentPatient, LastPatient : PatientPointer;
begin
TopOfList := nil;
CurrentPatient := nil;
LastPatient := nil;
reset (PatientFile);
while not eof (PatientFile) do
   begin
   new (CurrentPatient);
   read (PatientFile,CurrentPatient^);
   CurrentPatient^.next := nil;
   if TopOfList = nil
      then TopOfList := CurrentPatient
      else LastPatient^.next := CurrentPatient;
   LastPatient := CurrentPatient;
   end;
end;
```

The predefined identifier, **nil**, has been used to indicate when the end of the list has been reached. A pointer of *any* type may be assigned the value nil. This simply means that the pointer does not point to any dynamic variable. It is good practice to initialise pointer variables with the value nil rather than leaving them undefined, since then errors resulting from a failure to define their values are more likely to be detected.

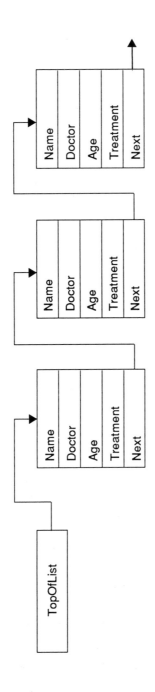

Figure 12.3

Values of pointer variables as records are read in from a file

	CurrentPatient	LastPatient	TopOfList
before reading	nil	nil	nil
after reading 1st record	^1st patient	^1st patient	^1st patient
after reading 2nd record	^2nd patient	^2nd patient	^1st patient
after reading 3rd record	^3rd patient	^3rd patient	^1st patient

Figure 12.4

Figure 12.4 shows how the values of the pointer variables vary as records are read in from the file.

ADDING RECORDS TO THE LIST

Now that we have created our list, we can add a new record by:

1) Creating a dynamic variable in which to store the record.
2) Finding the last record on the list so far.
3) Setting the **next** field of this record to point to the new dynamic variable.

We can, of course, find the last record on the list by starting at the top and working our way down until we find a record with **nil** as the value of its next field. But it will be more convenient if we store the address of the end of the list, so that we can go there immediately when we wish to add a record. So we will declare a global variable, **BottomOfList**, which will point to the record at the bottom of the list of patients. We will need to add a line to our procedure **InputList**, in order to assign the correct value to **BottomOfList** after all the records have been read in from the file:

BottomOfList := CurrentPatient;

This statement copies the *pointer* **CurrentPatient** into the *pointer* **BottomOfList**. The record to which **CurrentPatient** points is *not* copied, or, indeed, affected in any way by this assignment.

It is important to notice the distinction between assignments involving pointer variables, and assignments involving the variables to which they point. The following statement copies the *record*, **CurrentPatient** ^ into another space on the heap (**BottomOfList** ^):

    BottomOfList ^ := **CurrentPatient** ^;

This second kind of assignment is used much less frequently than assignment between pointers, since it is not usually necessary to keep more than one copy of a record on the heap.

You may like to think of the first assignment (between two pointers) as being a little like changing the name on the door of a room so as to make it the same as that on another door. Whereas the second assignment (between two variables on the heap) is like transferring the *entire contents* of one room into another.

You should be able to write a procedure, **InPatient**, which inputs all the necessary information about a new patient from the keyboard and stores it in a variable parameter, **NewPatient**, of type **PatientRec**. **NameType** can be a packed array of 20 characters, and **TreatmentCode** can be the subrange 'A'..'F'. Don't forget to assign the value nil to **NewPatient** ^.**next**.

The following procedure adds a record to the end of the list:

```
procedure AddPatient;
var ThisPatient : PatientPointer;
begin
new (ThisPatient);
InPatient (ThisPatient^);
If TopOfList = nil
  then TopOfList := ThisPatient
  else BottomOfList^.next := ThisPatient;
BottomOfList := ThisPatient;
end;
```

REMOVING A PATIENT FROM THE LIST

We can easily remove the topmost record from the list simply by making **TopOfList** point to the next record in the list:

    TopOfList := **TopOfList** ^.**next**;

However, the record which used to be at the top of the list does not cease to exist simply because there is now no pointer pointing to it. The space allocated for it on the heap is still treated as being 'in use' and so unavailable for storing other variables. It is easy to see that, if we continually add records to the bottom of the list and remove them from the top without 'clearing away' all the unwanted records, we will soon run out of memory.

Pascal allows us to 'reclaim' unwanted space on the heap using the predefined procedure **dispose**. The statement **dispose (TopOfList)** makes the area of memory pointed to by **TopOfList** available to be re-used, and makes the value of **TopOfList** undefined.

The following procedure removes the top record from the list:

```
procedure RemovePatient;
var
   OldTop : PatientPointer;
begin
OldTop := TopOfList;
TopOfList := TopOfList^.next;
Dispose (OldTop);
end;
```

Notice the use of the local pointer variable, **OldTop**, to store the address of the record which is being removed. This enables the space to be reclaimed, using **Dispose**, *after* **TopOfList** has been given its new value.

Extreme care must be taken when **Dispose**ing variables. It may be the case that two pointer variables are pointing to the *same* space on the heap (for example, **CurrentPatient** and **LastPatient** in procedure **Input-List**). If one of these pointers is **dispose**d then the area of memory which it points to is made available for re-use, but the *other* pointer is still pointing to that area. Before calling **dispose**, make sure that *none* of the pointers which are pointing to that heap space will be required later in the program.

Compilers vary enormously in the efficiency with which space on the heap is recovered by the **dispose** procedure. Indeed, it is not at all unusual for the procedure to have no effect whatever! Generally, however, some attempt is made to allow re-use of the memory occupied by **dispose**d variables; but, since the available space may be fragmented by the presence of other dynamic variables which are still in use, some of the space will almost certainly be wasted. So it is best to avoid creating unnecessarily large numbers of dynamic variables even if you **dispose** of them when they are no longer needed.

DISPLAYING A RECORD FROM THE LIST

You should be able to write a procedure, **DisplayPatient**, with a parameter, **PatientPtr**, of type **PatientPointer** to display the contents of a patient record. The following function searches for a patient by name, and returns a pointer to the appropriate record. If no patient of that name is found, a nil pointer is returned.

```
Function FindPatient (name : NameType) : PatientPointer;
var TempPtr : PatientPointer;
begin
TempPtr := TopOfList;
If TempPtr = nil
  then writeln ('List Empty')
  else begin
      while (TempPtr^.name < > name) and
               (TempPtr^.next < > nil) do
        TempPtr := TempPtr^.next;
      if TempPtr^.name < > name
        then TempPtr := nil;
      end;
FindPatient := TempPtr;
end;
```

Notice that we have used a local variable to store the value which will eventually be returned as the result of the function. This is to avoid any confusion between the use of the identifier **FindPatient** to represent the result of the function, and a *function call* to **FindPatient** from within its own body. (Calling a procedure or function from within its own body is called *recursion*. This is discussed in the more advanced section of Chapter 11.)

STORING THE LIST IN A FILE

We can store the list of records in a file simply by starting at the top and writing each record in turn to the file. The following procedure does this:

procedure StoreList;

```
var ThisPatient : PatientPointer;
begin
ThisPatient := TopOfList;
rewrite (PatientFile);
while ThisPatient < > nil do
  begin
  write (PatientFile,ThisPatient^);
  ThisPatient := ThisPatient^.next;
  end;
end;
```

COMPLETING OUR PROGRAM

We have now written all the components of our program except the main menu. You should be able to write a main menu procedure, and then join together all the constituent parts to make a complete program. Try to do this yourself before looking at the listing below. As usual, additional lines of code required by Turbo Pascal are marked {Turbo}.

```
program WaitingList (Input,Output,PatientFile);
const
  NameLength = 20;
type
TreatmentCode = 'A'..'F';
NameType = packed array [1..NameLength] of char;
PatientPointer = ^PatientRec;
PatientRec = record
                Name,Doctor : NameType;
                Age : integer;
                Treatment : TreatmentCode;
                Next : PatientPointer
              end;
var
  TopOfList,BottomOfList : PatientPointer;
  PatientFile : File of PatientRec;
procedure InputList;
var
  CurrentPatient,LastPatient : PatientPointer;
begin
TopOfList := nil;
CurrentPatient := nil;
```

```pascal
LastPatient := nil;
assign (PatientFile, 'a : Patients.rec'); {Turbo}
reset (PatientFile);
while not eof (PatientFile) do
  begin
  new (CurrentPatient);
  read (PatientFile,CurrentPatient^);
  CurrentPatient^.next := nil;
  if TopOfList = nil
    then TopOfList := CurrentPatient
    else LastPatient^.next := CurrentPatient;
  LastPatient := CurrentPatient;
  end;
BottomOfList := CurrentPatient;
close (PatientFile); {Turbo}
end;
procedure InName (var name : NameType);
var i : integer;
begin
for i := 1 to NameLength do
  name[i] := ' ';
i := 1;
repeat
  read (name [i]);
  i := i + 1;
until eoln or (i >= NameLength);
if not eoln then
  writeln ('Name truncated to : ',name);
readln;
end;
procedure ReadInt (var Int : integer);
var
  ch : char;
  FirstDigit,SecondDigit : integer;
begin
FirstDigit := 0;
SecondDigit := 0;
repeat
  read (ch)
until ch in ['0'..'9'];
```

```
SecondDigit := ord(ch)-ord ('0');
if not eoln
   then begin
        repeat
          read (ch)
        until eoln or (ch in ['0'..'9']);
        if ch in ['0'..'9']
           then begin
                FirstDigit := SecondDigit;
                SecondDigit := ord(ch)-ord ('0');
                end;
        end;
readln;
Int := 10*FirstDigit + SecondDigit;
end;
procedure InCode (var code : TreatmentCode);
var ch : char;
begin
repeat
  read (ch);
until ch in ['A'..'F', 'a'..'f'];
case ch of
    'a', 'A' : code := 'A';
    'b', 'B' : code := 'B';
    'c', 'C' : code := 'C';
    'd', 'D' : code := 'D';
    'e', 'E' : code := 'E';
    'f', 'F' : code := 'F'
end;
readln;
end;
procedure InPatient (var Newpatient : PatientRec);
begin
writeln;writeln;
writeln ('Enter patients''s name. Up to ',NameLength,'
letters allowed.');
InName (NewPatient.Name);
writeln ('Enter Doctor''s name. Up to ',NameLength,' letters
allowed.');
InName (NewPatient.Doctor);
```

```pascal
writeln ('Enter age (in years) up to a maximum of 99');
ReadInt (NewPatient.Age);
writeln ('Enter treatment code ("A" to "F") ');
InCode (NewPatient.Treatment);
NewPatient.next := nil;
end;
Procedure AddPatient;
var ThisPatient : PatientPointer;
begin
new (ThisPatient);
InPatient (ThisPatient^);
If TopOfList = nil
  then TopOfList := ThisPatient
  else BottomOfList^.next := ThisPatient;
BottomOfList := ThisPatient;
end;
procedure RemovePatient;
var
  OldTop : PatientPointer;
begin
OldTop := TopOfList;
TopOfList := TopOfList^.next;
Dispose (OldTop);
end;
procedure DisplayPatient (PatientPtr : PatientPointer);
begin
writeln;writeln;
if patientPtr < > nil then
  with patientPtr^ do
    begin
    writeln ('Details of patient ',name);
    writeln;writeln ('Doctor''s name : ',Doctor);
    writeln ('age :              ',age);
    writeln ('treatment :      ',treatment);
    end;
else writeln ('Patient not found');
end;
Function FindPatient (name : NameType) : PatientPointer;
var TempPtr : PatientPointer;
begin
```

```
TempPtr := TopOfList;
If TempPtr = nil
  then writeln ('List Empty')
  else begin
     while (TempPtr^.name < > name) and
             (TempPtr^.next < > nil) do
          TempPtr := TempPtr^.next;
     if TempPtr^.name < > name
             then TempPtr := nil;
     end;
FindPatient := TempPtr;
end;
procedure ChoosePatient;
var name : NameType;
begin
writeln ('Enter name of patient required.');
InName (name);
DisplayPatient (FindPatient (name));
end;
procedure StoreList;
var ThisPatient : PatientPointer;
begin
ThisPatient := TopOfList;
assign (PatientFile, 'a : Patients.rec'); {Turbo}
rewrite (PatientFile);
while ThisPatient < > nil do
  begin
  write (PatientFile,ThisPatient^);
  ThisPatient := ThisPatient^.next;
  end;
close (PatientFile); {Turbo}
end;
procedure MainMenu;
var
  choice : char;
  stop : boolean;
begin
stop := false;
repeat
  writeln;writeln;
```

```
writeln(' PLEASE CHOOSE OPTION');
writeln;
writeln ('1. Retrieve waiting list from file.');
writeln ('2. Add new patient to list in memory.');
writeln ('3. Remove patient from list in memory.');
writeln ('4. Display a patient''s records.');
writeln ('5. Store waiting list in file.');
writeln ('6. Stop');
writeln;writeln ('Enter number of option required.');
repeat
   readln (choice)
until choice in ['1'..'6'];
case choice of
     '1' : InputList;
     '2' : AddPatient;
     '3' : RemovePatient;
     '4' : ChoosePatient;
     '5' : StoreList;
     '6' : stop := true
  end;
 until stop;
 end;
 begin {main body}
 TopOfList := nil;
 MainMenu
 end.
```

MAKING OUR PROGRAM MORE REALISTIC

Our program is not, at present, very true-to-life. Patients on a waiting list do not, in fact, move up the list to the top in this orderly fashion. Some patients may need to be removed from the list before they reach the top, because they move away and go onto the waiting list of another hospital, or because they die or get better without treatment. Other patients may need treatment sufficiently urgently that they should be added to a place higher up the list than the very bottom.

We will now look at ways of modifying our program to allow records to be added or removed at *any* point in the list, not just at the bottom and top.

Removing a Record from the Middle of the List

We already have a function, **FindPatient**, which will search the list by name for a particular patient. So, we can find the record which the user wishes to remove; but how do we remove it?

To remove a record from a linked list we must:

1) Find the record immediately *before* the one which is to be removed.
2) Set the **next** field of this previous record to point to the record immediately *after* the one which is to be removed.
3) **Dispose** of the unwanted record.

The difficult bit is going to be finding the previous record in the list. There are three possible ways in which we could do this:

1) We could, at the point in the program where we remove a record, look down the list, starting from the top, until we find a record whose next field points to the unwanted record. The advantage of this approach is that we would not need to store any additional information. The disadvantage is that looking down the list may be time-consuming, especially if the list is long.
2) We could amend **FindPatient** so that it returns a value for the *previous* record as well as the required record.This would necessitate the addition of a variable parameter to **FindPatient**, in which to store this information. We would also need to declare a suitable variable to store the information returned by **FindPatient**.
3) We could declare an additional field of **PatientRec** in which to store a pointer to the previous record in the list. We would have to add code to assign the correct value to this new field whenever a new record is created. The advantage of this method is that it provides us with a quick and easy way of moving through the list in either direction. The disadvantage is that it adds to the size of *every* record in the list, whereas option 2 only requires *one* additional pointer variable to be declared.

In our present situation, option 2 is probably the most appropriate. Under some circumstances option 3 might be a better choice: if, for example, we were going to be required frequently to search for records starting at the bottom of the list.

So we will amend **FindPatient** like this:

```
Function FindPatient (name : NameType;
                var Previous : PatientPointer) : PatientPointer;
var TempPtr : PatientPointer;
begin
Previous := nil;
TempPtr := TopOfList;
If TempPtr = nil
  then writeln ('List Empty')
  else begin
      while (TempPtr^.name < > name) and
                (TempPtr^.next < > nil) do
          begin
          Previous := TempPtr;
          TempPtr := TempPtr^.next;
          end;
      if TempPtr^.name < > name
          then TempPtr := nil;
      end;
FindPatient := TempPtr;
end;
```

We can then use the following procedure to remove a record from the list:

```
procedure RemoveName (name : NameType);
var ThisPtr, LastPtr : PatientPointer;
begin
ThisPtr := FindPatient (name,LastPtr);
If ThisPtr = nil
  then writeln ('no patient of this name exists')
  else begin
      If ThisPtr = TopOfList {patient at top of list}
          then TopOfList := ThisPtr^.next
          else LastPtr^.next := ThisPtr^.next;
      If ThisPtr = BottomOfList {patient at bottom}
          then BottomOfList := LastPtr;
      Dispose (ThisPtr);
      end;
end;
```

Notice the special case where the patient is at the top of the list. We must treat this separately because, in this case, the value of **LastPtr** will be **nil**. An attempt to access the record pointed to by a nil pointer will cause a run-time error. When the patient is at the bottom of the list (don't forget that this same record may also be the *top* of the list!), we must take care to adjust **BottomOfList** to point to the previous record.

Adding Records to the Middle of the List

Let us suppose that all patients requiring treatment 'A' are to be given priority over all other patients. This means that, when we add a patient with treatment code 'A', we must add it *after* all the patients already waiting for treatment 'A', but *before* any other patients on the list.

To insert a patient into the list we need to:

1) Find the correct position in the list.
2) Set the **next** field of the new record to point to the record which is to come *after* it in the list.
3) Set the **next** field of the record which is to come *before* the new record to point to the new record.

The following procedure looks through the list, starting at the top, until it reaches a patient who does not require treatment 'A'. It then inserts a new record.

```
procedure PriorityAdd (patient : PatientPtr);
var LastPtr,ThisPtr : PatientPointer;
begin
If TopOfList = nil
  then begin {add to empty list}
     TopOfList := patient;
     BottomOfList := patient;
     patient^.next := nil;
     end
  else begin
     LastPtr := nil;
     ThisPtr := TopOfList;
     while (ThisPtr^.Treatment = 'A') and
                          (ThisPtr < > BottomOfList) do
        begin
        LastPtr := ThisPtr;
```

```
            ThisPtr := ThisPtr^.next;
            end;
        if (ThisPtr = BottomOfList) and
                        (ThisPtr^.Treatment = 'A')
            then begin {add to bottom of list}
                BottomOfList^.next := patient;
                patient^.next := nil;
                BottomOfList := patient;
                end
            else begin {add to top or middle of list}
                if ThisPtr = TopOfList
{add to top}        then TopOfList := patient
{add to middle}     else LastPtr^.next := patient;
                patient^.next := ThisPtr;
                end;
            end;
    end;
```

Here we have taken care to cater for the special cases where the patient is to be inserted at the top or bottom of an existing list, or into an empty list.

Try adding these new procedures to your program (you will need to add code giving the user the option of calling them!). Test them by adding and removing records from the top, bottom and middle of the list. (You may find it convenient to write a procedure which lists, on the screen, all the patients in order, so that you can check easily that the records are being added and removed correctly.)

MORE IMPROVEMENTS

You will be able to think of many more improvements and extensions to this program. You could, for example, include a facility to list all the patients with a particular doctor or all those requiring a particular treatment. Or you might allow an existing patient record to be changed if, say, he moves to a different doctor.

We will look in detail at one particular improvement which should be made before this package is released to ordinary users. At present, it is left entirely up to the user to make sure that he inputs any existing information from the disk when he starts using the program, and to store the new list before exiting from it. However, users cannot be relied upon to remember to do this. It is particularly important not to allow them to enter large quantities of information and then exit from the program without storing it.

It would be helpful if we were to insert a warning message before exiting from the program, and give the user the opportunity of storing the list of patient records. It might also be a good idea to remind the user that there may be an existing file of patient records which he should input at the start of the program. The main menu procedure could be amended like this:

```
procedure MainMenu;
var
  choice : char;
  stop : boolean;
begin
stop := false;
repeat
  writeln;writeln;
  writeln(' PLEASE CHOOSE OPTION');
  writeln; writeln ('1. Retrieve waiting list from file.');
  writeln ('2. Add new patient to list in memory.');
  writeln ('3. Remove patient from list in memory.');
  writeln ('4. Display a patient''s records.');
  writeln ('5. Store waiting list in file.');
  writeln ('6. Stop');
  writeln;writeln ('Enter number of option required.');
  repeat
    readln (choice)
  until choice in ['1'..'6'];
  case choice of
    '1' : InputList;
    '2' : AddPatient;
    '3' : RemovePatient;
    '4' : ChoosePatient;
    '5' : StoreList;
    '6' : begin
            stop := true;
            writeln(' WARNING!!!!');
            writeln ('Data not stored on disk will be lost!');
            writeln ('Store data? Enter y/n');
```

```
          if Yes then StoreList; {see below}
          end
     end;
   until stop;
   end;
```

The identifier, **Yes**, describes a function which may be defined as below:

```
Function Yes : boolean;
var ch : char;
begin
repeat
read (ch)
  until ch in ['y', 'Y', 'n', 'N'];
readln;
Yes := ch in ['y', 'Y'];
end;
```

It is useful to define a function such as this whenever yes/no questions are to be asked, so as to avoid repeated lines of code.

MORE ADVANCED TOPICS

Trees

Another common application of pointers is to link together records to form a 'tree'. A *tree* consists of a number of *nodes* linked together. The tree branches out from a single node (the *root*), which is connected to a number of other nodes. These in turn are connected to further nodes, and so on until the outermost nodes (or *leaves*) are reached. The *leaves* are distinguished by not having any further nodes attached to them Figure 12.5 shows the general structure of a tree.

Binary Trees

The most commonly used kind of tree is the *binary tree*.

In this case each node is directly connected to at most two branches. These branches are often labelled 'right' and 'left', or 'yes' and 'no'. A binary tree, where each node is a record, is a useful way of storing certain types of information. Figure 12.6 shows a binary tree.

We can construct a binary tree in Pascal by defining a record type

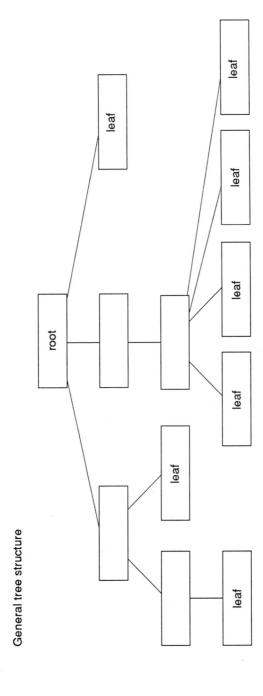

General tree structure

Figure 12.5

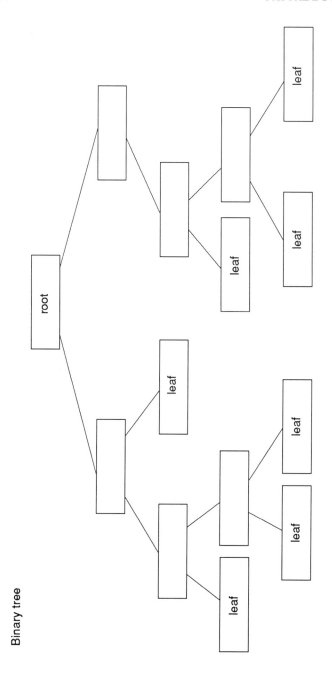

Binary tree

Figure 12.6

which includes fields giving pointers to each of the branches issuing from that record. We will illustrate this process by looking at an example.

'Animals'

In the game 'Animals' you are asked to choose the name of an animal. The computer then attempts to work out which animal you have chosen by asking a series of yes/no questions. If it fails to 'guess' correctly, you are asked to supply a suitable question which it could ask in order to distinguish that animal in the future.

We can implement this game using a binary tree. We will define a record type, **NodeType**, like this:

```
NodePtr = ^NodeType;
NodeType = record
                  question : packed array [1..50] of char;
                  yes,no : NodePtr
              end;
```

Adding and removing records from a binary tree can be done in a broadly similar way to the methods for a linked list. If you wish to find out more about this it is covered in detail in many books. Below is an implementation of 'Animals', which you may like to study:

```
program animals (input,output);
const
  QuestionLength = 50;
type
  QuestionType = packed array [1..QuestionLength] of char;
  NodePtr = ^NodeType;
  NodeType = record
                  question : QuestionType;
                  yes,no : NodePtr
              end;
var
  Root : NodePtr;
Function Yes : boolean;
var ch : char;
begin
repeat
  read (ch)
```

```
         until ch in ['y', 'Y', 'n', 'N'];
         readln;
         Yes := ch in ['y', 'Y'];
         end;
       procedure NewQuestion (node,previous : NodePtr);
       var
         NewNode,NewLeaf : NodePtr;
         animal1, animal2,question : QuestionType;
       procedure WriteName (Q : QuestionType);
         var i : integer;
         begin
         i := 9;
         while q[i] < > '?' do
           begin
           write (q[i]);
           i := i+1;
           end;
         end;
       procedure ReadQ (var q : QuestionType);
         var i : integer;
         begin
         i := 9;
         repeat
           read (q[i]);
           i := i+1;
         until eoln or (i = QuestionLength);
         if q[i–1] < > '?' then q[i] := '?';
         end;
       begin {NewQuestion}
       writeln ('I give up. What was your animal?');
       animal1 : node^.question;
       animal2 :=
       'Is it a                                    ';
       ReadQ (animal2);
       write ('What question should I ask to tell a ');
       WriteName (animal2);
       Write ('from a ');
       WriteName (animal1);
       writeln ('?');
```

```
question :=
'                                                   ';
ReadQ (question);
new (NewNode); {make new node to hold question}
NewNode^.question := question;
new (NewLeaf); {make new node to hold new animal}
with NewLeaf^ do
   begin
   question := animal2;
   yes := nil;
   no := nil;
   end;
write ('what answer would you give if it was a ');
WriteName (animal2);
writeln ('?');
if Yes
   then begin
      NewNode^.yes := NewLeaf;
      NewNode^.no := node;
      end
   else begin
      NewNode^.yes := node;
      NewNode^.no := NewLeaf;
      end;
   {link new node to its branches}
if (previous = nil) {node was root}
   then root := NewNode
   else
   if previous^.yes = node then previous^.yes := newnode
                           else previous^.no := newnode;
   {link new node to the tree if new node is not root}
end;
procedure play;
var
   ThisNode,LastNode,LastButOne : NodePtr;
   correct : boolean;
begin {play}
writeln ('Think of an animal');
writeln ('Press ENTER when ready');
```

```
readln;
correct := false;
LastNode := nil;
LastButOne := nil;
ThisNode := Root;
while ThisNode < > nil do
  begin
  LastButOne := LastNode;
  LastNode := ThisNode;
  writeln (ThisNode^.question);
  If Yes
    then begin
        ThisNode := ThisNode^.yes;
        correct := true
        end
    else begin
        ThisNode := ThisNode^.no;
        correct := false
        end;
  end;
if not correct then NewQuestion (LastNode,LastButOne);
end;
procedure MakeRoot; {give initial value to root node}
begin
new (root);
with root^ do
  begin
  question :=
  'Is it a porcupine?                          ';
  yes := nil;
  no := nil
  end;
end;
begin {main program}
MakeRoot;
repeat
  play;
  writeln ('again? enter y/n');
until not Yes;
end.
```

Binary trees also have many less frivolous uses. For example, Figure 12.7 shows how an arithmetic expression may be represented by a binary tree. A 'pocket calculator' program could use such a tree to store an expression while it is being typed in. Each leaf node contains a number. Each non-leaf node contains an operator. Each operator is defined to operate on the sub-expressions given by its left and right branches.

The calculation can be performed by *traversing* the tree, starting at the leftmost leaf (A, in Figure 12.7), which can be found by taking the lefthand branch at each node until a leaf is reached. From A we then move up to its 'parent' node (containing the operator +), and then take the righthand branch (B). In this case, this branch is also a leaf so the sub-expression A+B can now be calculated. Next we move back to the root (containing *), and then take the righthand branch from here. Continuing in this way, the expression can be evaluated as (A+B)*(C–D*E).

A good way of implementing this would be to call recursively a procedure which evaluates a sub-expression. The recursion would terminate when a leaf is reached.

A file of records may be sorted into order using a tree rather similar to the one for evaluating an arithmetic expression. The records are read in and linked to form a tree with the records which are to occur first in the

root

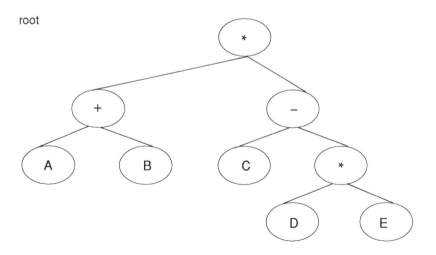

Figure 12.7

file being linked to the left of records which belong later. They can then be read from the tree in the correct order using the 'tree-traversal algorithm' described above.

If you are interested, there are many books which will tell you more about binary trees. You will be able to find algorithms for the creation and traversal of trees, and for storing them in a file and retrieving them again.

EXERCISES

1. Modify the estate agent package from Chapters 10 and 11 to allow the list of houses to be read in from the file and stored in a linked list within the computer memory, so that suitable houses may be selected more quickly.

2. A mail order company wishes to keep a record of orders which are waiting to be dispatched. The following information needs to be kept concerning each order:

  i)   The name and address of the customer.
  ii) The items required (up to a maximum of 20 items per order).
  iii) The date when the order was received.
  iv) Whether or not this is a 'priority order'.

Define a suitable record structure to enable you to store this information in a linked list.

Write a program which allows the user to:

  i)   Enter new orders as they arrive.
  ii) Print out invoices and address labels for batches of 10 items when they are required.

The items should be processed on a first-come-first-served basis, but 'priority orders' should be despatched before other orders.

When you have got this version working, modify your program so that any orders which have been awaiting despatch for a week or more are dealt with *before* any priority orders which may have been received more recently.

3. Write a program which sorts a list of examination marks into descending order by inputting the names and scores of a list of candidates, and storing them in a linked list of records. In order to store the

records in mark order, you will need to compare each new record with the existing members of the list until the correct place has been found.

*4. Write a program which stores data about your ancestry in a binary tree.
(Use a record such as this:

```
record
  name : NameType;
  Born,Died : DateType;
  mother,father : Person
end;
```

where **NameType** and **DateType** are suitably defined types, and **Person** is a pointer type.)

Appendix A

Solutions to Selected Exercises

Chapter 1

1. i), ii), v), vi), vii), ix)

Chapter 2

1. Result, x, a1b2, NAME

2. Alter the line where the error occurs to:

writeln ('I would like to say "welcome" to new users.');

Chapter 3

4. i), iv), vii)
i) **true** iv) **false** vii) **true**

Chapter 4

Program referred to on p.57.

```
program shortlist (input,output);
var
   score : integer;
   ch : char;
procedure GetYesOrNo;
   begin
   repeat
```

```
    readln (ch);
  until ch in ['y', 'Y', 'n', 'N'];
  end;
begin
score := 0;
writeln;
writeln ('Programming experience > 5 yrs?');
GetYesOrNo;
if (ch='y') or (ch='Y') then score := score + 3;
writeln;
writeln ('under 35?');
GetYesOrNo;
if (ch='y') or (ch='Y') then score := score + 2;
writeln;
writeln ('Car driver?');
GetYesOrNo;
if (ch='y') or (ch='Y') then score := score + 1;
writeln;
writeln ('Final score = ',score);
end.
```

2. Assuming that a variable, Digit, of type char has been declared in the variable declaration section of the program, an acceptable procedure is:

```
procedure AcceptDigit;
begin
repeat
  read (Digit);
until Digit in ['0'..'9'];
end;
```

Chapter 5

Program referred to on p.80.

```
program FindInfo (input,output);
var
  NameCode, AorT, ch : char;
procedure NameMenu;
begin
writeln;
```

```
writeln ('Which name do you require?');
writeln ('    (1) A. N. Other');
writeln ('    (2) N. O. One');
writeln ('    (3) Y. E. T. Another');
writeln ('Enter the number of the name you require');
repeat
      readln (NameCode);
until NameCode in ['1', '2', '3'];
end;
procedure AorTMenu;
begin
writeln;
writeln ('Do you require the address or telephone number?');
writeln ('Enter "A" for address or "T" for telephone');
repeat
      readln (AorT);
until AorT in ['A', 'a', 'T', 't'];
end;
procedure ShowResult;
begin
case NameCode of
    '1' : case AorT of
            'A', 'a' : begin
                        writeln ('1, Somewhere Street');
                        writeln ('Anytown');
                        end;
            'T', 't' :  writeln ('12345');
        end;
    '2' : case AorT of
            'A', 'a' : begin
                        writeln ('144, Nowhere Avenue');
                        writeln ('Nothingville');
                        end;
            'T', 't' :  writeln ('54321');
        end;
    '3' : case AorT of
            'A', 'a' : writeln ('73, Elsewhere Lane');
            'T', 't' : writeln ('24680');
        end;
end;
```

```
end;
begin {main program}
repeat
    NameMenu;
    AorTMenu;
    ShowResult;
    writeln ('Do you want to look up another?');
    writeln ('enter y/n');
    repeat
        readln (ch);
    until ch in ['y', 'Y', 'n', 'N'];
until ch in ['n', 'N'];
end.
```

2. There are a number of ways of doing this. Here is one:

```
program capital (input,output);
var ch : char;
begin
repeat
    read (ch);
    if ch in ['a'..'z'] then
        case ch of
                'a' : ch := 'A';
                'b' : ch := 'B';
    .
    .
    .
                'z' : ch := 'Z'
        end;
    if ch in ['A'..'Z'] then write (ch);
until not (ch in ['A'..'Z'] );
end.
```

3.

```
program add (input,output);
var
    ch : char;
    i, answer : integer;
procedure convert;
```

```
begin
repeat
  read (ch);
until ch in ['0'..'9'];
case ch of
  '0' : i:=0;
  '1' : i:=1;
  '2' : i:=2;
  '3' : i:=3;
  '4' : i:=4;
  '5' : i:=5;
  '6' : i:=6;
  '7' : i:=7;
  '8' : i:=8;
  '9' : i:=9
end; {case}
end; {convert}
begin
convert;
answer := i;
convert;
answer := answer+i;
writeln ('answer is : ', answer);
end.
```

5. See Figure A.1.

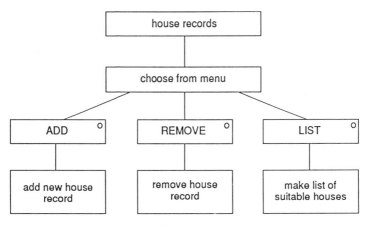

Figure A.1

```pascal
program HouseRecords;
var ch : char;
procedure AddHouse;
begin
end;
procedure RemoveHouse;
begin
end;
procedure GetList;
begin
end;
procedure menu;
begin
writeln ('What would you like to do?');
writeln;
writeln ('1: add a new house');
writeln ('2: remove a house');
writeln ('3: get list of suitable houses');
writeln;
writeln ('enter number to select option');
repeat
  read (ch)
until ch in ['1'..'3'];
case ch of
  '1': AddHouse;
  '2': RemoveHouse;
  '3': GetList
end; {case}
end; {menu}
begin {main program}
repeat
  menu;
  writeln ('Do you want another option?');
  writeln ('enter y/n');
  repeat
    read (ch);
  until ch in ['y', 'Y', 'n', 'N'];
until ch in ['n', 'N'];
end.
```

Chapter 6

1. a) **Age : array [1..35] of integer**
   b) **Price : array [1..150] of integer**
   c) **name : array [1..20] of char**
   d) **PIN : array [1..4] of char**

5. ii), iii), v), vi)

7. **i** is declared within the inner procedure **AddOne**, it is *not*, therefore, available to the main body of the program.

8. 3, 2

Chapter 7

1. iii), v)

Chapter 8

1. {2}, {3}, {4}, {5}, {6}, {7}

Chapter 9

1. i), iii), v)

2. **procedure stars (width,height : integer);**

var i,j : integer;
begin
for i := 1 to height do
   begin
   for j := 1 to width do write ('*');
     writeln;
     end;
   end;

3. Making the following type definition:

type MessageType = packed array [1..50] of char;

we can write this procedure:

ErrorMessage (message : MessageType);

```
begin
writeln;
writeln ('***************************************');
writeln;writeln;
writeln (message);
writeln;writeln;
writeln ('***************************************');
end;
```

Chapter 10

5 a) record
        name,tutor : packed array [1..20] of char;
        sex : (male,female);
        course : packed array [1..10] of char;
        year : 1..5
      end;
  b) record
        name : packed array [1..20] of char;
        age, height, weight : integer;
        sex : (female,male);
        fitness : 1..5
      end;
  c) record
        author : packed array [1..20] of char;
        title : packed array [1..200] of char;
        ISBN : packed array [1..10] of '0'..'9'
      end;

9. program PropertyData (input,output,propertyFile,TempFile);
const
  NameLength = 20;
  LineLength = 40;
  NumLength = 5;
type
  NameType = packed array [1..NameLength] of char;
  AddrLine = packed array [1..LineLength] of char;
  NumStringType = packed array [1..5] of char;
  MessageString = packed array [1..40] of char;
  AreaType = (Appleton,Walton,Grappenhall,Latchford,
  StocktonHeath);
```
```

```
PropertyInfo = record
                 identity : AddrLine;
                 price,beds,receps : integer;
                 area : AreaType
              end;
var
  PropertyFile,TempFile : file of PropertyInfo;
  exit : boolean;
  CurrentInfo : PropertyInfo;
  AreaNames : array [AreaType] of NameType;
procedure InitAreas;
begin
AreaNames [Appleton]            := 'Appleton           ';
AreaNames [Walton]             := 'Walton             ';
AreaNames [Grappenhall]        := 'Grappenhall        ';
AreaNames [Latchford]          := 'Latchford          ';
AreaNames [StocktonHeath]      := 'StocktonHeath      ';
end;
procedure EnterIdentity (var Ident : AddrLine);
var
  i : integer;
begin
for i := 1 to LineLength do
  Ident[i] :=' ';
writeln ('Enter first line of house address.');
i := 1;
repeat
  read (Ident[i]); i := i+1;
until eoln or (i >=LineLength);
readln;
end;
procedure Convert (NumString : NumStringType; var Total :
integer);
var
  i,TotalSoFar : integer;
begin
i := 1;
TotalSoFar := 0;
while (NumString[i] < > ' ') and (i<=NumLength) do
  begin
```

```pascal
    TotalSoFar := TotalSoFar*10 + ord (NumString[i]) – ord ('0');
    i := i+1;
    end;
Total := TotalSoFar;
end;
procedure EnterInt (Message1,Message2:MessageString; var
Result : integer);
var
  NumString : NumStringType;
  i : integer;
  ch : char;
begin
writeln (Message1);
writeln (Message2);
while not eoln do
  begin for i := 1 to NumLength do NumString[i] :=' ';
  i := 1;
  repeat
    read (ch);
    if ch in ['0'..'9'] then
      begin
      NumString [i] :=ch;
      i := i+1;
      end;
  until eoln or (i>NumLength);
  if not eoln then
    begin
    writeln ('Too long. Please enter 5-digit integer.');
    readln;
    end;
  end' {while not eoln}
  readln;
Convert (NumString,Result);
end;
procedure EnterPrice;
begin
EnterInt ('Please enter price                           ',
    'How many thousands of pounds?        ', CurrentInfo.Price);
end;
procedure EnterBeds;
```

```
begin
EnterInt ('Please enter number of bedrooms.        ',
            '                                  ', CurrentInfo.Beds);
end;
procedure EnterReceps;
begin
EnterInt ('Please enter number of reception rooms ',
            '                                  ',
            CurrentInfo.Receps);
end;
procedure EnterArea;
var
  Reply:char;
  Area:AreaType;
  found : boolean;
begin
found := false;
repeat
  writeln ('Which area is the house in?');
  writeln ('enter Y when correct area is displayed.');
  writeln ('enter N to move on to next area.');
  area := Appleton;
  while (area <= StocktonHeath) and not found do
    begin
    write (Areanames[area], '? ');
    readln (reply);
    if reply in ['y', 'Y'] then found := true
    else area := succ(area);
    writeln;
    end;
  if found then
    CurrentInfo.Area := area
  else writeln ('You must select one of the areas listed.');
until found;
end;
procedure InputInfo;
  begin
  EnterIdentity (CurrentInfo.Identity);
  EnterPrice;
  EnterBeds;
```

```
    EnterReceps;
    EnterArea;
    end;
procedure ShowCurrentRecord;
var
    i : integer;
    area:AreaType;
begin {ShowCurrentRecord}
writeln;writeln;writeln ('details of current property');
with CurrentInfo do
    begin {with}
    writeln;writeln ('IDENTITY ', identity);
    writeln ('PRICE ', price);
    writeln ('BEDROOMS ',beds);
    writeln ('RECEPTION ROOMS ',receps);
    writeln ('AREA ',AreaNames[area]);
    end {with};
end; {ShowCurrentRecord}
procedure CopyRestToTemp;
var TempRec:propertyInfo;
begin
while not eof (PropertyFile) do
    begin
    read (PropertyFile,TempRec);
    write (TempFile,TempRec);
    end;
end;
procedure CopyToTemp;
var TempRec : propertyInfo;
begin
if not eof (PropertyFile) then
    repeat
    read (PropertyFile,TempRec);
    if (TempRec.price > CurrentInfo.price) then
        write (TempFile,CurrentInfo);
    write (TempFile,TempRec);
    until eof (PropertyFile) or (TempRec.price>CurrentInfo.price);
while not eof (PropertyFile) do
    begin
    read (PropertyFile,TempRec);
```

```
    write (TempFile,TempRec);
    end;
end;
procedure CopyFromTemp;
var TempRec:propertyInfo;
begin
reset (tempFile) {prepare for input};
rewrite (propertyFile) {prepare for output};
while not eof (TempFile) do
  begin
  read (TempFile,TempRec);
  write (propertyFile,TempRec);
  end;
end;
procedure AddRec;
var ch : char;
begin
writeln ('Create new file or add to old one?');
writeln ('enter n for new or o for old');
repeat
  readln (ch)
until ch in ['N', 'n', 'O', 'o'];
if ch in ['O', 'o']
    then begin
            reset (propertyFile) {prepare for input};
            rewrite (TempFile) {prepare for output};
            CopyToTemp;
            CopyFromTemp;
            end
    else begin
            rewrite (propertyFile);
            write (propertyFile,CurrentInfo)
            end;
end;
procedure AmendMenu;
var
  ch : char;
  Stop : boolean;
begin {AmendMenu}
Stop := false;
```

```pascal
repeat
  writeln;writeln ('Which field do you wish to amend?');
  writeln ('enter number to select option.');
  writeln;writeln ('1. IDENTITY');
  writeln ('2. PRICE');
  writeln ('3. NUMBER OF BEDROOMS');
  writeln ('4. NUMBER OF RECEPTION ROOMS');
  writeln ('5. AREA');
  writeln ('6. no further amendments');
  repeat
    readln (ch);
  until ch in ['1'..'6'];
  case ch of
    '1' : EnterIdentity (CurrentInfo.Identity);
    '2' : EnterPrice;
    '3' : EnterBeds;
    '4' : EnterReceps;
    '5' : EnterArea;
    '6' : Stop := true
  end {case};
  If not stop then ShowCurrentRecord;
until Stop;
end {AmendMenu};
procedure AmendCurrentRecord;
var
  ch:char;
begin {AmendCurrentRecord}
writeln;writeln;
writeln ('Do you wish to amend this information?');
writeln ('Enter Y or N');
repeat
  readln (ch);
until ch in ['Y', 'y', 'N', 'n'];
if ch in ['Y', 'y'] then
  AmendMenu;
end {AmendCurrentRecord};
procedure StoreInfo;
begin
ShowCurrentRecord;
AmendCurrentRecord;
```

```
AddRec;
end;
procedure AddRecord;
begin
InputInfo;
StoreInfo;
end;
procedure FindInfo (PropIdent:AddrLine);
var
  TempRec:propertyInfo;
  Found:boolean;
begin
reset (propertyFile);
rewrite (TempFile);
found := false;
while not (eof (propertyFile) or found) do
  begin
  read (propertyFile,TempRec);
  if TempRec.Identity = PropIdent
    then found := true
    else write (TempFile,TempRec);
  end {while};
if found
  then CurrentInfo := TempRec
  else writeln ('property not found');
end;
procedure Delete;
begin
CopyRestToTemp;
CopyFromTemp;
end;
procedure Amend;
begin
AmendMenu;
write (TempFile,CurrentInfo);
CopyToTemp;
CopyFromTemp;
end;
procedure DisplayRecord;
var
```

```pascal
    RequiredIdent : AddrLine;
begin
EnterIdentity (RequiredIdent);
FindInfo (RequiredIdent);
ShowCurrentRecord;
end;
procedure RecordMenu;
var
    ch : char;
begin
writeln ('enter number to select option: ');
writeln ('1. delete record ');
writeln ('2. amend record');
writeln ('3. leave record unchanged');
repeat
    readln (ch);
until ch in ['1'..'3'];
case ch of
    '1' : delete;
    '2' : amend;
    '3' :
end;
end;
procedure MainMenu;
var
    ch : char;
begin
writeln ('PROPERTY INFORMATION');
writeln;writeln ('Do you wish to :');
writeln;writeln ('1. add a new property');
writeln ('2. display existing property');
writeln ('3. exit from this program');
writeln;writeln ('enter number to select option');
repeat
    readln (ch);
until ch in ['1', '2', '3'];
case ch of
    '1' :   AddRecord;
    '2' :   begin
            DisplayRecord;
```

```
        Recordmenu
        end;
 '3' : exit := true
end;
end;
begin {Main body}
exit := false;
InitAreas;
assign (propertyFile, 'b:Prop'); {Turbo}
assign (TempFile, 'b:temp');   {Turbo}
repeat
  MainMenu
until exit;
end.
```

Chapter 11

1. i)
```
        function length (x1,y1,x2,y2:real) :real;
        var xdiff,ydiff:real;
        begin
        xdiff := x2–x1;
        ydiff := y2–y1;
        length := sqrt (xdiff*xdiff+ydiff*ydiff);
        end;
```
  ii)
```
        function common (a,b: IntArray) :boolean;
        var i : integer;
        begin
        common := false;
        for i := 1 to 10 do
          if a[i] = b[i] then common := true;
        end;
```
  iii)
```
        function LowerCase (cap:char) :char;
        begin
        LowerCase := chr (ord(cap) + (ord('a') – ord ('A')));
        end;
```
  iv)
```
        function Largest (a : Int50Array) :integer;
        var i, max : integer;
        begin
        max := 1;
        for i := 2 to 50 do
```

```
           if a[i]>a[max] then max := i;
       Largest := max;
       end;
v)     function Pascal (str:StringType) :boolean;
       var
          PasString : packed array [1..6] of char;
          i,j : integer;
       begin
       Pascal := false;
       for i := 1 to 46 do
         if str[i] = 'P' then
           begin
           for j := 1 to 6 do
             PasString[j] := str[i+j–1];
           if PasString = 'Pascal' then Pascal := true;
           end;
       end;
```

2. Should use real arithmetic.
   Program still attempts to calculate mean when –1 entered as first integer.

Chapter 12

2. **type**
nameType = packed array [1..20] of char;
LineType = packed array [1..40] of char;
AddressType = array [1..6] of LineType;
DateIndexType = (day,month,year);
dateType = array [day..year] of integer;
CustomerPointer = ^Customer;
Customer = record
                name:NameType;
                address:AddressType;
                date : DateType;
                priority : boolean;
                next : CustomerPointer
            end;

Appendix B

Pascal Delimiter Words

and	function	program
array	goto	record
begin	if	repeat
case	in	set
const	label	then
div	mod	to
do	nil	type
downto	not	until
else	of	var
end	or	while
file	packed	with
for	procedure	

Appendix C

Standard Identifiers

Constant Identifiers

false   **maxint**   **true**

Type Identifiers

boolean   **char**   **integer**   **real**   **text**

Variable Identifiers

input   **output**

Procedure Identifiers

dispose	see Chapter 12
get	see Chapter 9
new	see Chapter 12
pack	see Chapter 7
page	see Chapter 7
put	see Chapter 9
read	see Chapter 7
readln	see Chapter 3
reset	see Chapter 9
rewrite	see Chapter 9
unpack	see Chapter 7
write	see Chapter 2
writeln	see Chapter 2

Function Identifiers

abs (x)
    returns the absolute value of x. The result is integer if x is integer, real
    if x is real.

arctan (x)
> returns the inverse tangent of x in radians.

chr (n)
> returns the character whose ordinal number is the integer, n.

cos (x)
> returns the cosine of x.

eof (f)
> returns **true** if, when reading in from file **f**, the end-of-file marker is encountered (see Chapter 9).

eoln (f) returns **true** if, when reading from text file, **f**, the end of the current line has been reached (see Chapter 9).

exp (x)
> returns the natural antilogarithm of x.

ln (x)
> returns the natural logarithm of x.

odd (n)
> returns **true** if the integer, n, is odd
>   **false** if n is even.

ord (q)
> returns the ordinal number of q, where q may be of *any* ordinal type.

pred (q)
> returns the item whose ordinal number is one less than that of q, where q may be of *any* ordinal type.

round (x)
> returns the nearest integer to x (x real).

sin (x)
> returns the sine of x, (x measured in radians).

sqr (x)
> returns the square of x. The result is integer if x is integer, real if x is real.

sqrt (x)
> returns the square root of x.

succ (q)
> returns the item whose ordinal number is one greater than that of q, where q may be of any ordinal type.

trunc (x)
> returns the largest integer less than x (x real).

Appendix D
Further Reading

Bishop J, *Pascal Precisely*, Addison-Wesley, 1989

Dwyer EP, Dodd FJ, *Learning Turbo Pascal*, NCC Blackwell, 1989

Dwyer EP, Dodd FJ, *Pascal on the BBC Microcomputer*, NCC Publications, 1988

Findley W, Watt D, *Pascal – An Introduction to Methodical Programming*, Pitman, 1982

Grogono P, Nelson SH, *Problem Solving and Computer Programming*, Addison-Wesley, 1982

Holmes BJ, *Pascal Programming*, DP Publications, 1987

Sand PA, *Advanced Pascal Programming Techniques*, Osborne/McGraw-Hill, 1984

Schildt H, *Advanced Turbo Pascal: Programming and Techniques*, Osborne/McGraw-Hill, 1988

Woods S, *Using Turbo Pascal*, Osborne/McGraw-Hill, 1988

Index